UNDERSTANDING INCLU

C000109025

Understanding Inclusion is a rich, comprehensive exploration of inclusion in education, challenging us to think about being 'inclusive' in its broadest sense. It unpacks a wide range of complex themes and issues that impact on educational practice, supporting educational professionals in helping teachers and learners understand difference as the norm, and not the exception.

Underpinned by the latest research, discussion is brought to life through vignettes of real experiences and examples of practice from a range of settings and across continents. Chapters consider crucial aspects of inclusion:

- Social inclusion and social class
- Global perspectives on culture and identity
- Aspirations and social mobility
- Relationships and sexual behaviours
- Gender equality and diversity
- Perceptions of ability and disability
- Barriers to learning
- Multilingualism in schools
- Religion and belief
- Restorative justice for inclusion
- Inclusion and the arts
- Teaching Assistants and inclusion
- The central role of leadership

Written by experts with extensive experience in a range of educational contexts, *Understanding Inclusion* is designed for all those engaged in understanding the complexities of teaching and learning. With reflective questions and selected reading designed to support further study, it will be essential reading for students on Education Studies and related courses, and pre- and in-service teachers.

Richard Woolley is Deputy Head of the Institute of Education at the University of Worcester, UK, and was Head of Centre for Education and Inclusion from 2011 to 2017. He is a Principal Fellow of the Higher Education Academy, UK.

UNDERSTANDING INCLUSION

Core Concepts, Policy and Practice

Edited by Richard Woolley

Routledge
Taylor & Francis Group

LONDON AND NEW YORK

First published 2018
by Routledge
2 Park Square, Milton Park, Abingdon, Oxon OX14 4RN

and by Routledge
711 Third Avenue, New York, NY 10017

Routledge is an imprint of the Taylor & Francis Group, an informa business

© 2018 selection and editorial matter, Richard Woolley; individual chapters, the contributors

The right of the editor to be identified as the author of the editorial material, and of the authors for their individual chapters, has been asserted in accordance with sections 77 and 78 of the Copyright, Designs and Patents Act 1988.

All rights reserved. No part of this book may be reprinted or reproduced or utilised in any form or by any electronic, mechanical, or other means, now known or hereafter invented, including photocopying and recording, or in any information storage or retrieval system, without permission in writing from the publishers.

Trademark notice: Product or corporate names may be trademarks or registered trademarks, and are used only for identification and explanation without intent to infringe.

British Library Cataloguing-in-Publication Data
A catalogue record for this book is available from the British Library

Library of Congress Cataloging-in-Publication Data
A catalog record for this book has been requested

ISBN: 978-1-138-24167-1 (hbk)
ISBN: 978-1-138-24168-8 (pbk)
ISBN: 978-1-315-27989-3 (ebk)

Typeset in News Gothic
by Apex CoVantage, LLC

Printed and bound by CPI Group (UK) Ltd, Croydon, CR0 4YY

CONTENTS

BIOGRAPHIES

All contributors to this book are members of the Centre for Education and Inclusion at the University of Worcester.

Editor

Richard Woolley was Head of the Centre for Education and Inclusion in the Institute of Education at the University of Worcester from 2011–2017. He is Deputy Head of Institute (Research) and a Principal Fellow of the Higher Education Academy (HEA). Richard's teaching and research interests relate to diversity and equality, children's spirituality, special educational needs and Relationships and Sex Education. He is the author of *Tackling Controversial Issues in the Primary School* (Routledge, 2010); co-author of *Relationships and Sex Education 5–11* (Continuum, 2012); and co-editor of *Values and Vision in the Primary School* (Open University Press, 2013), as well as a range of articles, papers and chapters on similar topics.

Contributors

Seán Bracken is a Principal Lecturer at the University of Worcester, and a Senior Fellow of the HEA. He has extensive experience in the fields of multilingualism, curriculum change management and inclusivity. In addition to supervising postgraduate researchers, Seán currently coordinates the PG Cert SENCO (the National Award for Special Educational Needs Coordinators) and also teaches on the PG Cert Higher Education Teaching and Learning.

Leela Cubillo is a Senior Lecturer at the University of Worcester. She teaches on the Education Studies degree and is the Pathway Leader for the master's degree in Educational Leadership and Management. Her research interests are in school leadership, gender and leadership and the management of change.

Gareth Dart joined the University of Worcester in 2007. He was Course Leader for the Education Studies degree for five years and continues to act as the Year Two lead as well as teach on various modules of the degree and on master's degree courses. He has specific interests in teacher education and special and inclusive education in the contexts of resource poor countries, particularly in southern Africa, where he worked for a number of years and where he continues to have professional interests.

Ruth Hewston is a Principal Lecturer at the University of Worcester and Head of Centre for Education and Inclusion. Her teaching interests are in areas of inclusive education, additional needs and learning support. Her research interests focus on the education of learners with high ability, the psychology of learning and teaching and special educational needs.

Ellie Hill is a Senior Lecturer in Education at the University of Worcester and Course Leader for Education Studies. She also leads the MA Pathway in Religion and Values. Her research interests are in the field of contemporary religion and values, and the higher education student experience. She is currently involved in a project evaluating the impact of RE Hubs on RE in schools.

Sophie King-Hill is a Lecturer in Education Studies at the University of Worcester. She teaches modules relating to radical education, controversial issues, relationships, policy, inclusion, research and evaluation. Her research interests include sex and relationships education, harmful sexual behaviour in children and young people, policy evaluation, teenage parents and social exclusion.

Teresa Lehane is a Senior Lecturer at the University of Worcester, teaching on a range of courses and specialising in aspects of 'special educational needs and disability' (SEND). Her research interests include the work of teaching assistants and SEND policy and the use of critical discourse analysis.

Wendy Messenger is a Senior Lecturer in Education and Course Leader for the MA Education degree. She teaches modules at undergraduate and postgraduate level that largely focus upon aspects of disadvantage in education. Her research interests include inclusion and inter-professional working.

Jane Owens is a Senior Lecturer at the University of Worcester and is also a practising career coach. Jane has a fascination with exploring influences upon people's learning and career decisions, and upon their employability. She teaches modules relating to mentoring and coaching and her research interests include career decision-making and career coaching.

Gwenda Scriven (1954–2014) was a Senior Lecturer in Education and Course Leader for FdA Learning Support. As a committed practitioner, she was very much involved in restorative practice, working with a range of organisations in the Worcester area. The chapter is included with the permission of her husband, Bill, and was updated by the editor.

Sharon Smith is a Senior Lecturer in Education Studies at the University of Worcester, and previously taught within further education. Her research interests are predominately in the areas of special education and inclusion and the use of virtual learning environments. She has engaged with a number of JISC projects and has undertaken research as part of a team on a European Union Comenius-funded project.

Simon Taylor joined the University of Worcester's Centre for Education and Inclusion in 2016. His background is within the arts and cultural sector and he has worked with adult learners, prisoners and young offenders and children with special educational needs. He currently teaches undergraduate modules on education policy, work experience and creative and expressive arts.

Philip Woodward is a Senior Lecturer in Education Studies at the University of Worcester and Phase Lead for the first year of the undergraduate Education Studies degree. He teaches on a range of undergraduate and postgraduate modules specialising in the sociology of education and critical theory. His research interests include intra-class differences in university choice and access to university with particular reference to elite HEIs.

ACKNOWLEDGEMENTS

This book grew out of its contributors' shared experience of working in the Centre for Education and Inclusion in the Institute of Education at the University of Worcester, UK. We express our gratitude to colleagues, both students and staff, for their support during this project, and particularly members of the team who acted as critical friends.

The University of Worcester has a long-held commitment to inclusive education, in a broad understanding of the phrase. Indeed, it was founded in 1946 to meet the need for additional teachers in post-war Britain, with the aspiration to 'win the peace' through education. In 2016, it was shortlisted as University of the Year by the *Times Higher Education* for its work in the area of inclusion.

It goes without saying that all shortcomings in the text are our own. Every effort has been made to contact copyright holders for their permission to reprint material in this book. The publishers will be grateful to hear from any copyright holder who is not here acknowledged and will undertake to rectify any errors or omissions in future editions.

Finally, our thanks to the colleagues, students and others who contributed to the research projects of varying sizes included in this book. We are grateful for their time and commitment, and hope that the elements of original research, case studies and other accounts from practice bring the issues to life. Where appropriate their contributions have been anonymised. Primary research received ethical approval from the University of Worcester.

1 Introducing inclusion

Richard Woolley

I remember being a child and thinking how odd it was that no one else (or at least it felt like no one else) lived in a flat or apartment like me and my family. The conversations that I heard in class, and the stories that were shared in lessons, all seemed to include families that lived in houses of varying sizes and styles. Indeed, even the literature that I enjoyed reading for pleasure seemed to present living in a house as the norm.

For my living space to be unusual, perhaps atypical, gave a strange feeling. That said; our home was lovely, spacious and comfortable. No doubt it was nicer than many of my peers', it was just that it was "upstairs" and happened to be above the place where my parents worked.

Introduction

Inclusion is a term that is interpreted in many ways. For some working in the field of education, it indicates a focus on special educational needs. Others would add disability or disabilities to this focus. A broader definition is to include areas relating to diversity and equality, including gender, age, sexual orientation and other areas that resonate with equalities legislation such as the Equality Act (2010) in the UK. This book embraces that breadth of understanding, adding areas such as social class, leadership for inclusion, meritocracy and career aspiration.

Understanding inclusion

The *UN Convention on the Rights of the Child* (1989) outlines how children and young people should be enabled to have a voice and to express their views and opinions. This essentially involves ensuring that children and young people are involved actively in the educational organisations in which they find themselves. Such activity is not always particularly inclusive, and sometimes trying to involve children in decision-making processes can be superficial or tokenistic. However, the intention and vision for their involvement is of note, and needs to be considered in a book of this nature.

United Nations (UN) Article 1 of the *Universal Declaration of Human Rights* (UN, 1948a) states that:

> All human beings are born free and equal in dignity and rights. They are endowed with reason and conscience and should act towards one another in a spirit of [kinship].

This suggests that an approach to including all in society, in schools and educational establishments, and in constructive and supportive human relationships, is important. Whilst the language is of its era, and fails to be gender inclusive (referring to "brotherhood" in the original), the spirit of the statement interpreted decades later provides a sense of equality that requires that we are all included. This is particularly significant as this is Article 1: the first of all the articles.

As I have argued elsewhere (Woolley, 2010: 60–61) the notion of children having influence and a voice, in other words democracy, can be difficult to specify clearly. On first consideration, such a democratic contribution may be described as the way in which the political systems work in many parts of the world. Political systems may be regarded in two ways: first, the formal structures of governance and secondly, a values base that informs personal opinion and action. These two approaches may be characterised by:

structures, which involve
- representative and accountable government, elected from a choice of political parties;
- protection of human rights and by the rule of law; and
- freedom of speech and expression, including free and diverse mass media;

a values base, which includes
- mutual respect between individuals and groups, including valuing diversity;
- willingness to be open to changing one's mind, and basing one's opinions in evidence; and
- regarding all human beings as having equal rights.

Being inclusive requires openness to the differences found in others, and indeed to recognising the differences within oneself. We are all unique and therefore all different. If we could only develop a society and a wider world that appreciated that difference as the norm, and not the exception, surely the world would be a better place. We are not naturally homogenous: heterogeneity is the norm.

In the context of the United Kingdom, the *Crick Report* (QCA, 1998: 44) outlined eight key concepts relating to having a voice that children should understand by the end of compulsory schooling:

- democracy and autocracy;
- co-operation and conflict;
- equality and diversity;
- fairness, justice, the rule of law and human rights;
- freedom and order;
- individual and community;
- power and authority; and
- rights and responsibilities.

These eight facets are notable in their focus on requiring an inclusive approach to valuing other people, and indeed valuing oneself. Whilst now somewhat dated, *Crick* set out enduring values and principles that have informed policy development in subsequent years, and its influence should not be underestimated.

In an international context, the second section of Article 26 of the *United Nations Declaration of Human Rights* relates directly to education and to the issues addressed throughout this book:

> Education shall be directed to the full development of the human personality and to the strengthening of respect for human rights and fundamental freedoms. It shall promote understanding, tolerance and friendship among all nations, racial or religious groups, and shall further the activities of the United Nations for the maintenance of peace.

Furthermore, Article 12 of the United Nations *Convention on the Rights of the Child* (1989) states that:

1   Parties shall assure to the child who is capable of forming his or her own views the right to express those views freely in all matters affecting the child, the views of the child being given due weight in accordance with the age and maturity of the child.
2   For this purpose, the child shall in particular be provided the opportunity to be heard in any judicial and administrative proceedings affecting the child, either directly, or through a representative or an appropriate body, in a manner consistent with the procedural rules of national law.

The child's voice is therefore important, as are their views and their rights. These are core principles in ensuring that children and young people are included in decisions relating to themselves and their own welfare, and also to decisions affecting provisions made for them.

These principles and values relate particularly to children and young people, and this book is not concerned with just the young. However, setting our inclusive approaches to the voices of children suggests that those often considered to be the inexperienced and vulnerable in society have a say, and from this we should conclude that all must have a say. Whatever our need or difference, we have a right to be included by and in society, and a responsibility to accept and appreciate the contribution of those different to ourselves. In fact, everyone is different to ourselves: there has never been anyone in the history of the world who has been me.

Experiences of inclusion

Case study

Jake was born in 1967, coincidently the year homosexuality was legalised in the UK (between two consenting men in private). Now in his fiftieth year, he is planning his wedding to his partner Steve. They have been together for six years, and have lived together for the past two. Reflecting on his life, Jake is glad to live in a place where he is able to make a public, legally recognised commitment to the person he loves. He knows that even in his early 20s sex with a man in a hotel room, or a house where a guest was in another room, would have been illegal (because this was not defined as being "in private"). Although Jake and Steve are still careful about holding hands when out in public, something that they often discuss and lament, Jake talks about the freedom he feels in being able to plan their honeymoon together without having to pretend to be just friends or work colleagues. For him the world has moved on significantly, but he is very aware that this is not true for all gay men around the globe.

Carline has just been appointed to her first post as head teacher in a primary school. She entered the teaching profession eight years ago, after undertaking a three year degree in primary education. She is currently working to complete her master's degree, and has taught in two schools, taking a middle leadership position as the Special Educational Needs Coordinator (SENCo) in the last one. Carline was the first in her family to go to university, and the only one from her group of friends at school to undertake a degree. Her careers advisor at school suggested that she train to be a teacher, as she had volunteered with uniformed organisations and as a Sunday School teacher in her local church for several years. She now has a highly responsible job, and a salary higher than her parents ever dreamed of earning themselves.

Reflect on:

- Your responses to the experiences of Jake and Carline.
- How might the concept of inclusion relate to their situation?
- What facets of them as individuals might affect their experience?

When considering inclusion, it can be all too easy to focus on visible or obvious aspects of what we see in other people. For example, we may see someone as being in a wheelchair and make simple, and perhaps superficial, assumptions about their needs. However, their social class, age, gender, sexual orientation and non-visible health needs (to suggest just a few examples) also impact on who they are and how they relate to the world. In the case study above, Carline's socio-economic or class background may not be known to those with whom she works, and Jake's sexual orientation may not be known or visible to others. In both cases, the issues they face in day to day life in terms of feeling included in society may not be known to those around them. Creating an inclusive environment is essential in order to aim for all people to feel included, whatever their differences. It is not just a case of responding to differences when we come across them. This is reflected in a small incident from my own experience:

> After a meeting I was engaged in conversation with a woman who suddenly turned her interest to my own background: "Do you have a family?" she asked. "Yes I do," I replied, "my mum and dad live locally and I have a brother." "No," she replied, "I meant do you have a family of your own?"

> (Woolley, 2010: 1)

This brief example shows how others can make assumptions about us, and how sometimes they filter their expectations of us through their own experience. The woman did not understand that as a single man I still have a family. I find it interesting how often it is assumed in general conversation that all present have partners and children. Whilst I do not feel particularly excluded in such situations, it does interest me that often people assume that everyone is just like them.

Broadening inclusion

The *Crick Report* (QCA, 1998) considered how whole-school approaches could contribute to the development of active citizenship and an understanding of democracy. It suggested that such issues needed to be understood in terms of the whole-school ethos, the ways in which a school is organised, its structures and daily practices (Woolley, 2010):

> In particular, schools should make every effort to engage pupils in discussion and consultation about all aspects of school life on which pupils might reasonably be expected to have a view, and wherever possible to give pupils responsibility and experience in helping to run parts of the school. This might include school facilities, organisation, rules, relationships and matters relating to teaching and learning. Such engagement can be through both formal structures such as school and class councils and informal channels in pupils' daily encounters with aspects of school life. To create a feeling that it is 'our school' can increase pupil motivation to learn in all subjects.
>
> (QCA, 1998: 36)

Crick also identified three strands that make up effective education for citizenship, with the intention that these should develop progressively as children move through the school system, namely:

- social and moral responsibility;
- community involvement; and
- political literacy.

Democracy suggests engagement, an interest in the common good, a concern for others and a belief that things can be better than they are. Readers will want to reflect on their own views of democracy and democratic values, and whether they reflect such principles. They certainly have the potential to engage individuals with decision-making processes and to encourage them to care about what happens in the wider world. Such values can constitute part of inclusion, in a broad definition.

Gregory (2000: 447, drawing on Gilligan, 1993) outlines six elements that contribute to an ethic of care and thereby, I argue, the building of communities: acquaintance, mindfulness, moral imagining, solidarity, tolerance and self-care, to which I have added my own interpretations (Woolley, 2010: 67):

- *Acquaintance* is concerned with the ways in which we develop contact with others, noticing their existence, naming and communicating with them. It is difficult to measure the ripple effects that acquaintance has on others, but it is important to note that our contact and reactions have impact.
- *Mindfulness* considers the ways in which our conduct affects others. It includes developing respect for others because they are fellow humans, whilst also appreciating that they are unique and individual. Thus, it is fundamentally concerned with equality, understanding that this does not mean that we all have to be the same. It considers the attention we give to those around us.

- *Moral imagining* provides the opportunity to develop pro-social behaviours such as empathy and altruism. It provides the opportunity to think about what it might be like to be in someone else's position and to face their circumstances, without actually becoming like them.
- *Solidarity* involves helping others to achieve their goals and dreams and exercising a commitment to work on behalf of others. It infers that we are acquainted with and mindful of them. However, we are also able to empathise with and care for strangers.
- *Tolerance* may be viewed as a negative virtue: "Behaviourally, tolerance is evidenced as much by the absence of repressive actions as by the practice of non-discriminatory procedures" (Gregory, 2000: 450). It provides opportunities to work towards inclusiveness and to accommodate each other's divergent needs and aspirations. However, I feel that the term *respect* encompasses these attributes and find this a more positive (and less begrudging) word.
- *Self-care* stands in contrast to the notion of being selfless. To be selfless implies that one does not matter oneself (it is not the direct opposite of selfishness). Being able to articulate one's own wants and needs is a part of caring for oneself, and negotiating this with others is a fundamental part of existing in relationship with them. Citizenship does not require people to deny themselves; it requires the development of a sense of people's equally valuable contribution to and place in society.

Gregory suggests that these facets provide the *soil* in which both personal and communal growth can take place through the development of mutual care.

Pause for thought

Reflect on the vignette at the start of this chapter.

Children in our schools and other education settings may find themselves in a very similar position to that which I experienced as a child. They may not live in an apartment, but they might live in a trailer or a caravan or on a boat. They might live in a house but share it with varying combinations of family members, and perhaps others. They may live with one or two parents, with a grandparent or an uncle or aunt. Some will live in an extended family covering three or more generations, and other may have those other than their blood relatives living with them. Some children have siblings and these can be of varied ages. Given this diversity, it is important for those designing and sustaining a school environment to acknowledge difference and diversity, and to ensure that all children feel welcome, safe and supported no matter what the pattern and format of their home "space".

When considering inclusion as both a term and a concept we need to consider:

- Who and what are we seeking to include?
- What is the opposite of inclusion, and what are the implications if our approach is not inclusive?
- How broad is our understanding of inclusion? For some the term relates particularly to those with special educational needs; for others it is an all-encompassing term that challenges us to consider how everyone's differences are acknowledged and celebrated.
- What is your view of and vision for the term inclusion?

Perspectives and practice

Research I have undertaken with final year student teachers in England identified a range of issues relating to a broad understanding of inclusion that caused them concern. Electronic questionnaires were distributed to student teachers in the spring of 2016, with Course Leaders and Heads of Schools of Education in universities acting as gatekeepers. One hundred and five responses were received from across all regions of England. Eighty-nine per cent of respondents identified as female, which generally reflects the gender balance on training courses. One third was undertaking first degrees in primary education, and others were on a one year postgraduate course. Participants were asked to identify three areas that caused them concern when anticipating their first teaching post, and to provide reasons.

Research

Consider the responses provided by participants in the 2016 study. What issues do they identify that relate to inclusion?

> Due to what is currently happening in the media I think that many children could be possibly influenced by this and if not educated properly about other religions many children may judge others based on what they see in the media.
>
> *Female final year undergraduate (3 year degree), training to*
> *teach children aged 5–11 years, North West England*

> How do you begin to explain to a child what is happening in the world? People are committing horrendous crimes in the name of Islam. But how can this be explained to a child without causing religious hatred or unnecessary fear?
>
> *Female final year undergraduate (3 year degree), training to*
> *teach children aged 5–11 years, West Midlands*

> Children refusing to play with others due to religion/ethnicity has already been witnessed by myself during placement. I assume it will happen again and I understand how to deal with it although I feel it is an issue because the children are learning this behaviour from home.
>
> *Female PGCE student, training to teach children*
> *aged 5–9 years, London & South East*

> Because we are still in a society where heterosexuality is the "norm" and other sexualities are outside of that "norm". This is shown when we discretely teach sexualities rather than having one lesson where we talk about possible relationships – that could include m-f, m-m, f-f etc. (including family structure). By secluding out sexualities and difference (rather than simply acknowledging and celebrating all possible differences) we are still inferring that heterosexuality is the "norm" and that we have to make the others explicit. Therefore, tackling negative views of sexualities (homophobia/transphobia/biphobia) is difficult and the approach to addressing it is unknown.
>
> *Male undergraduate (4 year degree), training to*
> *teach children aged 5–11 years, East Midlands*

> At primary age I have found that children may display non-heteronormative behaviours and mannerisms however they tend to be too young to identify as LGBT, making it difficult to address homophobia as children may not realise that specific bullying is homophobic if they do not know they are gay etc. or if another child is.
>
> *Female PGCE student, training to teach children*
> *aged 5–11 years, North East of England*

> — I think that there are so many instances where gender stereotypes are present in the schools and it is not noticed and considered normal. It is also something that children encounter a lot at home and if this is something that children are struggling with then this is really going to affect their progress in their education. As a teacher, it is a subject that is really hard to get children to think about what it means to be a particular gender as they are so ingrained in our society and there is not a lot of awareness within schools themselves. I don't expect that there would be a great deal of support in a school for teachers should a situation arise.
>
> *Female PGCE student, training to teach children*
> *aged 5–11 years, North East of England*

> This is frequent at a low level (you can't do that because you're a girl) and almost excepted [sic] so will be hard to know when to confront it
>
> *Male PGCE student, training to teach children*
> *aged 5–11 years, London & South East*

The experience of student teachers shows key apprehensions as they anticipate the commencement of their careers. Readers may want to consider their own views on what newly trained teachers may worry about, what parents and carers may feel apprehension about with their children and what issues they are concerned about in wider society.

I was a pupil in schools in the late 1970s and early 1980s. We used to debate what we would do if the warning sounded for the imminent detonation of a nuclear bomb. It was a real concern, and our teenage discussions often centred around making sure we had enjoyed sex before we died, and standing out in the street to ensure that we were killed immediately and avoided suffering. As it turned out, neither opportunity happened. Into the 1980s we discussed the high-profile government television advertising that told us not to "die of ignorance" from HIV/AIDS, with a tombstone crashing to the floor. Every home was sent literature with this message. Each generation faces its own range of issues, and the situation today is very different from the one in which I grew up.

Perhaps the current visions in society are founded around racism, including non-colour-coded racism (for example, European Union nationals living and working in the UK) and Islamophobia (fuelled by minority terrorist activity). In each generation there seems to be a new threat to undermine inclusion and harmonious living and a new "demon" to scare the population and create stereotypes, encourage prejudice and always provide a reason to highlight division in the news media, undermining an accepting and inclusive society. It is almost as though human beings thrive on identifying the "other" and grouping together to feel a sense of "us" and "them" rather than just "us".

In my own schooling I remember the impact of bullying behaviours that were endemic in the education system. There was what we may term the "low level" general name calling (which in later life I would now term persistent bullying), and then there was the more systematic cruelty that testosterone fuelled young men inflicted on each other. I have sometimes reflected (taking imagery from a sketch by the comedian Victoria Wood) that in my secondary school bullying was part of the uniform.

Using more recent information, collected more formally and systematically, one way in which a sense of difference is highlighted is through bullying behaviours that ensure that some people are treated differently to others, excluded and made to feel inferior. This recent research has explored the issues with children in the relatively early years of their lives, and with the staff who care for them.

Research

In research undertaken in 16 schools in the East of England in 2016 with anti-bullying organisation GR8 AS U R (www.gr8asur.com), members of staff were asked to identify how they help children to learn to be safe and to look after the safety and wellbeing of others. This is a key area of being inclusive and ensuring that no one is excluded, ostracised or treated in a negative way. The responses were coded and grouped, with 145 specific areas identified, and nine participants choosing not to answer. Of the nine, five were teachers, two administrators and two teaching assistants. The results showed that circle time and/or talking with one another were the most used strategies:

> Circle time and/or talking with one another 38
> Role modelling, school ethos and class rules 34
> Through the curriculum (e.g. PSHE lessons) 33
> Assemblies 7
> Using visits or visitors (e.g. police or fire service) 7
> Monitoring or celebrating good behaviour 4
> Systems (e.g. school council, house system or prefects) 4
> Other (fewer than 4 responses) 18

Staff members were also asked in what ways they help children to be welcoming and to accept, value and celebrate difference; in other words, how they encourage children to be inclusive. The results identified:

> Discussions, including circle time 25
> Lessons including RE and PSHE 25
> Role modelling/example/ethos 24
> Cultural activities (including multicultural weeks/days) 17
> None/not sure 17
> Assemblies and collective worship 16
> Celebration of achievements, uniqueness and languages 16
> Diversity books and stories 7
> Instilling British Values 5
> Other (fewer than 4 responses for a particular approach) 27

It is interesting that in response to both questions, members of staff focussed on relationship-based responses including discussion, being a role model and using specific lessons to explore issues. These are opportunities to build bridges, create links and cement connections between individuals.

Reflecting on your own experience of schooling, consider:

- What strategies you feel were effective in addressing situations where division or social exclusion occurred.
- Which members of staff you felt were key in developing a harmonious, inclusive and safe learning and social environment.
- What made you feel included, welcomed and special at school?

Alongside the research undertaken with staff in schools, short interviews were also undertaken with children in the same settings. From the 16 schools in the East of England engaged with the GR8 AS U R project, 161 children took part in face-to-face interviews conducted by the project team. Ninety-two of the children were male, and sixty-nine female. The numbers by chronological age were:

Age 4   31
Age 5   87
Age 6   32
Age 7   10

The mean average age was five years and one month.

The children were asked: What do you like most about coming to school? Their answers are summarised in Figure 1.1.

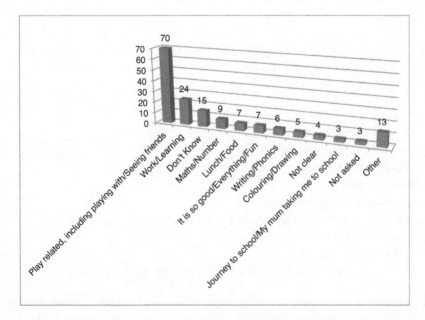

Figure 1.1 Children's responses to the question "What do you like most about coming to school?"

It is very interesting that the children identified social and relational elements as being their favourite aspects of attending school. One child misunderstood the question, and took "coming to school" as undertaking the physical journey itself: they enjoyed that experience with their parent. Whilst the negative construction of the question was not asked, which for ethical reasons is totally appropriate (we did not wish to ask very young children what they particularly disliked about coming to school), it is clear that being included in play, conversation and relationships plays a significant part in children feeling accepted, positive and included in school. This will probably come as no surprise to readers; but it is certainly worth noting. It appears that inclusion matters to children even from their early years.

Exploring a diverse range of aspects of inclusion

This book explores inclusion in a way not commonly found in similar texts. Many books relating to inclusion, education studies and allied areas focus on inclusive education. By this they mean children's special educational needs, and sometimes aspects of disability. A review of the contents lists and indexes of many books shows that inclusion is a niche term, and over past years the niche has narrowed. This book challenges that concept. For us as authors, inclusion is inclusive.

Exploring the chapters

Each chapter stands as an individual consideration of an aspect of inclusion. Cross-references are included to guide readers to other, complementary chapters and pointers to further reading provide additional views and ideas.

In Chapter 2, Philip Woodward explores issues relating to social inclusion, with a particular focus on social class and the work of Bourdieu. He explores the extent to which educational policies and initiatives can reduce social class inequalities in education and the degree to which social class intersects with other characteristics in influencing educational outcomes. He provides a thoughtful consideration of the extent to which we allow, or ignore, the *othering* of those in low social class groups. He is also concerned with the place of the independent sector in the education system in England, and its impact.

Chapter 3 focusses on the global dimension, with Gareth Dart drawing on his extensive experience in sub-Saharan Africa to bring to life issues relating to inclusion. He asserts that there is often no single story and affirms that we need to become more knowledgeable about situations that are "distant" but also reflect honestly on our assumptions about situations that are "near". Gareth suggests that questions of culture and identity are crucial in many contexts with regard to more inclusive practice (including our own culture and identity and our own assumptions about the culture and identity of others).

Wendy Messenger explores learners and learning in Chapter 4, drawing upon her extensive experience in special and inclusive education and as a school governor. She affirms that it is essential to understand the nature of learning and to know the factors that contribute to successful learning. Wendy argues that we need to actively identify barriers to learning in order for them to be overcome, and to take into account diversity and difference with reference to family, culture, ethnicity, religion, socio-economic status, gender and ability or disability, providing rich learning opportunities that do not limit achievement or expectations.

Seán Bracken's discussion of identity in Chapter 5 is distinctive in its focus on multilingualism and the ways in which policy relating to English as an additional language impacts on this. He questions who should be involved in determining what languages a school might wish to include in its curriculum, and what knowledge, skills and values will be required by the teaching workforce in order to facilitate the further enhancement of multilingualism within schools. Seán raises the issue of the resources that will be required to assist in the enhancement of multilingualism and questions how communities external to the school can be included.

Religion and belief provide Ellie Hill the opportunity to consider in Chapter 6 the experience of recent university graduates to reflect on how they experienced university as a safe space to consider issues. Ellie questions how recent graduates view their experiences positively in the area of religion and belief, ethnicity, stereotyping and prejudice, and what we can learn from their experience. She is concerned to explore how university campuses can include safe spaces where key issues of the day can be explored in a safe and constructive environment. She gives voice to recent students, and their responses to engaging with a degree in Education Studies, that has a strong focus on inclusion and inclusive practices.

In Chapter 7, Sharon Smith explores both medical and social models of disability, questioning the use of language, perceptions of ability and disability and whether a more challenging and wide-ranging perspective is required. Drawing on her own personal experiences and research with partners across the European Union, Sharon considers social and medical models of disability and highlights experiences from those with personal experience of specific challenges.

Ruth Hewston's exploration of gender (Chapter 8) is inclusive in its approach to non-binary expressions and experiences of gender. She considers the interaction of gender with a learner's social background and ethnicity; the individual needs of the learner, irrespective of their gender identity; and a setting's culture and ethos in supporting gender equality and diversity, including in relation to the curriculum, teaching and learning, assessment and accessibility to facilities.

In Chapter 9, Jane Owens draws on her own career journey to explore nurturing and mentoring, with a focus on Careers Information Advice and Guidance (CIAG). From an initial plan to become a librarian, to an academic career with patchwork careers alongside, Jane reflects on the impact of guidance and support for young people. Jane presents a powerful argument for the role of educational support in providing life-changing experiences for those with little cultural or social capital.

Sexual behaviours and development are explored by Sophie King-Hill and Richard Woolley in Chapter 10. Sophie has previously worked for the sexual health charity Brook in the UK, and Richard has written about relationships and sex education in the context of primary education. They explore teenage pregnancy and its impact and the importance of understanding the concept of consent alongside sexual identities and behaviours. In particular, they explore how education professionals can be enabled to identify both acceptable and risky sexual behaviours, according to the age and stage of those in their care; how the influence of the media can impact on young people, and what strategies can be used to support healthy development, including positive self-identity; and what is meant by inclusive relationships and sex education.

In Chapter 11, "Inclusion and Teaching Assistants", Teresa Lehane explores her research in the area of how learning support professionals are trained, prepared, supported and deployed and what the aims of learning support are. She notes that research indicates that default and dependency models are likely to work less well and that models based on careful deployment and clear focus are likely to work more effectively. Teresa argues that we are asking a huge amount from Teaching Assistants and their professional work has evolved in a relatively ad hoc way, responding to different drivers, over the last 50 years or so. They have made and continue to make an enormous contribution. We need to think this through fully in the light of current research and knowledge and provide the support that is required.

In Chapter 12, Simon Taylor provides insight as an arts educator with experience in galleries as well as in prison education and a university setting. "Inclusion and the Arts" explores the "safe space" that participatory arts can offer through a non-threatening environment to explore issues and cultivate imagination. Simon discusses issues relating to agency; freedom from constraints; dialogue and discussion; interpretation; being comfortable with ambiguity and debate; and experiential learning and making meaning. He argues for the importance of unexpected outcomes, as using the arts can have wider significance to excluded learners beyond educational progression and development, including social skills, cultural identity, economic status, health and wellbeing.

In Chapter 13, Gwenda Scriven's work on restorative justice explores how we can develop inclusion through healing relationships. She explores opportunities to put key decisions in the hands of those most affected by the wrongdoing; promoting a victim oriented approach in which s/he takes an active role in the restorative process; ensuring that the concerns of the victim are central; and helping the wrongdoer take ownership and responsibility for their own actions. All these areas are central to the concept of restorative practice, to which Gwenda was so committed in her professional life.

In the final chapter, Leela Cubillo considers the role of leadership in taking forward many of the issues and principles outlined in this book, and Richard Woolley explores potential next steps in effective practice, values and vision for inclusion, considering how school leaders are prepared and equipped to understand, appreciate and celebrate difference in their schools and how teachers can be enabled to look beyond the obvious or superficial and see the real needs of children, young people and their families. He concludes that education can be appreciated and celebrated as a transformative experience that enables all people (learners and staff) to feel valued as unique individuals, and to develop in a safe and supported environment.

Using the chapters in this book

Each chapter shares a similar structure, with an opening vignette (a short example or illustration) to whet the appetite and set the scene for the chapter. After an introduction to the chapter's focus, there are variously a collection of primary or secondary research materials, opportunities for reflection and examples presented in research, pause for thought and case study boxes, alongside accompanying narrative and questions to raise interest and issues.

Each chapter concludes with suggestions for developing future practice and policy, in the form of next steps for consideration, and a conclusion. Further reading identifies key texts that can extend and complement the chapter, in addition to the references to published sources used within the book itself.

Readers will note that whilst we share similar formats, and a common editor, our individual voices still come through. We are a diverse team, we work closely together, we have many beliefs and values in common, but yet we are still individuals and are included in our own right. We do not always agree.

Acknowledgements

Thanks are expressed to the project team at GR8 AS U R for undertaking data collection with members of staff and children in primary schools in the East of England, and to the National Lottery *Reaching Communities* funding for their support. (www.gr8asur.com)

Thanks must also be expressed to the student teachers who engaged with the national survey of views on sensitive issues faced in primary education.

Further reading

Woolley, R. (2010) *Tackling Controversial Issues in the Primary School: Facing Life's Challenges with Your Learners.* London: Routledge.

References

Gilligan, C. (1993) *In a Different Voice: Psychological Theory and Women's Development.* Cambridge, MA: Harvard University Press.
Gregory, M. (2000) 'Care as a Goal of Democratic Education', *Journal of Moral Education* 29 (4): 445–461.
Legislation.gov.uk. (2010) *Equality Act 2010.* [Online]. Available at: www.legislation.gov.uk/ukpga/2010/15/contents
QCA. (1998) *Education for Citizenship and the Teaching of Democracy in Schools: Final Report of the Advisory Group on Citizenship (Crick Report).* London: Qualifications and Curriculum Authority.
UN. (1948a) *Universal Declaration of Human Rights*, United Nations. [Online]. Available at: www.un.org/Overview/rights.html (accessed 10 January 2009).
United Nations General Assembly. (1989) *The UN Convention on the Rights of the Child.* New York: United Nations.
Woolley, R. (2010) *Tackling Controversial Issues in the Primary School: Facing Life's Challenges with Your Learners.* London: Routledge.

2   Social inclusion and social class

Philip Woodward

Tyler, like many young men on the estate, had been involved in various "runnings"; however, unlike many of his friends, he had left that behind, and was trying to set up his own business. He had real ability to use computers and write programmes – he was completely self-taught, and he wanted to set up a social enterprise, teaching children to write their own computer games rather than play them. He had no qualifications but he had an infectious curiosity for everything . . . Tyler was determined he was going to university, and he wanted to go to the University of Nottingham. Why? Because he knew that people like him and me found it difficult to get in there . . . He enrolled on an Access course, still determined to go to the University of Nottingham, but half-way through the year he was told that the university would not accept the Access course as he also needed a maths A-level at grade A or A* . . . Tyler did the maths A-level in his spare time – he used books and lectures on YouTube and attended the Access course at the same time. Tyler passed the course, and passed the maths A-Level, but he got a grade B. The University of Nottingham decided to give him a chance despite the B grade . . . [Tyler] is in his first week of lectures. He is so proud of himself, and regularly posts pictures of himself on Facebook, sitting in lectures, in his University of Nottingham sweatshirt, but he often messages me, and tells me about the difficulties he encounters . . . He is doing brilliantly in class, and his studies are going well, but he is struggling with "feeling out of place".

(McKenzie, 2015: 95–97)

Introduction

Recent years have seen marked improvement at different levels of education for many of those who were in the past marginalised. The desire, and pressure, to create a more inclusive society has been reflected in recent legislation in the United Kingdom, in particular through the Equality Act (2010). This foregrounds a range of protected characteristics that are enshrined in anti-discrimination law and aims to ensure that those with the said characteristics are not discriminated against or disadvantaged. Initially, when formulated in a draft stage by the Labour administration, the Act also sought to tackle socio-economic disadvantage through a 'socio-economic duty' aimed at narrowing inequalities. However, this was removed by the subsequent Conservative administration, despite continuing and pervasive socio-economic or social class inequalities, which are consistently mirrored in the education system.

This chapter explores the persistent correlation between social class and degree of educational success. If we are living in a time where all should be included in society and where all are perceived to have equal opportunities regardless of social and economic origins, it seems contradictory that legislation might ignore, or at least diminish, the marked differences that social class engenders. Moreover, dominant public discourse concerning those perceived to be in the lowest social class groups appears to ignore conventions of respect and decency, and 'allows' discrimination on this basis. Those in the lowest groups appear vilified and are consistently blamed for their own failings, not least in terms of educational success. Arguably an acceptance of social class inequalities in educational settings is implicit and is rooted in a discourse that gives primacy to individual or familial cultural explanations for educational success.

To explore some of the issues discussed in the chapter, higher education is examined as a case study to consider the impact of social class on access to university, the application of Bourdieusian social theory and the possibility of intervention.

Inequalities in education: social deprivation or social class?

The correlation between social class position and educational attainment has long been established and discussed in a broad range of sociological literature (Halsey et al., 1980; Halsey et al., 1997; Cassen and Kingdon, 2007; Gewirtz and Cribb, 2009). Whilst over time achievement has improved for many sections of society, including those in different social class groups, a persistent gap remains between those at the bottom and the top end of the social class spectrum (Dearden et al., 2010; Department for Education, 2012). In addressing such differences, a range of sociological explanations have been proposed that, broadly speaking, link to material or cultural explanations. These in turn relate to the *structure* and *agency* debate. This debate hinges between the ways our lives, and so our educational experiences and outcomes, are subject to social forces that are largely beyond our control – *structure* – and alternatively a position that emphasises our degree of choice – our *agency*.

Those suggesting material explanations point to economic reasons to explain inequalities, giving primacy to the inequitable structure of society (Halsey et al., 1980). Some of those adopting cultural explanations suggest that individuals and families lack the appropriate values to embrace education (Douglas, 1964; Sugarman, 1973), giving primacy to human agency. Whilst others suggest they are unable to sufficiently access cultural resources to successfully or equitably participate in the field of education – these approaches acknowledge a combination of structure and agency (Bourdieu and Passeron, 1998).

A broad range of literature explores the nature and significance of socio-economic status or social class. In addition, commentators often point to social deprivation, poverty and the relationship to social exclusion. Many of these terms appear to be used interchangeably, and here it is suggested that an overemphasis on social deprivation or poverty can be overly reductive, diminishing a significant focus on and understanding of the structural significance of social class and its detrimental impact on equality in society. So here it is not suggested that social deprivation or poverty are not significant, but that they are the consequence of a stratified social class system.

Through focussing too much on the educational consequences of social deprivation or poverty, one can lose sight of the way the position of people in such circumstances might be caused by the structure of society. This also might diminish an overview of society as a whole and potentially contribute to a negative label. This seems to be of particular significance when it is suggested that a particular group constitutes a sub-culture or an *underclass*. This appears to remove them from the broad structure of society and positions them as *the other* or *them* (*othering*). This kind of labelling has become prevalent in the media in recent years in the United Kingdom and in the USA (Skeggs, 2005) and has been rightly condemned for the way it vilifies some sections of the working class (Skeggs, 2005; Swann, 2013). This debate is exemplified by Jones (2011) in his examination of social class hatred and labelling in *Chavs* (Jones, 2011). The term *chav*, which stems from a Romany word for child (Jones, 2011), has come to refer negatively to a particular section of the working class and positions them as culturally forming an underclass. This is reminiscent of cultural explanations for inequality (Murray, 1990) and the notion that particular groups have no interest in the wider context of society, and in this case education. These kinds of explanations, which appear to have limited empirical support, at best diminish or reduce the structural significance of social class, and at worst encourage or contribute to a narrative that encourages hatred and ridicule for particular working-class groups. Whilst this kind of discourse might appear benign, it nevertheless may well impact on education policies that give credence to the notion of an underclass (Swann, 2013) at the expense of structural interventions.

Pause for thought

Reflecting on the discussion so far in this chapter, consider:

- Whether you feel social inequality stems mainly from economic differences (advantage or disadvantage) or whether you feel other factors play a part.
- Whether you identify an underclass within your social context and in the region and country in which you live.
- To what extent do you identify social class as existing within the context in which you live? If you do identify it, how does it manifest itself?

What is particularly worrying (Jones, 2011) is the way that labelling and prejudice appear to be increasingly socially acceptable, where in other areas, such as in relation to ethnicity, this kind of treatment would be termed racism and would be both socially and legally unacceptable. Apportioning blame to sections of society for their own circumstances is nothing new, although the venom which working class groups have recently been subject to has been particularly vicious. A good way to question the validity of such cultural and individual accounts is through exploring the reality of working-class life. Here the work of Lisa McKenzie (2015) is of particular significance (see the Research Box later in this chapter); it offers an indispensable insight into the real experiences of working-class communities. In the light of such concerns, one wonders why the Equality Act (2010) did not explicitly provide appropriate protection in relation to socio-economic status.

Defining social class

Social class can be examined within the context of some notable theoretical traditions, including Marxist approaches that look at an economic basis for class and Weberian approaches that, whilst acknowledging economic factors, also introduce notions of status and power (Ritzer, 1996b). In more contemporary philosophical and sociological debate, postmodern approaches negate the significance of social class, suggesting that such a concept is redundant as we create our identity through our consumption (Ritzer, 1996b). However, whilst this is an interesting debate, in the context of educational inequalities outlined below, a working concept or definition of class is required.

Social class can be defined in a number of ways, and such definitions are regularly discussed, contested and adapted over time. In relation to educational research, many practitioners adopt a broadly Weberian approach to social class in terms of an occupational definition that encompasses a range of criteria linked to employment. Weberian conceptions of social class do not wholly give primacy to economic factors, such as ownership of the means of production (as Marx suggests) or remuneration, but also consider issues of status or standing that an occupation confers as well as the degree to which political power or influence is linked to a particular role (Ritzer, 1996b; Woodward, 2000). In the last hundred years or so, two occupational schemes have been utilised by the British government when defining social class. At the turn of the last century, the Registrar General Classification (Iannelli, 2007; Savage et al., 2015) divided the population into six occupational groups – although these also broadly corresponded to middle-class (non-manual) and working-class (manual) occupations. Whilst this was ostensibly based on occupation, this also linked to perceived cultural characteristics of different groups and hence formed a cultural and moral judgement (Savage et al., 2015).

The second approach, The National Statistics Socio-Economic Classification (NS-SEC) system (Office for National Statistics, 2009), is derived from earlier work by Goldthorpe (1980) and is the government scheme employed from 1998 in its current form. This also utilises an occupational class-based system, but broadens the occupational groups to reflect changes to the labour market and differences between employers and employees (Savage et al., 2015). This scheme also encompasses a classification that considers not only pay, but also factors such as tenure, autonomy at work, promotional prospects and life chances as a means to assess relative accumulated advantage (Rose et al., 2005). However, it still distinguishes a clear hierarchy, ranging from employers and higher managerial occupations in group one, to those who have never worked in group eight (Office for National Statistics, 2009). Adaptations of this scheme are broadly used internationally (Savage et al., 2015).

Whilst the different occupational schemes have clear variations, as they have tried to reflect the changing nature of the labour market, they nevertheless point to clear hierarchies in terms of employment. This does present its own problems, however, as making a comparison across time is made more difficult. Comparisons are also problematic, as no consensus emerges linking particular classifications to the middle or working class. In research that utilises the Registrar General Classification, some studies define the middle class in terms of classes one and two, who constitute the professional and managerial groupings (Power, 2000), whilst other studies also add class three non-manual (Connor, 2001). However, whilst helpful in identifying broad and often significant differences between occupations, these definitions do not capture the complexity, dynamism and nuances of the impact of social class in different contexts and situations. One might suggest that regardless of scheme, it is the relative benefit of those at the top and the relative disadvantage of those at the bottom that is significant.

Bourdieu and the concept of capital

One way to explore these kinds of differences lies in considering the relative significance of, and access to, economic, cultural and social resources, or *capital*, that can be employed to gain advantage in different circumstances. These ideas stem from the work of Pierre Bourdieu and have been used extensively within educational research to examine different explanations for experiences and inequalities.

Bourdieu suggests that those in higher social class positions wish to define themselves as such through distinctive cultural norms that distinguish them from lower social class groups – he terms this *distinction* (Bourdieu, 1998: 22). Not only do specific cultural traits provide such distinction, but they also facilitate the exclusion of those lacking such culture and maintain privilege and social inequality (Winkle-Wagner, 2010). However, this is not solely rooted in an economic relationship of advantage; Bourdieu points to a more conscious process where individuals through their agency gain advantage. This links to the quite specific notion of *cultural capital*, which refers to the mechanisms by which individuals are socialised into accepting specific class-based norms, values and tastes which will later enable social reward and increase power. Bourdieu highlights three different types of cultural capital:

> Cultural capital can exist in three forms: in the embodied state, i.e. in the form of long-lasting dispositions of the mind and body; in the objectified state, in form of cultural goods (pictures, books, dictionaries, instruments, machines, etc.), . . . and in the institutionalized state, a form of objectification which must be set apart because . . . [as] . . . in the case of educational qualifications, it confers entirely original properties on the cultural capital which it is presumed to guarantee.
>
> (Bourdieu, 2003: 47)

The child can then utilise such embodied cultural resources during schooling. Objectified cultural capital could include educational resources such as books. Institutionalised cultural capital links to both values within education and the qualifications obtained from education. This is not simply a case of passing on economic capital, but involves familial and educational socialisation in terms of cultural resources. In this way, social class background can be transmitted from one generation to another.

Education compounds this situation as educators, consciously or not, reward high status cultural capital, which can be inferred from the clear correlation between higher socio-economic groups and higher educational qualifications and higher status, better paid employment (Ball et al., 2002; Metcalf, 1997). The corresponding credentials that are accrued can then be utilised to gain high status and rewarding employment. This gives the illusion of meritocracy in terms of outcomes.

To further explain the situation of dominance, Bourdieu introduces the concepts of *field* and *habitus*. A *field* is an arena where cultural knowledge of specific "tastes, dispositions, or norm, is both produced and given a price" (Winkle-Wagner, 2010: 7). It could also be described as a "type of competitive marketplace in which various kinds of capital . . . are employed and deployed" (Ritzer, 1996a: 406). For example, both family and education, or the school, are examples of a *field*. Within a specific field, and multiple fields exist, cultural capital has a particular value. Consequently, within a given context, or field, such as a college, "a field is simultaneously a space of conflict and competition . . . in which participants vie to establish monopoly over the . . . effective capital within it" (Bourdieu and Wacquant, 1992: 17). The value given to any cultural capital is dependent on the particular field in question. What is high value in one field may not be appropriate to another.

Bourdieu also employs the concept of *habitus* to describe the way that individuals internalise specific dispositions, rules and values through their primary socialisation. Swartz terms this a "deep structuring cultural matrix" (Swartz, 1997: 104), whilst Vandenberghe terms the process as "deposited [or] incorporated within individuals" (Vandenberghe, 2002: 8). What does seem significant is the way that such deep-rooted notions of value operate, at least partly at a subconscious level. They also seem to create a habitus that is reluctant to change and to some degree might constrain agency. Habitus also represents the internalisation of a specific social class position. Consequently, "one's seemingly benign dispositions are actually integral to the reinforcement and creation of the social stratification and one's location within it" (Winkle-Wagner, 2010: 9). So social class position, dispositions and corresponding disadvantage "can be transmitted intergenerationally through socialization and produce forms of self-defeating behaviour" (Swartz, 1997: 104). As Bourdieu suggests, "habitus . . . is embodied" (Bourdieu, 1998: 437). Habitus links to the degree of cultural capital one 'recognises', even if subconsciously, in a given social situation.

In tandem with cultural capital, social capital is also explored by Bourdieu as "a capital of social connections, honourability and respectability" (Bourdieu, 1998: 122). Social capital is employed, or functions, through networks. This also links to the acquisition and utilisation of cultural capital through social connections.

Whilst a range of students can acquire cultural capital in education, those who have a head start through familial influence – of cultural tastes valued by higher social class groups – will gain more reward. So choosing to send your child to prestigious institutions, such as Eton or Harrow, will have the effect of both recognising cultural capital acquired through familial influence as well as adding additional cultural capital from the institution. Whilst it might appear that students have 'gifts' or skills, in reality they are rewarded for the tasks that are derived from their social class origin: "school today succeeds, with the ideology of natural 'gifts' and innate 'tastes', in legitimating the circular reproduction of social hierarchies and educational hierarchies" (Bourdieu and Passeron, 1998: 208).

In Bourdieusian terms social class, whilst a central concept, is often 'implicit', and Bourdieu does not engage in his own classification system (Crossley, 2011). Whilst Bourdieusian approaches are often broadly linked to a critical or Marxist perspective, Bourdieu moves to a position that, one can argue, is closer to Weber, where he considers that a range of factors contribute to a 'social class' position, also suggesting that social class is relational. These factors link to the access, acquisition and utilisation of different types of capital (Crossley, 2011) and better reflect the nuances of a highly differentiated labour market. Some of these differences are discussed below.

The impact of social class can be experienced across a broad range of educational sectors and levels. Here higher education forms the focus for social class inequalities. Such inequalities can be considered in relation to participation rates as well as the different higher education institutions (HEIs) attended and the choices made in relation to this. Here a particular focus is provided in relation to choice.

Higher education and social class

Participation rates for higher education have improved significantly over the last 60 years and currently 40 per cent of the population attends university, compared with less than 4 per cent in 1950 (Social Mobility Commission, 2016). Whilst this is encouraging, increased access has not removed inequalities in terms of participation and access to the most prestigious HEIs. The current picture points to improved participation for ethnic minority groups, women and students aged over 30 (Crawford and Greaves, 2015; Higher Education Statistics Agency, 2012; Social Mobility

Commission, 2016). However, those in lower social class groups have not benefitted in the same way. Only a minority of those from the poorest groups attend university and, when doing so, they do not access degrees that provide the most benefit in terms of subsequent employment (Social Mobility Commission, 2016). This concern over participation and choices linked to social class form the basis of the following section.

Despite some claims that differential advantage in higher education is decreasing, a large scale research project in the early 1990s points to a continuous and consistent link between higher social class and attendance at prestigious institutions over time. In addition, those from lower social class groups are also more likely to attend as mature students (Egerton and Halsey, 1993). This links to attendance at lower prestige institutions, probably as a result of lower school-leaver qualifications, which is corroborated by HEFCE, who demonstrate that those who are less likely to participate are also found in more deprived neighbourhoods and achieve poorer GCSE results (Higher Education Funding Council England, 2005). The situation in the early 1990s suggests multiple disadvantages, with those in lower social class groups being less likely to attend university, less likely to obtain prestigious qualifications and more likely to attend later in life (Egerton and Halsey, 1993).

In terms of prestige, entrants to first degrees from lower socio-economic groups disproportionately enter post-1992 universities, and correspondingly are not proportionally represented in 'old' (pre-1992) universities (Keep and Mayhew, 2004). Also, participation from those with manual backgrounds is low with limited access to Oxbridge. The economic significance is clear: those from higher socio-economic backgrounds enter higher status institutions and gain more favourable employment opportunities (Keep and Mayhew, 2004). Additionally, "candidates applying to 'blue chip' jobs [jobs in companies with highly rated stocks] from Oxford University were 29 times more likely to be appointed to such work than someone applying from a 'new' (post-1992) university" (Keep and Mayhew, 2004: 308). Government attempts to investigate and redress such a situation have been rebuked by the independent sector and labelled as 'social engineering' (Lucas, 2003).

Pause for thought

Reflecting on your own experience of the education system:

- Do you feel that social class plays a part in people's decision to apply for university?
- What other factors affect the decision to apply for university?
- What factors might make accessing higher education easier for some individuals and less easy for others? Might it be possible to mitigate such factors?

Research

Getting By: Estates, Class and Culture in Austerity Britain (McKenzie, 2015) is a good example of the way that ethnographic research can shed light on the reality of the way a group of people experiences life. McKenzie's study provides rich insight into the lives of those living on the St Ann's housing estate in Nottingham, in the Midlands in the UK. Whilst many different areas are highlighted in the study, an interesting perspective is provided regarding education.

McKenzie notes the significant levels of deprivation and social disadvantage experienced on the housing estate, with high numbers of children eligible for free school meals (FSM), a proxy measure for low income. She also identifies high levels of children with special educational needs and disabilities and a population who are predominately from ethnic minority backgrounds. Nevertheless, within this context, it is highlighted that the four primary schools on the estate deliver a high standard of education, considered outstanding in some areas, with pupils performing particularly well in standardised tests at age 11. However, as children get older and move into secondary education, their educational performance diminishes, and by the age of 16 "only 7 per cent of pupils at the local comprehensive school in St Ann's achieved five or more 'good' GCSEs" (McKenzie, 2015: 41).

This certainly suggest that the children from the estate have the potential to achieve a great deal in education, but in their later years of compulsory schooling something is preventing this. This might give the impression that those from St Ann's do not value education as highly; however, the example of Tyler, detailed in the vignette at the start of this chapter, questions this. Tyler is one of the young adults who participated in the research. When he met McKenzie, he was fascinated by the prospect of going to university and keen to engage in conversation over different aspects of university life.

Reflecting on the research undertaken by McKenzie:

- What factors impact on Tyler's experience?
- What factors might affect children's attainment after the age of 11? Could anything be done to support their continued progress?
- What does the example of Tyler tell us about the impact of formal and informal education for particular learners?

Now consider the issues that form your own perspective:

- What are your views on moves to expand the higher education system and make university degrees accessible to many more people?
- What issues might first generation students encounter that are different to those whose parents attended university?
- Thinking of the different ways of identifying social class detailed above, which definitions do you feel are most appropriate?

Whilst a number of different measures are used to determine social class in different jurisdictions, one can nevertheless consider some of these criteria as more or less significant in terms of progression to higher education. Thomas and Quinn note the significance of economic capital – wealth – but also highlight access to cultural capital. What appear to be significant in this respect are parental experiences of education and the way these influence access to higher education.

Thomas and Quinn (2007) note that while income is significant as a determinant of progress, parental education in higher education is arguably more significant. This is demonstrated through evidence from Canada and the US. In contrast, those who are 'first generation' entrants, whose parents have no experience of higher education, are less likely to progress to higher education, but are also more likely to experience higher education in a negative way through feeling "a lack of entitlement" and diminished self-confidence (Thomas and Quinn, 2007: 77). What seems to be suggested is that those from lower social class groups, with less likelihood of having a parent with high levels of education, find it more difficult to 'fit in' and adapt to university life as they lack the middle-class cultural capital to do so.

Strategies to mitigate the impact of social class inequalities

Addressing inequalities in education is a complex process. At its broadest this requires a consideration of the intersection between variables such as social class, special educational needs and disability (see also Chapters 4 and 7), ethnicity and gender (see Chapters 6 and 8) and the extent to which these impact on outcomes. Simultaneously, one also needs to consider these variables in relation to the specific ways that they are impacted by familial and structural factors that sit outside of education as well as the impact of formal education. Evidently, educational policy alone cannot tackle structural inequalities. However, some policy initiatives and legislation in the United Kingdom have sought to support those who are most disadvantaged.

The extent to which one can mitigate for significant structural social class-based inequalities is debatable, certainly in a United Kingdom context where 7–8 per cent of the school population is privately educated and gains a significant and demonstrable advantage. State intervention has the potential to address such inequalities, and in the extreme could challenge the model of private education; however, in the current and recent political climate this seems unacceptable to the major political parties. The emphasis in policy has also shifted, in relation to HE entry, from *equal opportunities* to *widening participation* (Matheson and Woodward, 2015).

Subsequent to the general election in the United Kingdom in 2010, the coalition government (Conservative and Liberal Democrat) introduced a raft of legislation, some of which claimed to address socio-economic inequalities in education, and significantly aimed to diminish the gap between 'rich' and 'poor'. The primary policy offered to deliver this was the *Pupil Premium*. This initiative targets 'disadvantaged' pupils in England and provides additional 'ring fenced' funding to schools to provide support. The funding is aimed at families that are entitled to free school meals (FSM), used as a proxy for low income, as well as other vulnerable groups (Abbott et al., 2015). The way the funding is utilised is at the discretion of the schools, although a range of advice is available through the Education Endowment Foundation. However, schools have to show impact in relation to learner outcomes. The policy commenced in 2011–12 with schools receiving £488 per free school meal eligible pupil (Lupton and Thomson, 2015), but this figure has risen to £1,320 (primary) and £935 (secondary) for the 2016–17 financial year (Department for Education, 2017). Whilst funding was intended for those eligible, during early implementation it appears to have been utilised where required to compensate for diminishing funding rather than as a focus for disadvantaged pupils (Lupton and Thomson, 2015). However, the tightening of regulations and the need to show impact as part of the regulatory framework aims to address this issue.

Although the real impact of *Pupil Premium* is quite difficult to assess at this relatively early stage of implementation, nevertheless some research points to advantages and limitations in practice. It is evident that schools do not restrict the use of *Pupil Premium* funding to the targeted pupils, but often utilise this to support those with educational rather than purely economic need (Carpenter et al., 2013). When *Pupil Premium* funding is utilised it funds a range of interventions, although these are often associated with additional support from staff through extra teaching, tutoring and mentoring (Carpenter et al., 2013). What is noteworthy is that the kinds of interventions identified by schools were those being implemented in any event (Carpenter et al., 2013), but *Pupil Premium* funding provides extra support for these. On this basis, one might reasonably assume that these extra resources could make an important impact on learning.

Whilst the aims of the *Pupil Premium* may be laudable, on an early assessment it seems to have delivered limited 'overall' impact in terms of pupil outcomes. In overall terms it has managed to redistribute funding to poorer pupils to some extent, although this distribution is not uniform and does not adequately address the full extent of social class inequalities (Lupton and Thomson, 2015). Within a broad context, Lupton and Thomson note that *Pupil Premium* is "a rare example of investment in the life chances of disadvantaged children among a broader range of policies which have reduced family incomes and depleted services" (Lupton and Thomson, 2015: 10). Consequently, any assessment of *Pupil Premium* must be tempered by wider structural considerations. In a time of austerity and currently significant spending cuts in social welfare and overall education budgets, it is unlikely that *Pupil Premium* can dent social inequalities. *Pupil Premium* might 'grab' the political headlines, but it can do little to reduce profound educational inequalities when other aspects of pupils' lives are significantly disrupted.

Moving forward

In order to work towards inclusion with regards to social class we need to consider:

- The extent to which educational policies and initiatives can reduce social class inequalities in education. Can education make an impact independently? Or do we need to consider broader policies linked to social welfare and communities?
- The degree to which social class intersects with other characteristics in influencing educational outcomes.
- The extent to which we allow, or ignore, the *othering* of those in low social class groups. Consequently, we need to ensure that individuals and institutions do not subsequently discriminate on the basis of social class.
- How we can avoid the potentially exclusionary impact of different forms of *capital?* Additionally, how can we help pupils, and families, to access and utilise different resources?
- How we might diminish the way the independent sector monopolises elite higher education.

Conclusion

This chapter has explored the way that social class continues to have an impact on education, both in the United Kingdom and elsewhere. Although social class is not the only criteria that impacts on educational outcomes and experiences, and the intersection with other criteria is important, it nevertheless appears to be highly significant in determining the resources that can be accessed and the opportunities that are available.

Whilst to a large extent the structure of society might limit the extent to which educators can make an impact, this does not mean that agency is redundant. It is our duty as educators to challenge negative labelling and prejudice both in relation to social class and elsewhere. Learners' resources can be augmented through local and national policy initiatives and individuals empowered to maximise the benefit from education. However, education does not operate in a vacuum, and social welfare and the redistribution of wealth are also concerns that need addressing if we are to offer genuine equal opportunities to all in society. It is the role of the educator to remain critical, challenge orthodoxy and advocate for all.

Further reading

Archer, L., Hollingworth, S. and Mendick, H. (2010) *Urban Youth and Schooling*. Maidenhead, Open University Press: McGraw-Hill Education.

Gewirtz, S. and Cribb, A. (2009) *Understanding Education: A Sociological Perspective*. Cambridge, Polity.

Savage, M., Cunningham, N., Devine, F., Friedman, S., Laurison, D., McKenzie, L., Miles, A., Snee, H. and Wakeling, P. (2015) *Social Class in the 21st Century*. London, Pelican.

Ward, M. (2015) *From Labouring to Learning: Working-Class Masculinities, Education and De-Industrialisation*. Basingstoke, Palgrave Macmillan.

References

Abbott, I., Middlewood, D., and Robinson, S. (2015). "It's not just about value for money: A case study of values-led implementation of the Pupil Premium in outstanding schools." *Management in Education*, 29(4), 178–184.

Ball, S. J., Davies, J., David, M., and Reay, D. (2002). "'Classification' and 'judgement': Social class and the 'cognitive structures' of choice of higher education." *British Journal of Sociology of Education*, 23, 51–72.

Bourdieu, P. (1998). *Distinction: A Social Critique of the Judgement of Taste*, R. Nice, translator. Cambridge, MA: Harvard University Press.

Bourdieu, P. (2003). "The Forms of Capital", in A. Halsey, H. Lauder, P. Brown and A. Wells (eds.), *Education: Culture, Economy and Society*. Oxford: Oxford University Press, pp. 46–58.

Bourdieu, P., and Passeron, J.-C. (1998). *Reproduction in Education, Society and Culture*, R. Nice, translator. London: Sage.

Bourdieu, P., and Wacquant, L. (1992). *An Invitation to Reflexive Sociology*. Chicago: University of Chicago Press.

Carpenter, H., Papps, I., Bragg, J., Dyson, A., Harris, D., Kerr, K., Todd, L., and Laing, K. (2013). *Evaluation of Pupil Premium*. London: Department for Education.

Cassen, R., and Kingdon, G. (2007). *Tackling Low Educational Achievement*. York: Joseph Rowntree Foundation.

Connor, H. (2001). "Deciding for or against participation in higher education: The views of young people from lower social class backgrounds." *Higher Education Quarterly*, 55(2), 204.

Crawford, C., and Greaves, E. (2015). *Socio-Economic, Ethnic and Gender Differences in HE Participation*. BIS Research paper No. 186. London: Department for Business Innovation and Skills.

Crossley, N. (2011). "Social Class", in M. Grenfell (ed.), *Pierre Bourdieu: Key Concepts*. Durham: Acumen, pp. 87–99.

Dearden, L., Sibieta, L., and Sylva, K. (2010). *The socioeconomic gradient in child outcomes: The role of attitudes, behaviours and beliefs from birth to age 5: Evidence from the millennium cohort study*. Available at www.ifs.org.uk

Department for Education. (2012). *GCSE and Equivalent Attainment by Pupil Characteristics in England, 2010/11*. London: Department for Education.

Department for Education. (2017). *Pupil Premium: Funding and Accountability for Schools*. London: Department for Education. Available at www.gov.uk/guidance/pupil-premium-information-for-schools-and-alternative-provision-settings. Accessed on 23 April 2017.

Douglas, J. (1964). *The Home and the School*. St Albans: Panther.

Egerton, M., and Halsey, A. H. (1993). "Trends by social class and gender in access to higher education in Britain." *Oxford Review of Education*, 19(2), 183–196.

Equality Act 2010, c.15. Available at www.legislation.gov.uk/ukpga/2010/15/pdfs/ukpga_20100015_en.pdf. Accessed on 28 July 2015.

Gewirtz, S., and Cribb, A. (2009). *Understanding Education: A Sociological Perspective*. Cambridge: Polity.

Goldthorpe, J. (1980). *Social Mobility and Class Structure in Modern Britain*. Oxford: Clarendon Press.

Halsey, A. H., Heath, A. F., and Ridge, J. M. (1980). *Origins and Destinations: Family, Class and Education in Modern Britain*. Oxford: Oxford University Press: Clarendon.

Halsey, A. H., Lauder, H., Brown, P., and Wells, A. (eds.). (1997). *Education: Culture, Economy and Society*. Oxford: Oxford University Press.

Higher Education Funding Council England. (2005). *Young Participation in Higher Education*. Bristol: Higher Education Funding Council England.

Higher Education Statistics Agency. (2012). *Statistics – Students and Qualifiers at UK HE Institutions*. Bristol: Higher Education Statistics Agency.

Iannelli, C. (2007). "Inequalities in entry to higher education: A comparison over time between Scotland and England and Wales." *Higher Education Quarterly*, 61(3), 306–333.

Jones, O. (2011). *Chavs: The Demonization of the Working Class*. London: Verso.

Keep, E., and Mayhew, K. (2004). "The economic and distributional implications of current policies on higher education." *Oxford Review of Economic Policy*, 20(2), 298–314.

Lucas, G. (2003). "Beware the social engineers." *The Times Educational Supplement*, 7 November, p. 25.

Lupton, R., and Thomson, S. (2015). "Socio-economic inequalities in English schooling under the coalition government 2010–15." *London Review of Education*, 13, 4–20.

Matheson, C., and Woodward, P. (2015). "Post-Compulsory Education: Further and Higher Education", in D. Matheson (ed.), *An Introduction to the Study of Education*. London: Routledge, pp. 259–291.

McKenzie, L. (2015). *Getting By: Estates, Class and Culture in Austerity Britain*. Bristol: Policy Press.

Metcalf, H. (1997). *Class and Higher Education: The Participation of Young People from Lower Social Classes*. London: Council for Industry and Higher Education.

Murray, C. (1990). *The Emerging British Underclass*. London: Institute of Economic Affairs.

Office for National Statistics. (2009). *The National Statistics Socio-Economic Classification (NS-SEC)*. Office for National Statistics. Available at www.ons.gov.uk/about-statistics/classifications/current/ns-sec/index.html. Accessed on 3 October 2009.

Power, S. (2000). "Educational pathways into the middle class(es)." *British Journal of Sociology of Education*, 21(2), 133–145.

Ritzer, G. (1996a). *Modern Sociological Theory*. New York: McGraw-Hill.

Ritzer, G. (1996b). *Sociological Theory*. New York: McGraw-Hill.

Rose, D., Pevalin, D., and O'Reilly, K. (2005). *The National Statistics Socio-Economic Classification: Origins, Development and Use*. London: Palgrave Macmillan: HMSO Crown Copyright.

Savage, M., Cunningham, N., Devine, F., Friedman, S., Laurison, D., McKenzie, L., Miles, A., Snee, H., and Wakeling, P. (2015). *Social Class in the 21st Century*. London: Pelican.

Skeggs, B. (2005). "The making of class and gender through visualising moral subject formation." *Sociology*, 39(5), 965–982.

Social Mobility Commission. (2016). *State of the Nation 2016: Social Mobility in Great Britain*. London: HMSO.

Sugarman, B. (1973). *Sociology*. London: Heinemann Educational Books.

Swann, S. (2013). *Pupil Disaffection in Schools: Bad Boys and Hard Girls*. Farnham: Ashgate.

Swartz, D. (1997). *Culture and Power: The Sociology of Pierre Bourdieu*. Chicago: University of Chicago Press.

Thomas, L., and Quinn, J. (2007). *First Generation Entry into Higher Education: An International Study*. Maidenhead: Open University Press.

Vandenberghe, F. (2002). "Obituary symposium: The sociological ambition of Pierre Bourdieu." *Radical Philosophy*, 113(May/June), 7–9.

Winkle-Wagner, R. (2010). *Cultural Capital: The Promises and Pitfalls in Educational Research*. Hoboken, NJ: Wiley Periodical.

Woodward, K. (2000). *Questioning Identity: Gender, Class, Nation*. London: Routledge: The Open University.

3 Education and global dimensions

Gareth Dart

A young teenager herds his father's cattle on the edge of his village at the end of the 20th century, 25 km up the road from the headquarters of one of the richest mining organisations in Africa and indeed the world. Each day he watches his friends go to school and one morning, against his father's wishes, he joins a class of 6- and 7-year-olds in the local primary school. A decade later, having leapfrogged his way through the various standards and levels of school, he studies as a student teacher in a college of education and points out to me the fields where his father's cattle still graze as I give him a lift into town. He burns with a quiet enthusiasm to get into schools as a teacher so that he can listen to the stories of pupils like himself and inspire them to get on in their education.

Introduction

This chapter challenges our propensity to see the world in one dimension (our world), or even in two (our world; their world). The chapter title deliberately uses the plural form 'dimensions' because the world is arguably more multi-dimensional in nature than ever. Single dimensional thought only allows one point of view or, at best, travel from one point to another. Two dimensional thought at least allows for an expanded horizon but only ever in a space that is flat with no texture. Multi-dimensional thought is challenging because it can be disorienting (think of looping the loop in an aeroplane) but has the potential for richer experiences and understandings. Using examples from my experiences in Botswana, a country in southern Africa, juxtaposed with examples from literature in Western contexts, this chapter will ask you to explore a number of issues that illustrate the manner in which the world challenges our assumptions about the nature of difference and differences.

The two examples are examples often discussed with regard to inclusive practice: the education of groups from minority cultures and the impact of identity on acceptance. We start by examining perceptions of cultural norms through research about the educational experiences of minority groups, and then explore challenges to identity as personified in the experiences of people with characteristics that set them apart from mainstream norms. Throughout we reflect on how these discussions might shape our practices as students of education and educators in Western contexts.

Pause for thought

Before continuing, read the vignette at the start of the chapter again. Are there any statements in that account that challenge accepted perceptions? You will find my response to that question at the end of this thought box. But before you read that, write down or discuss with another your own thoughts.

If you have access to the internet, view the TED talk by Chimamanda Ngozi Adichie, 'The danger of a single story.' You can find it here: www.ted.com/talks/chimamanda_adichie_the_danger_of_a_single_story

Consider:

- What examples of a 'single story' does Adichie reveal that she held about others? What examples does she tell of the 'single stories' that others had about her and Africa?
- What single stories are told about you that should be challenged? What single stories might you tell about others that you need to challenge yourself about?

Now consider my own response to the vignette from the start of the chapter:

Three issues stand out for me:

- The first is the mention of the wealthy diamond-mining company (DeBeers). Botswana was one of the fastest growing economies in the world for at least two decades, and though these rates have recently fallen, there is still huge wealth in the hands of the state (much of which is spent on social development) and a small percentage of individuals (Carnoy, Chisholm & Chilisa 2012: xii).
- The second is the fact that as a boy Thuto was kept at home. The gender gap in educational engagement in Africa tends to get discussed in terms of girls not accessing schools. In Botswana, it was the boys who were kept at home because of the need to look after the family cattle (Mgadla 2003: 144). (In recent times, the great majority of both girls and boys attend school in Botswana.)
- Thirdly, and you would have to know quite a lot about education in Africa to spot this one, is the fact that Thuto sees himself as being a teacher who will 'listen' first and foremost. Perceptions of teachers in Africa (reinforced by much of the literature) posit African education as teacher-centred and African teachers as didactic and authoritarian (Stephens 2012: 95).

Consider which elements stood out for you and how your own reflections have similarities or differences with my own.

Learning about global issues

Bourn (2014: 23) notes that learning about global issues is sometimes seen as being adequate to allow for a genuine understanding of the global context to emerge. However, he argues that:

this is not necessarily the case. Learning about poverty and development could be seen as being about other places and peoples, of no direct relevance to the teachers and learners.

This chapter illustrates how our thinking about 'other places and peoples' would benefit from deeper understandings and reflection and that these can be fostered by considering more carefully the 'other' that often goes by outside, or even inside, our own (classroom) door. To take it a step further, and going back to the analogy of looping the loop in the introduction, we could represent this as a diagram that encourages us to use our growing understandings of one space to more critically interrogate our assumptions of another:

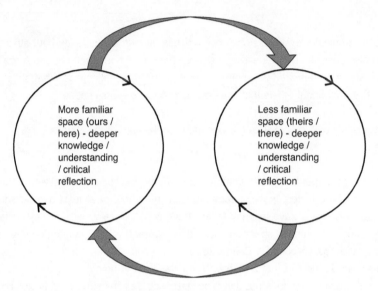

More familiar space (ours / here) - deeper knowledge / understanding / critical reflection

Less familiar space (theirs / there) - deeper knowledge / understanding / critical reflection

Figure 3.1 Engaging with global dimensions: a model for enquiry

Nussbaum (1997: 9–11) suggests that we need to develop three skills or capacities: a critical examination of ourselves and our own traditions; a capacity to see ourselves as human beings mutually bound by ties of recognition and concern; and an empathetic skill that allows us to consider what it might be like to walk in the footsteps of someone different from ourselves. This chapter argues that this 'someone different' might be a distant other but might equally be a close-by other and that either has the potential to teach us about the other, and ourselves.

The impact of local culture on national education practice

A superficial reading of statistics and reports on education regarding the global south can lead us to think that there is a single picture of provision. For example: 58 million pupils are still out of school globally; gender parity has been achieved in lower secondary education in 48% of countries; adult literacy rates have increased by 4% between 2000 and 2015 (UNESCO 2015: xii–xiii). These, of course, hide many variations with regard to educational processes and outcomes, not just between countries in the global south, but within countries. In Botswana, one issue that has been of ongoing concern for a number of decades is the poorer achievement of learners from minority groups in the west of the country.

Case study

Whilst working in teacher education in Botswana I accompanied my colleague Kelone (Khudu-Petersen) to a school where she was conducting fieldwork for her PhD. The school was in a 'remote area' in Botswana, and the children who attended it were from 'remote area dweller' families. The terms 'remote area' and 'remote area dwellers' (RADs) are official policy terms in Botswana. They indicate a certain set of environmental circumstances (accessibility, distance from common amenities, level of resources) and also have cultural connotations in that RADs are predominately from minority groups in Botswana culturally different to the majority Setswana peoples. Many RADs are from San/Bushmen or BaKgalagari groups who live in parts of the Kalahari Desert region.

After a long drive along dirt roads, we arrived at a village close to the school we were to visit in the morning and found Kelone's relatives. The village was small and 'traditional' in that nearly all the dwellings were small rondavels made of mud with grass thatch for roofing. There was no mains electricity, and as night fell, we sat round a large fire outside Kelone's cousin's rondavel drinking hot, sweet tea and eating large slabs of bread and jam from the supplies we had brought for the family. Outside the light of the fire the night was pitch black but full of the noises of the village children playing all manner of games that involved clapping, shouting, chanting, dancing and singing.

The next morning, we arrived at the school a few kilometres away and spent the morning in the class with the same children who had been so lively and active the night before. Here, in the new, modern school building, they were as if dumb, silently sitting at their desks, barely whispering responses to the questions posed by the increasingly frustrated teacher.

Reflecting on this account, consider:

* What might have been the factors that caused such a change in behaviour from the children between their village context and their school context?

Despite a number of attempts by educational authorities to improve education experiences for minority groups such as the San and BaKgalagari of western Botswana, there remains concern regarding poor educational experiences and outcomes (Sekere 2011). Issues include:

* low achievement rates;
* high rates of drop-out;

- abuse of a variety of sorts in schools and boarding hostels towards the learners;
- unwillingness of teachers to engage with local communities; and
- the apparent reluctance of parents to engage with the schools and staff.

Khudu-Petersen's work (2007, 2012) explores the role of Intercultural Community Arts and Education (ICAE) projects in challenging and addressing some of the practices and beliefs that have shaped educational experiences of these minority groups. She notes:

> Botswana's education system presents *the Batswana* culture as the culture of the nation and uses their language, *Setswana* (alongside English), as a medium of communication for all. This arrangement has been identified by researchers as a point of grievous disadvantage for members of non-*tswana* ethnic groups.
>
> (2012: 195)

Differences between the cultural norms expressed in school settings and local cultures include those regarding the nature of childhood itself and ideas about the relationship between child and adult. An authoritative, didactic style is often privileged in Tswana-dominated school culture (Tabulawa 2013: 91). In schools, this has led to relationships based on overtly expressed disrespect for local norms and practises, including violence against pupils, and in particular the sexual harassment of female pupils. Khudu-Petersen reports the manner in which this situation has been internalised by some who, rather than seeking to challenge such practices in school, blame themselves:

> Another group . . . accepted the teachers' actions as based on legitimate authority. In interviews learners justified poor academic results and harsh punishment received, like being caned, as a result of 'giving wrong or no answers' or for 'arguing in class.'
>
> (2012: 198)

In studies in similar schools, Ketsitlile (2011) and Sekere (2011) note how school staff apportion blame to the families for not being willing to come to school to discuss the progress of their children. Khudu-Petersen (2012) describes how parents have become suspicious of being treated as culturally inferior when they do visit schools, with the blame for their children's perceived lazy attitude, stupidity and bad behaviour being laid at the door of that culture's deficient norms and practices.

With the agreement of all parties in an attempt to bridge the gap the between the school and local communities, Khudu-Petersen set up an ICAE initiative bringing arts practitioners from the village into classrooms and curriculum-based lessons to share their knowledge and skills. She acted as a mentor to the teachers, modelling and supporting the integration of such activities into the formal curriculum. Despite the issues reported in the research above, all sides agreed to the project, expressing the desire that it would lead to an improvement in stakeholder engagement and interactions. There was also a clear wish for a better understanding across the cultures. Interestingly, this bridged a gap between the locally valued apprentice style of traditional education in the village communities and the more didactic, authoritarian Tswana culture typified in the schools.

Case study

Storytelling and crafts near the Kalahari Desert

Craftspeople with skills in carving, pottery, singing, dancing, poetry, wire sculpting and dramatisation were engaged. The account below comes from a session involving a local story teller (Khudu-Petersen 2012: 200):

> When the learners were settled, the storyteller gave each child a piece of grass to stick in their hair. She then asked children to explain why the gesture was necessary. The children were excited and eager to answer: In the local culture, it is a taboo to tell stories during daytime because it is believed the activity could offend the ancestors. If you still do so, some evil could befall you. But the gods could be appeased by sticking a piece of grass in the hair during daytime storytelling. The elderly lady told the . . . story in a lively voice, making gestures and encouraging children to join her. The learners . . . happily chanted and dramatised as they were shown . . . The story involved a song, which . . . the whole class sang with her. The atmosphere was informal and relaxed.
>
> At the end of the story, the teacher took over. She divided the children into groups and allocated them a scene of the story to perform in mime to the class. . . . The class carried out the task with great enthusiasm. The children were then asked to remain in their groups and to draw significant characters and actions of the story.
>
> In the next lesson, the groups were guided by the teacher to paint a background for their scenery . . . All the while, the children were singing the song of the story. In a following Setswana lesson the children comprehended scenes of the story, in an English lesson they answered simple questions of understanding regarding the story. At the end of the mini-project, the teacher was impressed by the interdisciplinary nature of the activity, the level of learner participation and the quality of the artworks. She confessed that these were the best paintings her class ever made.

The account above comes from a school on the edge of the Kalahari Desert, involving pupils whose parents grew up still learning the skills necessary to live as hunter-gatherers and keepers of cattle. It would seem as distant an experience as most of us could reasonably contemplate. Consider:

- What might we learn from Kelone's work with regard to the situation in the UK's schools?
- Are there some general principles?
- Are there even some specific ideas?

Gypsy, Roma and Traveller (GRT) achievement in Leeds, UK

> We recognised a need in our Early Years Foundation Stage to reach Gypsy, Roma and Traveller families isolated from our provision and who may not know what we can offer. We needed to develop relationships strong enough to overcome the barriers created by

experiences of sustained prejudice and to ensure Gypsy, Roma and Traveller children feel safe and cared for.

(Leeds City Council 2015)

Staff began to explore needs of children in the Foundation Stage (FS) by developing a resource pack. This was also shared with parents, carers and other members of the Gypsy, Roma and Traveller (GRT) community. The teacher participated in focussed in-service training in order to develop the skills needed to support children from GRT families. The resources that were developed were not only used in the classroom, but also taken home so that the children and their parents/carers could use them whilst travelling. On their return, the photos and the album of 'talking photographs' that they had developed became a focus for discussion and sharing of information:

> The impact of this work was a visible increase in self-esteem among both children and adults from the Gypsy Traveller community, an increased attendance leading to higher literacy levels plus higher levels of achievement in Personal, Social and Emotional Development (PSED). The children also had an increased interest in reading, particularly sharing books reflecting Traveller heritages and cultures while the parents developed a greater willingness to speak with teachers. The culmination of the positive links and renewed relationships was a week long, whole school focus on Gypsy and Traveller lifestyle and culture, when a family brought their old wagon/vardo and horse to the school playground for all to see confirming the high status given to this project, and to the community. Practitioners were effective when they were seen to: . . . know or find out about the community and local dynamics; involve Gypsy, Roma and Traveller fathers and mothers; take time to listen to people from different backgrounds and to be open about differences of language and approach; make time to listen to parents and their feelings and concerns; ensure parents have regular opportunities to add to children's records; ask, and respond to the views of Gypsy, Roma and Traveller parents on the care and education they provide.

(Leeds City Council 2015)

This account comes from a school that could be like a school near you or indeed a school that you went to. The experiences described could well be close to home. The juxtaposition of the Botswana case study and the one above involving GRT learners in a British school is not meant to imply that the experiences of the participants in each are equivalent. However, they do allow us to engage critically with our understanding of what we might learn about the complexities of more distant (in terms of knowledge, space and culture) contexts than our own and to examine how we might learn more about our own closer experience. Or, as Edwards and Usher (2008: 158) put it, such an endeavour 'challenges traditional continuities and bounded senses of identity through an increased and intensified engagement with the other.'

Consider:

- What sort of discussions would parents from the Botswana schools in Kelone's work have with parents from the UK initiative above?
- What might we learn from each of the examples?
- In what way have the examples challenged your thinking?

By engaging with these questions, you are using the model of enquiry set out in Figure 3.1 earlier in this chapter.

Skin deep can be very deep indeed

In this section, using two single case studies, we are going to consider the multi-dimensional challenges that differences in individual characteristics can make, in this case albinism and aspects of the experiences of people in what is often termed the Lesbian, Gay, Bisexual and Transgendered (LGBT) community. We will briefly consider what albinism is, some of the challenges faced by people with the condition in southern Africa, particularly in an education context, and consider what their experience might have to tell us about our perceptions of difference in our own contexts using a particular question of identity from within the LGBT community.

Albinism occurs the world over, but its prevalence in populations varies widely (Baker, Nyathi & Taylor 2010). It is caused by a reduction or absence of the pigment melanin. Skin cancer is a major risk as with reduced levels of melanin the skin is highly susceptible to burning. Because melanin is also needed for the proper development of the optic nerve, all people with albinism also have problems with sight: these include short sightedness and sensitivity to bright light (Lynch & Lund 2011).

Case study

Tiro (now a teacher but formerly a student of mine) describes his childhood experiences and his albinism. He uses the word 'albino' to describe himself:

> During standard one [Tiro] sat at the back of the class, self-conscious, taking very little in, being teased by many of his classmates. Often treated very harshly by his teachers who would sometimes beat him for not being able to copy from the board or understand what was going on in class. After standard one he left school and went to the cattle post for two years as a herd boy. This he enjoyed as he was away from the stress of the classroom. Herding cattle under the hot Botswana sun is not the ideal choice of occupation for an albino but Tiro notes that it is a common occupation for

young albino boys to enter into (later in life he developed serious skin cancer that he continues to need regular radiation treatment for, often having to travel long distances to access it). It was only after strong encouragement from his family that he decided to re-enter school.

(Dart, Nkanotsang, Chizwe & Kowa 2010: 84)

Tiro's elderly aunt motivated him to return to school, and pointed out that the American doctor in the village lived in a beautiful house and had a nice car. She noted that he was white (like Tiro) and suggested that Tiro might succeed like the doctor had done. Tiro returned to school and:

fearlessly entered into fights with anyone who mocked him or opposed him in any way and became infamous in the village for leading a gang of young boys. He refused to be bowed by the punishments of teachers and determined that he was going to succeed. This effort was not without cost: he developed bad stomach ulcers and eventually was referred to a psychiatrist who prescribed drugs to try and calm his temper.

(Dart, Nkanotsang, Chizwe & Kowa 2010: 84)

This is a very clear illustration of the difference between 'integration' and 'inclusion.'

Entering secondary school he was determined to prove himself by being at the top of the class for every subject. This he achieved by gathering around him fellow pupils who were academically bright and with whom he discussed the lessons of the day. He also continually approached his older sister at home for help. He placed himself in positions in the classroom where he could see the board more easily (he did not get any spectacles until he came to the teacher training college).

(Dart, Nkanotsang, Chizwe & Kowa 2010: 84)

Reflecting on these experiences, Tiro notes that although attitudes have changed over time, he still detects barriers in many social contexts. When he visits government offices, he still senses that members of staff feel reticent to give him their full attention until he has had the opportunity to show his own personality and skills, establishing himself as a 'normal' person. He still feels that he has to earn the respect of others and show that he deserves the consideration that others receive as a right.

Lynch and Lund (2011: 3) note that 'Children and young people with albinism are doubly vulnerable: they are visually impaired and their striking difference in appearance, looking "white" in a black population, makes them the target of bullying and name-calling.' There is a third vulnerability in that the lack of pigmentation in the skin makes them highly vulnerable to skin cancer, an ever present danger in a context such as Botswana where the sun is often very hot and there is little access for many poorer people to adequate sunscreen protection. Indeed, Tiro's story above illustrates all these challenges. For the purposes of this chapter, however, we concentrate on the issue of identity caused by the 'striking difference' that Lynch and Lund note above.

This chapter has stressed from the start that it is dangerous to assume that there is a 'single story' even when a group of people share a common characteristic, and this is as true for people with albinism as it is for any others. Nevertheless, there are certain commonly experienced situations for people with albinism in countries in southern Africa that relate to beliefs and practices about their identity and that shape their engagement in society. These range from questions as to their identity as fully fledged human beings to their legitimate claims to know the experiences of being 'black' Africans.

Blankenberg (2000) provides a deep and wide ranging discussion of the complexities of identity and albinism in the African context, and in particular the added layer of complication caused by having albinism during the time of apartheid in South Africa. She notes that a fundamental issue of identity is the belief amongst many that people with albinism inhabit a world somewhere between the living and the dead, which is of course a major threat to their being identified as 'human.'

In Setswana (the official language of Botswana), the common term for someone with albinism is 'leswahe': the prefix 'le' in the language denotes a thing rather than a human. In Dart, Nkanotsang, Chizwe and Kowa (2010: 40), Tiro noted that:

> It is said that albinos simply disappear. He reflected that this might be because in the past a mother who gave birth to such a child would be encouraged to put the baby in a pot with some herbs and place it out into the forest for the animals to take. . . . Also albinos traditionally would not be seen at the normal community celebrations such as weddings, village meetings and funerals. Even today he states that if he walks through a village many small children will spit on their own clothing, a practise that arises from the belief that spitting out saliva when you see an albino ensures that any babies that you might have will not be albino.

Although many of these beliefs are starting to disappear, particularly in towns and cities, Tiro claims that he still needs to 'prove' himself to strangers as a full human being worthy of respect when he walks into an office or other public space instead of being granted that respect. This giving of respect, symbolised mainly through forms of speech and particular manners, is a very important part of Tswana society, and normally those who fail to show it are considered to be extremely rude (Denbow & Thebe 2006).

For most of us reading this chapter, understanding the perceptions of people with albinism with regard to its impact on their identity in southern parts of Africa will be very far from our grasp, and the very brief discussion above will barely scratch the surface. Nevertheless, the fact that an issue is complex should certainly make us wary of claiming any great understanding, but not of being willing to try and comprehend it in at least a little more detail. Similar issues are likely to confront us in other guises if we are interested in deepening inclusive practices, even in contexts that we are more familiar with.

LGBT perspectives from the context of Canada

One such context which might help shed a mutual light is the experience of certain groups in the LGBT community. Speciale, Gess and Speedlin (2015) use autoethnography (an ethnographic study of themselves) to examine their experiences as lesbians in the LGBT counselling community:

> When I first became licensed as a mental health counselor, I planned to offer a few hours per week of pro bono counseling at a local LGBTQQIA community center located on a college campus. I contacted the director of the center and she responded immediately, seeming delighted by my eagerness to hang up my rainbow-clad shingle. I was beside myself with excitement when she invited me to the center for a tour and to meet the students before I set up shop. As soon as I arrived, however, I noticed that the once cheerful and excited demeanor the director had portrayed in e-mails had become more distant and muted. I introduced myself, shaking her hand with excitement, and began to ask her about the current needs of the center and its constituents. She answered with caution, in one- or two-word responses; it was clear that something had upset her. I slowed myself down, thinking that I may have overwhelmed her with my rapid-fire enthusiasm. She then began to ask me questions – What are your thoughts about lesbian and gay people? How do you feel about same-sex marriage? Do you use religion in your counseling sessions? – and I perplexedly answered, wondering what I had done to initiate such palpable skepticism. I quickly understood when she asked me the final question, "Now, how do you think you'll be able to relate to LGBT individuals?" In that moment, I realized that when she had seen me – long blonde hair in curls, mascara, and a close-fitting cardigan – she saw a White, feminine, cisgender woman and had presumed I was straight, and that I had no idea what it meant to be marginalized, oppressed, or silenced.
>
> (Speciale, Gess & Speedlin 2015: 261–262)

Pause for thought

Reflecting on the account from Speciale, Gess and Speedlin above, consider:

- What caused the initial dysfunction of the relationship between the writer and the director of the counselling centre? (Note: the word 'cisgendered' means to have 'a gender identity or perform a gender role society considers appropriate for one's sex.')

  (Crethar & Vargas 2007: 59)

- What was the director expecting to see?
- Referring back to Tiro's experiences above, what does he imply office workers are expecting to see when he enters the room?
- What do both stories have in common with regard to the views of the outsiders (director/office worker) on the subject's (counsellor/Tiro) identity?
- How do these reactions hinder inclusive practice?

Have you ever been in a similar place to any of the four characters (outsiders/subjects)?

Moving forward

In order to work towards inclusive practice in the context of global dimensions, we need to consider:

- That there is often no single story.
- That we need to become more knowledgeable about situations that are 'distant' but also reflect honestly on our assumptions about situations that are 'near.'
- That there might be occasions when becoming more knowledgeable about the one gives added insight about the other, as long as we pass that potential insight through a critical lens.
- That questions of culture and identity are crucial in many contexts with regard to more inclusive practice (including our own culture and identity and our own assumptions about the culture and identity of others).

Conclusion

Almost inevitably, this chapter falls into its own trap. It assumes a 'single story' of its readership, that for readers the experiences of people with albinism are 'other/there' whilst those of GRT pupils in UK schools are 'ours/here.' I might be entirely wrong (indeed, I hope that in some cases I am) and that there are some readers for whom the experience of a child in a classroom on the edge of the Kalahari Desert is far more real to them than of a student in the LGBT community in a western university.

I hope that some of the underlying principles will be of use whatever your position as a reader (for example, Nussbaum's notion of the need for criticality, awareness of mutuality and empathetic open-ness or the visual framework presented in Figure 3.1) in regard to the manner in which we consider the manner in which actions, assumptions and beliefs of ours/others' work toward the exclusion or inclusion of ourselves/others, be they here or there. Distance does not have to be geographical. It can be many dimensional – social, cultural, economic, attitudinal, biological – which is why we need to think and act in regard to multiple dimensions when considering more inclusive practice, both glob-ally and locally, for learners, including ourselves.

Further reading

The Great Dance – A Hunter's Story – www.isuma.tv/intezam/the-great-dance-a-hunters-story
    This documentary follows the lives of three hunters from a community similar to the one discussed in Kelone's work earlier in the chapter. Although it is not explicitly about education or inclusion, it raises questions about the impact of assimilation of cultures. Towards the end, one of the men talks of his desire for a 'modern' education for his children but also the opportunity for them to learn about their traditional skills, knowledge and culture.

The Traveller's Times – http://travellerstimes.org.uk/About.aspx
    This a good source for information, news and ideas regarding the GRT community. Its founding editor, Damian Le Bas, is from a Traveller family and an Oxford graduate, and so a clear example of the challenge to the 'single story.'

Search for the term 'albinism' at https://curve.coventry.ac.uk/open/searching.do for various items about aspects of albinism in southern and eastern Africa from very practical, pictorial information pamphlets, to radio drama to empirical research papers.

Check out the Global Alliance for LGBT Education (GALE) – www.lgbt-education.info/en/association/mission 'GALE is a learning community focusing on education about lesbian, gay, bisexual and transgender (LGBT) issues. We promote the full inclusion of people who are disadvantaged because of their sexual orientation, sexual identity and their expression by identifying, enhancing and sharing educational expertise. The membership of the community is free and open to anyone actively involved in education about LGBT issues.'

References

Baker, C., Lund, P., Nyathi, R. & Taylor, J. (2010) The myths surrounding people with albinism in South Africa and Zimbabwe. *Journal of African Cultural Studies*, 22(2), 169–181. DOI: 10.1080/13696815.2010.491412

Bhopal, K. & Myers, M. (2009) Gypsy, Roma and Traveller pupils in schools in the UK: Inclusion and 'good practice'. *International Journal of Inclusive Education*, 13(3), 299–314.

Blankenberg, N. (2000) That rare and random tribe: Albino identity in South Africa. *Critical Arts*, 14(2), 6–48. DOI: 10.1080/02560040085310081

Bourn, D. (2014) *The theory and practice of global learning*. DERC Research Paper No. 11 for the GLP. London: IOE.

Breidlid, A. (2013) *Education, indigenous knowledges, and development in the global south*. London: Routledge.

Carnoy, M., Chisholm, L. & Chilisa, B. (2012) *The low achievement trap: Comparing schooling in Botswana and South Africa*. Cape Town: HSRC Press.

Crethar, H. C. & Vargas, L. A. (2007) The counselor's companion: What every beginning counselor needs to know. In Gregoire, J. & Jungers, C. (Eds.), *Multicultural intricacies in professional counseling*. Mahwah, NJ: Lawrence Erlbaum, p. 59.

Dart, G., Nkanotsang, T., Chizwe, O. & Kowa, L. (2010) Albinism in Botswana junior secondary schools – a double case study. *British Journal of Special Education*, 37(2), 67–77.

Denbow, J. & Thebe, P. C. (2006) *Culture and customs of Botswana*. Westport: Greenwood Press.

Edwards, R. & Usher, R. (2008) *Globalisation and pedagogy: Space place and identity*. Abingdon: Routledge.

Florian, L. (2014) Inclusive pedagogy: An alternative approach to difference and inclusion. In Florian, K. & Hausstatter, R. S. (Eds.), *Inclusive education twenty years after Salamanca*. Oxford: Peter Lang, pp. 219–229.

Ketsitlile, L. (2011) San junior secondary students' home-school literacy disconnection: A case study of a remote area dweller school in Botswana. *Diaspora, Indigenous, and Minority Education*, 5(2), 88–99.

Khudu-Petersen, K. (2007) *Intercultural Arts Education: Initiating Links between Schools and Ethnic Minority Communities Focussing on the Kweneng West Sub-District in Botswana*. Unpublished doctoral dissertation, United Kingdom. Scotland, Edinburgh University.

Khudu-Petersen, K. (2012) The involvement of ethnic minority communities in education through the arts. *Intercultural Arts Education in Action*, 6(6), 194–208.

Leeds City Council. (2015) Gypsy Roma Traveller Achievement Service: Good Practice guide. Available at: http://travellerstimes.org.uk/UserFiles/Resources/GRTAS-good-practice-guide.pdf (Accessed: 10/04/2017).

Lynch, P. & Lund, P. (2011) *Education of children and young people with albinism in Malawi*. London: Commonwealth Secretariat. Field report for Commonwealth Secretariat. [Online]. Available at: https://curve.coventry.ac.uk/open/file/aced2b3f-539d-2ef0-1b2c-7adccfc29ab9/1/Education.pdf (Accessed: 10/04/2017).

Mgadla, P. T. (2003) *A history of education in the Bechuanaland Procterate to 1965*. Lanham, MD: University Press of America.

Nussbaum, M. (1997) *Cultivating humanity: a classical defense of reform in liberal education*. Cambridge, MA: Harvard University Press.

Sekere, B. (2011) Secondary education for san students in Botswana: A new xade case study. *Diaspora, Indigenous, and Minority Education*, 5(2), 1559–5706.

Speciale, M., Gess, J. & Speedlin, S. (2015) You don't look like a lesbian: A coautoethnography of intersectional identities in counselor education. *Journal of LGBT Issues in Counseling*, 9(4), 256–272. DOI: 10.1080/15538605.2015.1103678

Stephens, D. (2007) *Culture in education and development: Principles, practice and policy*. Oxford: Symposium Books.

Stephens, D. (2012) A critical overview of education for sustainable development with a particular focus on the development of quality teacher education in Sub-Saharan Africa. In Griffin, R. (Ed.), *Teacher education in Sub-Saharan Africa: Closer perspectives*. Didcot: Symposium Books, pp. 72–91.

Tabulawa, R. (2013) *Teaching and learning in context: Why pedagogical reforms fail in Sub-Saharan Africa*. Dakar: CODESRIA.

UNESCO. (2015) *Global monitoring report, education for all 2000–2015: Achievements and challenges*. Paris: UNESCO.

4   Learners and learning

Wendy Messenger

Tariq, aged 7, is of Bangladeshi heritage; English is an additional language for him. He comes from a large family and attends mosque school most evenings. His parents are keen for him to do well at school and support him with homework whenever they can, although his mother is still learning English.

Introduction

This chapter explores what we mean by learners and learning with reference to schooling and education. The notion of diversity and difference between learners as well as commonalities between them will be considered. With this in mind, the ideas surrounding inclusive policies and practice will be considered alongside some of the dilemmas and tensions associated with them.

It is widely acknowledged that most humans have the capacity to learn, whether they are children or adults; Bruner (1960) believed that anyone could be taught to do anything given the right kind of support. If learning is the ability to acquire new knowledge, skills and understanding through experience or being taught, then the conditions under which these processes can take place are very much the business of education professionals, parents/carers and the learners themselves. Most societies globally have provision for an education system whereby children attend educational settings that, for some, are from as early as two or three years old until sixteen or eighteen, and in some cases longer. It is also widely acknowledged that the most powerful influences on children's lives in terms of learning and education are likely to be their parents or carers, and so their significance to and influence on a child's ability to learn cannot be overestimated. Furthermore, some parents may choose to educate their children at home through 'home schooling'; according to Hopwood et al. (2007) home educated children are represented across all phases of schooling in the UK with the majority being white British, although there are also high proportions of Gypsy, Roma and Traveller children.

Factors affecting learning

Learning takes many forms, including cognition, social learning and physical learning. Whilst Piaget (1952) considered the child themselves to construct their own learning from their environment around them and progress through a series of cognitive stages, Vygotsky (1978) emphasises the importance of social interaction with a 'more knowledgeable other' who can help support the child in the zone of proximal development where optimum learning takes place.

Pause for thought

Using your own experience and knowledge of schools and other learning environments, consider:

- What factors contribute to successful learning for children?
- How do schools and parents facilitate successful learning? Can you think of specific examples?
- A time when you learned something quickly. What influenced your ability to be able to do this?
- Think about something you have recently learned. Using Bloom's taxonomy (see Figure 4.1), try to identify the layers of learning. How did the dispositions discussed below help you to learn?

1 Knowledge (acquiring information/remembering);
2 Comprehension (understanding);
3 Application (using and applying);
4 Analysis (identifying and analysing patterns);
5 Evaluation (comparison of ideas).

Figure 4.1 Bloom's taxonomy of learning

According to Bertram and Pascal (2002), positive dispositions to learn can be defined as frequent habits of thinking and doing, and include such attributes being curious, self-motivated, resilient and independent. We can all think of either children or adults who may display these dispositions in abundance and who are indeed successful learners; therefore, it is important to understand how these dispositions can be nurtured and what factors may inhibit their development. Bloom (1956) suggested there were layers to learning, and his taxonomy (Figure 4.1) illustrates how learning can become embedded.

The best learning occurs when the learner has been able to go through all five stages. Education professionals will be frequently mindful of these stages when planning learning experiences in order for the learner to have exposure to them. It is clear there is a relationship between these stages of learning and the learning attributes mentioned above, because successful learning will take place when there is a positive interaction between both.

All learners have common needs in order for them to learn, and children and young people in particular have very specific ones. Consider the list of such needs detailed below and think about ways in which these needs might be met.

All children need:

- to feel safe emotionally and physically;
- to have secure attachments;
- to enjoy a stable home life;

- to have a nutritious diet;
- to be healthy physically and emotionally;
- to feel they belong and to experience positive relationships;
- to feel listened to; and
- to understand information they are given and make sense of concepts and ideas they are learning.

According to Maslow's hierarchy of needs (1968), the need to feel safe is one of the basic human needs, which if unmet prevents the ability for a person to reach their full potential. Twemlow et al. (2002) suggested the factors that influenced a child feeling safe included the quality of the caregiver relationship, the degree of exposure to family violence, good relationships with peers and family and the presence of a 'safe haven', as well as a sense of belonging. Furthermore, any presence of emotional, sexual or any other form of abuse would be influential. Moore and McArthur (2016) conducted a study in relation to what Australian children thought about feeling safe and how they experienced feeling being safe. The children defined safety as the absence of unsafe people and experiences and things. Importantly, the children distinguished *feeling safe* from *being safe* and gave examples of when they had experienced one without the other. They believed adults were often too focussed on making things safe rather than ensuring the children felt safe at the same time (2016: 5). Furthermore, the children sometimes discussed safety in relation to power and particularly with reference to bullying. It is important to remember that all forms of physical, emotional and sexual abuse, as well as some online activity, including engagement with social media, are normally associated with imbalances of power. John Bowlby's seminal work on attachment theory (1969) has led to a greater understanding of the need for all children to have secure, stable attachments. Attachment can be described as an emotional bond to a 'significant person' who responds sensitively and appropriately to the needs of the child. Recent developments in neuroscience have led to a greater understanding of the significance of attachment in relation to brain development. There is now strong evidence to suggest that the development of some of the neural pathways in the brain of a child who has experienced poor attachment or trauma may remain under-developed, which may lead to possible social and emotional difficulties. Attachments not only form within the family but are desirable within a professional capacity within education as well and may take the form of a key worker, teaching assistant or teacher.

Good nutrition has long been identified as necessary for healthy physical and emotional development. The World Health Organisation (2016) regards childhood obesity as one of the most serious global health challenges for the 21st century, and poor diet lacking sufficient balance of nutrients may impede cognition and therefore learning. Parenting has a large role to play in ensuring children adapt healthy eating habits and lifestyles, and schools also support and educate children in leading a healthy life.

Bronfenbrenner (1979) considered the process of human development and suggested that it was influenced by an interaction between the individual and their environment. His Ecological Systems Theory (Figure 4.2) helps to exemplify some of the influences on children's development and learning. Bronfenbrenner suggests these systems interact with each other as well as with the child interacting with them.

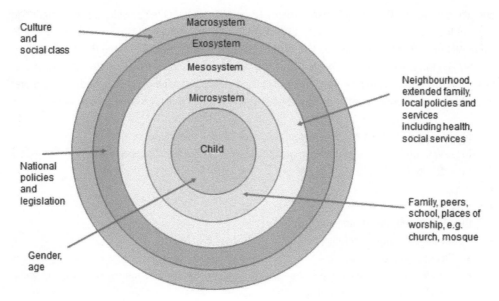

Figure 4.2 Ecological Systems Theory

Source: Bronfenbrenner, 1979

Pause for thought

Using Bronfenbrenner's Ecological Systems Theory (Figure 4.2), consider the experience of Tariq (in the vignette at the start of this chapter) and Molly (below).

Think about all the layers of influence in their lives and how this might have an impact upon their learning.

Molly, aged 13, has four younger siblings and lives with her mother, who has two jobs in order to support her children. This means Molly is often left to care for her brothers and sisters whilst her mother is at work. They live in a neighbourhood where there is much social and economic deprivation, and Molly often feels unsafe.

How useful is the theoretical model in helping you to reflect on their experience?

What other aspects of the factors might influence a child's experience and could potentially be added to the model?

Learning and difference

All children need to be taught in a way that is relevant and appropriate to their age and ability in order for them to learn and engage in the learning processes identified above. In order for this to take place, not only is it necessary to consider the commonalties between learners, but also the diversity and differences. The Ecological Systems Theory (Bronfenbrenner, 1979) provides a good insight into some of the factors that have an impact upon diversity and difference between learners and ability to learn. All human rights legislation, including the *United Nations Convention on the Rights of the Child* (1989) and the *United Nations Convention on the Rights of Persons with Disabilities* (2006), identifies difference in relation to race, gender, disability and ethnic and religious background. Furthermore, in England, the schools inspectorate Ofsted (2016: 34) extends this list further and includes:

- pupils with disabilities and those who have special educational needs (SEND);
- those with protected characteristics, including Gypsy, Roma and Traveller children as defined by the Equality Act (2010);
- boys;
- girls;
- the highest and lowest attainers; and
- disadvantaged pupils, including
  - looked after children;
  - pupils known to be eligible for free school meals (i.e. those who may be experiencing social and/or economic disadvantage); and
  - those attending alternative provision.

Diversity and difference can be considered in relation to 'the difference from the norm', and according to Lawson et al. (2013), they are often referenced by disadvantage or deficit, particularly when they refer to disability or special educational needs. This may be problematic, however, because there is an assumption that everyone understands what the norm is, and that we are identifying diversity in terms of 'otherness'. Booth et al. (2011: 23) view diversity in terms of respecting and valuing others and recognising the contributions they make *because* of their individuality. Growing diversity in societies generally has been reflected in the education systems globally. In many countries, fairly stable and apparently homogenous populations and family structures are no longer necessarily the norm. Figure 4.3 shows the ethnic groups in England and Wales in 2011.

Pause for thought

Consider the statistical profile shown in Figure 4.3.
   What implications does this data raise in relation to education and schooling?
   Consider issues that relate particularly to:

- newly arrived children and families
- language
- cultural differences
- educational achievement
- identity
- religion

Are there other factors that might be relevant when considering the data?

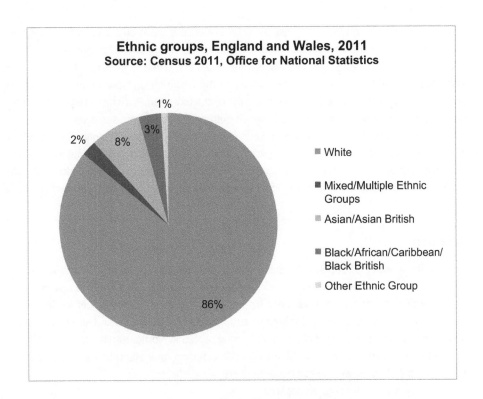

Ethnic groups, England and Wales, 2011
Source: Census 2011, Office for National Statistics

- White
- Mixed/Multiple Ethnic Groups
- Asian/Asian British
- Black/African/Caribbean/ Black British
- Other Ethnic Group

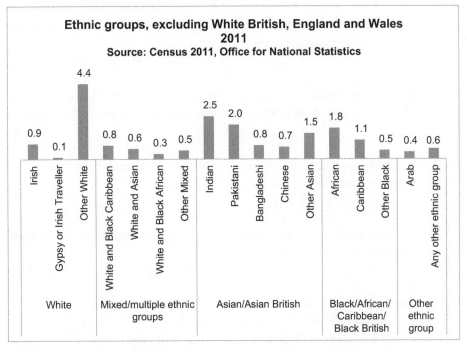

Ethnic groups, excluding White British, England and Wales 2011
Source: Census 2011, Office for National Statistics

Figure 4.3 Ethnicity in England and Wales

Source: Office for National Statistics (2011)

It is often acknowledged that the most powerful influence in children's lives is the family, and therefore understanding the family make-up and ensuring it is valued and acknowledged are important aspects of inclusive practice in education. Differences and diversity in terms of different types of family help us further to understand the context for the whole child. Types of family include the nuclear family, extended family, lone-parent family, restructured family (which may include step-parents and/or step-children) and families in which both parents are of the same sex.

Family income, social status and occupation are also complex factors that influence the lives of children; Frederickson and Cline (2015) suggest that children who have disabilities are more likely to live in workless households. This may be because it is difficult for parents to sustain work whilst caring for a child with a disability. Cultural differences can also have a large impact upon children's learning.

Research

Consider the research undertaken by Bloomer and Hamilton (2014) entitled *Challenges and barriers in primary school education: the experiences of Traveller children and young people in Northern Ireland*. It was commissioned by the Northern Ireland Commissioner for Children and the Equality Commission for Northern Ireland to assess the adequacy and effectiveness of education provision for Traveller children and young people in Northern Ireland.

The research participants were 63 Traveller children from rural and urban areas. Through interviews, the children were asked about their experiences of school.

An overview of the findings shows that:

- Some children discussed that their dislike of school stemmed from how they were treated by fellow pupils in terms of bullying and racial prejudice.

(Bloomer and Hamilton, 2014: 7)

- For some children, attending school and learning to read and write was important, but Traveller and family traditions inhibited them from pursuing educational opportunities.

(2014: 8)

- Many travellers noted how their traditions and 'way of life' could impact on their school life, for example, absence from school to attend family gatherings.

(2014: 8)

- One boy noted his desire to start working within the family business, stating 'Travellers don't like staying in school too long'.

(2014: 9)

Consider how the needs of Travellers can be embraced in schooling.

What challenges and opportunities might arise?

The National Curriculum for England (DfE 2014: 4.2) states that:

Teachers should take account of their duties under equal opportunities legislation that covers race, disability, sex, religion or belief, sexual orientation, pregnancy and maternity,

and gender reassignment . . . and lessons should be planned to ensure there are no barriers to every pupil achieving.

Children and young people who have special needs and disabilities have been a particular
focus of legislation and government guidance for a long time, and it is interesting to consider
how the language has changed over time, particularly with reference to labelling such pupils
(see also Chapter 7 on Dis/ability and Chapter 11 on Teaching Assistants and Inclusion).
Farrell (2014: 58) defines labelling as 'a way of summarising a perceived characteristic or
attribute of a person or a group in a word or a phrase'. Labelling within the context of special
educational needs and disability is strongly related to the medical and social model of disability whereby the former views the child as having problems which need to be treated and the
latter takes into consideration the child's wider social environment, including discrimination,
with regard to meeting their needs. Over time, the language has changed from labels that
imply deficit and problems that need to be overcome to ones that imply meeting needs. The
Warnock Report of (1978) and the subsequent Education Act of (1981) for the first time used
the term special educational needs.

In contrast, consider the 'categories of handicap' that were associated with the Education
Act of 1944 and compare this to the 'broad areas of need' in the Code of Practice (Department
for Education and Department of Health 2015: 97 (Table 4.1).

Using the information in Table 4.1:

- Compare both lists and consider the differences in the use of language.
- Do you consider that either or both lists have the potential to encourage and maintain
  mind-sets associated with discrimination and segregation?
- What might be the implications of the terminology with reference to the child's potential
  for learning?
- How do you think these labels influence expectations of teachers and parents/carers?

Table 4.1 'Categories of handicap' and broad areas of need

Categories of handicap Education Act 1944	Broad areas of need Special Education and Disabilities Code of Practice 2015
• Blind • Partially sighted • Deaf • Partially deaf • Delicate • Diabetic • Educationally sub-normal • Epileptic • Maladjusted • Physically handicapped • Children with speech defects	• Communication and interaction • Cognition and learning • Social, emotional and mental health difficulties • Sensory and/or physical needs

The dilemma of difference

Booth et al. (2011) suggest that by using labels, even using the term 'special educational needs' can lead to a lowering of expectations towards groups of children. They suggest this practice can lead to fragmentation of provision in attempting to address the diversity of learners. Norwich (2007) goes further and suggests that in relation to children with special educational needs, a system has been constructed in an effort to meet their needs, but in so doing this has the effect of reinforcing exclusionary practices within mainstream schools because of its focus on difference, and yet there is a need to recognise difference in order to meet individual needs.

Exclusion or segregation could take the form of education in a different physical location, for example in a special school or unit. But it could also take the form of being grouped by ability or need and taken out of the classroom to be taught on occasions.

Pause for thought

Consider the settings listed below in relation to the dilemma of difference. What might be the advantages and disadvantages in relation to learning?

- special school
- residential schooling for specialist provision
- setting or grouping by ability in a classroom
- intervention groups whereby children are taken out of their regular class for a short period of time before returning.
- individual support within the classroom

Norwich (2010) acknowledges the tension between the educational values of meeting individual needs and promoting inclusion for all in his international study examining the dilemma of difference in England, the USA and the Netherlands. Dilemmas existed in the identification of needs, placement in educational provision and within the curriculum. Kerins (2014) also identified dilemmas in relation to resources and teacher expertise.

Booth et al. (2002, 2011) consider it to be unhelpful to contextualise inclusion with reference to an aspect of student identity such as impairment or ethnicity. Rather, students should be seen as having multiple, complex identities and should not be 'categorised' by one identity alone. Consider their views below with reference to diversity and think about how this may be enacted and what challenges may arise:

Inclusive respect involves valuing others and treating them well, recognising the contributions they may make to a community because of their individuality as well as through positive actions. Diversity encompasses everyone, not just those seen to depart form the illusory normality, however its use is sometimes corrupted in this way so that diversity becomes linked to *otherness*, those not like us . . . Diversity is a rich resource for life and learning rather than a problem to be overcome.

(Booth et al., 2011: 23)

Inclusion can be interpreted in a variety of ways:

- Inclusion is about participation and access to meaningful learning experiences.
- Inclusion is concerned with human rights and is strongly associated with equality of opportunity.
- Inclusion is about belonging and accepting difference and diversity.
- Inclusion encompasses everyone associated with a school, including the wider community.
- Inclusion is associated with all children attending mainstream schools.

Reflect on these interpretations of inclusion:

- Consider these broad definitions above and think about how these may have relevance academically and socially for all children.
- Think about how these interpretations may be interrelated.
- Think about any barriers that might be associated with any of them.
- Think about challenges for implementation from a global perspective.

Successive international and national agreements around the world have long espoused and acknowledged the importance and the need for inclusive education; the rationale is frequently associated with human rights, equality and successful learning. Its importance is frequently also linked to integration into the wider society of which we are all a part. The problem with inclusion is that it is often a contested concept, and therefore it is difficult to establish an agreement of what it might look like. Booth and Ainscow (2002) consider it to be about developing inclusive cultures, policies and practices, whereas for others it might be associated with the type of school the child attends, the curriculum offered or degree of access to resources.

In England, Warnock (1978) was instrumental in beginning to change thinking with regard to the association with labelling children according to their 'problems' and types of educational provision. Instead, she advocated viewing children in terms of their needs, and argued that as far as possible children should be educated in a mainstream school. However, in 2005 she questioned the wisdom of this blanket policy, noting that feeling different for long periods of time was in itself a disabling experience and inclusion must be seen to be about the *quality of learning* experience rather than where the schooling takes place. Ofsted (2007: 7) described an educationally inclusive school as one in which the teaching and learning achievements, attitudes and well-being of every young person meant taking into account pupils' varied life experiences.

Embracing diversity and difference in the classroom

In England, the Teachers' Standards (DfE, 2011) include a section on teachers being able to adapt teaching to the strengths and needs of all pupils, listing the following requirements:

- know when and how to differentiate appropriately, using approaches which enable pupils to be taught effectively;

- have a secure understanding of how a range of factors can inhibit pupils' ability to learn, and how best to overcome these;
- demonstrate an awareness of the physical, social and intellectual development of children, and know how to adapt teaching to support pupils' education at different stages of development; and
- have a clear understanding of the needs of all pupils, including those with special educational needs; those of high ability; those with English as an additional language; those with disabilities; and be able to use and evaluate distinctive teaching approaches to engage and support them.

Teachers' professional capability can be measured against these standards, and Ofsted inspections will consider the extent to which Teachers' Standards are being met as well as consider how equality of opportunity and recognition of diversity are promoted through teaching and learning (Ofsted Handbook, 2016). Developing inclusive pedagogical approaches is complex and multi-faceted, which was demonstrated by the research carried out by Florian and Hawkins (2011).

Research

Two questions shaped research undertaken by Florian and Hawkins (2011), which explored inclusive pedagogy:

1   What teaching strategies help to increase the participation and achievement of all children, including those identified as having special educational needs or requiring additional support for learning?
2   How can examples of inclusive pedagogy in action be articulated in ways that are useful to other teachers and supportive of their practice?

The context of the research was two primary schools in Scotland; data was gathered through interviews and observation and focus groups of 11 class teachers in addition to learning support staff.

The research identified two key findings:

- How teachers address the issue of inclusion in their daily practice determines their pedagogical approach. This is reflected in their knowledge, attitudes and beliefs about learners and learning, as well as the responses they make when students encounter barriers to learning.
- Teachers are often committed to the principles of inclusion but have to work within systems that rely on developmental norms to assess learning, identification and categorisation of learners by ability level. Florian and Hawkins suggest this serves to limit rather than enhance learning and achievement.

Florian and Hawkins suggest there needs to be a shift in approaches that work for most learners existing alongside something additional or different for those experiencing difficulties. This needs to be towards one that involves providing rich learning opportunities that are available to everyone so that all learners can participate (2011: 826).

Raising achievement

Working towards providing rich learning opportunities that are accessible to all has been part of the work of Swann et al. (2012), who use the term 'learning without limits'. They consider that working within a framework of predefined views of achievement limits learning and teacher expectations. Targets, objectives and outcomes are, in their view, all ways of conceptualising learning that require teachers to behave as if learning potential is predictable; learning is always linear, quantifiable and measurable (2012: 1) and, furthermore, that ability is fixed. They call this *deterministic thinking* and suggest it is rooted in the legacy that grouping children by ability is the best way to educate them. Instead, they propose a model that is based on learning free from unnecessary limits imposed by ability based practices, and have implemented such a pedagogy in Wroxham primary school in Hertfordshire with great success. The school was once in the Special Measures Ofsted category and is now deemed to be Outstanding.

Raising achievement, or what is commonly known as the 'standards agenda', has gained momentum for governments across the world; external accountability sets the discourse for performance and standards. Pupils' individual progress and attainment are measured alongside their progress in comparison with their peers within the school, and the attainment and progress in one school is compared against others through publication of data in the form of what has become to be known as league tables. Whilst it may be seen to be done in the interests of transparency and accountability, the stakes are high for all schools in order for them to remain competitive with others. Through recent studies, tensions have been detected between the effort for schools to become more inclusive and yet mindful of the standards agenda.

Pause for thought

Reflecting on the ideas in previous paragraphs, consider:

- What tensions might there be between inclusion and the standards agenda?
- What might be the impact of some of these tensions?
- How might schools or settings be pressured by the tensions between focussing on inclusion and focussing on standards?

Ainscow et al. (2006) suggested that this was the reason the general progress towards inclusion had been painfully slow, and that some schools generally remain ambivalent to inclusion. However, it was found that whilst many teachers were concerned about the impact on their work in relation to the standards agenda, in that it narrowed and subverted their work towards inclusion, teachers nevertheless sought ways to intertwine the two. One of the more positive aspects of the standards agenda has been that in some cases, the relentless focus on attainment has prompted teachers to examine issues in relation to achievement and participation that may have previously been overlooked.

The effect of labelling

A question that is often asked by parents and professionals with reference to inclusion and achievement is about the impact on the achievement of student who may not be identified within a minority group. Farrell et al. (2007: 124), in their study in relation to the impact of inclusion of children with special educational needs, were unable to find any meaningful evidence of a negative impact upon overall levels of attainment in schools. They suggested this could be because schools deemed to be inclusive have a range of strategies for driving up achievement which is not dependent upon or hampered by pupils who have special educational needs, and this was because they employed flexible and individualised provision. However, it is acknowledged that managing an inclusive classroom is not an easy task; it is a delicate balance between being mindful of the standards agenda, the resources available and the skills and capacities of the teacher.

The Centre for Studies in Inclusive Education (CSIE) (2016), an influential organisation in relation to inclusion policy in England, has put forward some strong arguments for inclusion which have formed the basis to their publication an Index for Inclusion.

Pause for thought

Consider the following reasons for inclusion suggested by the CSIE:

- Valuing some people more than others is unethical.
- Maintaining barriers to some students' participation in the cultures, curricula and communities of local schools is unacceptable.
- Preserving school cultures, policies and practices that are non-responsive to the diversity of learners perpetuates inequalities.
- Thinking that inclusion mostly concerns disabled learners is misleading.
- Thinking that school changes for some will not benefit others is short-sighted.
- Viewing differences between students as problems to be overcome is disrespectful and limits learning opportunities.
- Segregated schooling for disabled learners violates their basic human right to education without discrimination.
- Improving schools only for students is disrespectful to all other stakeholders.
- Identifying academic achievement as the main aim of schooling detracts from the importance of personal and moral development.
- Isolating schools and local communities from one another deprives everyone of enriching experiences.
- Perceiving inclusion in education as a separate issue from inclusion in society is illogical.

CSIE [online] available from www.csie.org.uk/inclusion/why.shtml

With reference to the above, can you provide a rationale as to why you might agree with some or all of these statements?

Consider whether some of the tensions raised through this chapter may have relevance to some of these statements.

Moving forward

In order to develop effective practice relating to learning and inclusion we need to:

- Understand the nature of learning.
- Know the factors that contribute to successful learning.
- Develop inclusive cultures, policies and practices that are based upon meaningful partici-pation and foster a sense of belonging for everyone.
- Actively identify barriers to learning in order for them to be overcome.
- Take into account diversity and difference with reference to family, culture, ethnicity, religion, socio-economic status, gender and ability or disability.
- Provide rich learning opportunities that do not limit achievement or expectations.

Conclusion

Diversity and differences between learners are a fundamental consideration for educators and present many opportunities for a rich learning experience for all. It can be seen that external drivers, as well as frames of thinking and pedagogical considerations, influence how inclusive policies and practice are implemented. The tension between giving consideration to what separates children and distinguishes them as individuals, and yet also giving consideration to what they have in common, challenges educators and policy makers because paying greater attention to one may lead to insufficient attention to the other. However, it is widely acknowledged that good teaching is good for all children whatever their differences and commonalties; therefore, the focus of paramount importance is to agree on what constitutes good teaching and how it may be best implemented.

Further reading

Booth, T., Ainscow, M. & Centre for Studies on Inclusive Education (Bristol, England) (2011) *Index for inclusion: Developing learning and participation in schools*, 3rd edn. Bristol: Centre for Studies on Inclusive Education. The Centre for Studies on Inclusive Education [online] www.csie.org.uk
Norwich, B. (2013) *Addressing dilemmas and tensions in inclusive education: living with uncertainty*. London: Routledge.
Swann, M., Peacock, A., Hart, S. & Drummond, M. J. (2012) *Creating learning without limits*. Maidenhead: Open University Press.

References

Ainscow, M., Booth, T. & Dyson, A. (2006) Inclusion and the standards agenda: Negotiating pressures in England. *International Journal of Inclusive Education*, vol 10, no. 4, pp. 295–308.
Bertram, T. & Pascal, C. (2002) What counts in early learning. In *Contemporary perspectives in early childhood curriculum*, eds. O. N. Saracho & B. Spodek, 241–256. Greenwich, CT: Information Age.
Bloom, B. S. (1956) *Taxonomy of educational objectives, Handbook I: The cognitive domain*. New York: David McKay Co. Inc.
Bloomer, F. & Hamilton, J. (2014) Challenges and barriers in primary school education: The experiences of Traveller children and young people in Northern Ireland. *Education, Citizenship and Social Justice*, vol 9, no. 1, pp. 3–18.

Booth, T. & Ainscow, M. (2002) *Index for inclusion*, 2nd edn. Bristol: Centre for Studies in Inclusive Education.

Booth, T., Ainscow, M. & Centre for Studies on Inclusive Education (Bristol, England) (2011) *Index for inclusion: Developing learning and participation in schools*, 3rd edn. Bristol: Centre for Studies on Inclusive Education.

Bowlby, J. (1969) *Attachment and loss, Vol. 1: Loss*. New York: Basic Books.

Bronfenbrenner, U. (1979) *The ecology of human development: Experiments by nature and design*. Cambridge, MA: Harvard University Press.

Bruner, J. S. (1960) *The process of education*. Cambridge, MA: Harvard University Press.

Centre for Studies on Inclusive Education (2016) Why inclusions? [online] available from www.csie.org.uk/inclusion/why.shtml accessed 21.12.16.

Department for Education (2011) The teachers' standards [online] available from www.gov.uk/government/uploads/system/uploads/attachment_data/file/283566/Teachers_standard_information.pdf accessed 15.01.17.

Department for Education (DfE) (2014) National curriculum in England: Framework for key stages 1–4. Statutory Guidance [online] available from www.gov.uk/government/publications/national-curriculum-in-england-framework-for-key-stages-1-to-4/the-national-curriculum-in-england-framework-for-key-stages-1-to-4 accessed 10.01.17.

Department for Education & Department of Health (2015) Special educational needs and disability code of practice 0–25 years [online] available from www.gov.uk/government/uploads/system/uploads/attachment_data/file/398815/SEND_Code_of_Practice_January_2015.pdf accessed 28.11.16.

Education Act 1981 [online] available from www.legislation.gov.uk/ukpga/1981/60/enacted accessed 20.01.17.

Equality Act (2010) [online] available from www.gov.uk/guidance/equality-act-2010-guidance accessed 20.01.17.

Farrell, M. (2014) *Investigating the language of special education*. Basingstoke: Palgrave Macmillan.

Farrell, P., Dyson, A., Polat, F., Hutcheson, G. & Gallannaugh, F. (2007) Inclusion and achievement in mainstream schools. *European Journal of Special Needs Education*, vol 22, no. 2, pp. 131–145.

Florian, L. & Hawkins, K. (2011) Exploring inclusive pedagogy. *British Educational Research Journal*, vol 37, no. 5, pp. 813–828.

Frederickson, N. & Cline, C. (2015) *Special educational needs, inclusion and diversity*, 3rd end. Buckingham: Open University Press.

Hopwood, V., O'Neill, L., Castro, G. & Hodgson, B. (2007) The presence of home education in England: A feasibility study. Research Report 827. York Consulting [online] available from http://webarchive.national archives.gov.uk/20130401151715/www.education.gov.uk/publications/eOrderingDownload/RR827.pdf accessed 10.01.17.

Kerins, P. (2014) Dilemmas of difference and educational provision for pupils with mild general learning disabilities in the Republic of Ireland. *European Journal of Special Needs Education*, vol 29, no. 2, pp. 47–58.

Lawson, H., Boyask, R. & Waite, S. (2013) Construction of difference and diversity within policy and practice in England. *Cambridge Journal of Education*, 43(1), 107–122.

Maslow, A. H. (1968) *Toward a psychology of being*. New York: D. Van Nostrand Co.

Moore, T. & McArthur, M. (February 2016) You feel it in your body: How Australian children and young people think about and experience feeling safe and being safe. *Children and Society*, 31(3), 206–218.

Norwich, B. (2007) *Dilemmas of difference, inclusion and disability: International perspectives and future directions*. London: Routledge.

Norwich, B. (2010) Dilemmas of difference, inclusion and disability: International perspectives on placement. *European Journal of Special Needs Education*, vol 23, no. 4, pp. 287–304.

Office for National Statistics (2011) Ethnicity in England and Wales [online] available from www.ons.gov.uk/peoplepopulationandcommunity/culturalidentity/ethnicity/articles/ethnicityandnationalidentityinenglandandwales/2012-12-11#ethnicity-in-england-and-wales accessed 27.11.16.

Office for Standards in Education (Ofsted) (2016) School inspection handbook [online] available from www.gov.uk/government/uploads/system/uploads/attachment_data/file/553942/School_inspection_handbook-section_5.pdf accessed 21.11.16.

Ofsted (2007) Evaluating educational inclusion [online] available from www.naldic.org.uk/Resources/NALDIC/Teaching%20and%20Learning/EvaluatingEducationalInclusion.pdf accessed 20.01.17.

Piaget, J. (1952) *The origins of intelligence in children*. New York: International University Press.

Swann, M., Peacock, A., Hart, S. & Drummond, M. J. (2012) *Creating learning without limits*. Maidenhead: Open University Press.

Twemlow, S. W., Fonagy, P. & Sacco, F. C. (2002) Feeling safe in school. *Smith College Studies in Social Work*, vol 72, no. 2, pp. 303–326.

United Nations Convention on the Rights of the Child (1989) [online] available from http://353ld710iigr2n4po7k4 kgvv-wpengine.netdna-ssl.com/wp-content/uploads/2010/05/UNCRC_PRESS200910web.pdf accessed 20.01.17.

United Nations Convention on the Rights of Persons with Disabilities (2006) cited in Centre of Human Rights for people with disabilities [online] available from www.disabilityaction.org/fs/doc/publications/summary-of-unconvention-on-the-rights-of-persons-with-disabilities.pdf accessed 20.01.17.

Vygotsky, L. S. (1978) *Mind in society: The development of higher psychological processes*. Cambridge, MA: Harvard University Press.

Warnock, M. (1978) *Special educational needs*, Report of the Committee of Enquiry into the education of handicapped children and young people. Cmnd. 7212 London: HMSO.

Warnock, M. (2005) *Special educational needs: A new look*. London: Philosophy of Education Society of Great Britain.

World Health Organisation (2016) Commission on ending childhood obesity [online] available from www.who.int/end-childhood-obesity/final-report/en/ accessed 20.01.17.

5 Multilingualism

Overcoming policy constraints

Seán Bracken

The atmosphere in Mr. Taylor's Year 5 class is engaging and welcoming. There are 26 children in the class. There is an air of collaboration and cooperation among the groups of children who are busily interacting around tables in the classroom. The groups comprise four groups of five children and one group of six children. The children are working on figuring out written problem based tasks allowing them to practice adding and subtracting fractions in complex problems. On closer examination, it appears that the children have been placed in groups according to perceptions about their abilities. Each of the tables is engaging with a task on a different level of cognitive challenge.

Introduction

Educational research is about finding suggested solutions to real challenges that teachers and learners face within schools. In the context of English as an Additional Language (EAL), there is significant scope to investigate the experiences of learners and their teachers and to come to an understanding as to how policy and practice might be strengthened. There is an increasing body of research focusing upon the acquisition of English among learners for whom English is an additional language. However, accessing and learning from the cultural and linguistic capital that children have in home or community languages is less frequently explored. This may be because of the ambiguity surrounding the place of heritage and community languages and the lack of mention of these languages within the national curriculum in England.

National policy provides little guidance concerning students for whom English is an additional language (Bracken et al., 2017). For some schools wishing to be inclusive, a natural response may be to seek equality by 'treating all students the same'. This approach could be referred to as cultural and linguistic 'elision', where the distinctive attributes of individual learners and groups of learners are ignored or supressed. This response has the potential to negatively impact upon learners' identities. When learners' identities are ignored, this may affect their motivation to engage and a resulting unintended consequence will be that learners fall short in realising their full learning potentials. An alternate approach would seek to consider and incorporate the multiple aspects of bilingual learners' cultural and language learning experiences. Fortunately, there is an established tradition of such multilingual practice, so there are good examples of what it might look like, especially in primary schools (Bracken et al., 2008; Stille and Cummins, 2013; Cummins, 2014).

In order to better understand the nature of the learning and social requirements of the diversity of bilingual and multilingual learners in early years, as well as in primary and secondary schools, we need to pose some key questions. The responses to these questions will frame the remainder of this chapter.

- To what extent is there a national policy perspective on EAL, and how was this developed?
- In light of current policy, what are the best ways for schools to develop research-informed practices?
- What are some of the inclusive practices that could be used to insure that these learners are socially and academically engaged within schools and classrooms?

In responding to these questions, the chapter draws upon research involving two primary schools in the English Midlands (Bracken, 2014). The research design used narrativity, or a form of experienced stories, to reflect the realities of some learners' lives in school (Clandinin and Connelly, 2000). In doing so, the aim was to provide an insight into the educational lives of learners whose perspectives might otherwise remain on the peripheries of educational research (Cole, 2008; Youdell, 2011). A further aim of the research was to illustrate how 'things could be done differently' through praxis and teacher development (Cole, 2008, 2011). Praxis here refers to the critical capacity to change pedagogical practices based on the realisation that through the educational empowerment of minority groups, the cultural, social and educational learning of all students is strengthened.

Inclusive linguistic diversity can become an important feature in a school's curriculum when the study of cultural and linguistic differences and similarities are posited at the heart of the curriculum. There is latitude for schools to use multilingualism as an intellectually challenging way to prompt learning about the form, structures and semantics of English as well as other languages (Hyltenstam, 2015). An ethical appeal is made to engage pupils and teachers in a 'pedagogy of becoming' (Marble, 2012; Semetsky, 2006, 2012) which strives to negotiate shared meanings from within a diversity of linguistic and cultural experiences.

In this way, students can learn about and through the English language when there is a focus on the grammar and on the form of the language. Teachers consciously and consistently bring linguistic forms and features to the attention of those for whom English is an additional language. Likewise, students for whom English is an additional language have scope to share their linguistic heritage and to discuss how this language might compare and contrast with the language of English. In so doing, these learners heighten the awareness of teachers and other students regarding the nature of how languages are constructed and learned. At the heart of this chapter lies the argument that engaging learning is always dynamic and multidimensional rather than being a process of unidirectional transmission; there is much more to EAL than teaching immigrants English.

Case study

Consider the scenario outlined in the vignette at the start of this chapter, and its continuation below, and reflect on the questions raised below:

> Within the class, there are ten children from a diversity of ethnic and linguistic backgrounds. These include three girls and two boys from Poland, two boys and one girl from Pakistan, a boy from the Philippines and a girl from Lithuania. All have arrived in the UK

within the past six years. All of the other children are White British. Within the "weakest performing" group, four of the six children are immigrants. An additional four are in the next lowest group and only one sits within the 'top performing' group.

Mrs Jeynes, a teaching assistant, provides support for Mr Taylor; in addition, Ms Merrick, a trainee teacher, is also guiding the learning. Whilst on placement, Ms Merrick has been asked by her university to keep a log about her experiences and has asked Mr Taylor about the rationale for how the class is set up. Mr Taylor shares that it is important to differentiate the learning according to ability so that 'weaker' students can be provided with support and 'brighter' learners can be challenged and stretched in their learning. Ms Merrick has noted that those who are learning English tended to be in the groups where cognitive learning demands were not as challenging.

Ms Merrick asked if she could reorganise the groups for the maths class on the following day. She has suggested mixing the groups. For the next lesson, Ms Merrick has provided instructions that each of the groups should write two of their own challenging mathematics problems. One of these problems should be written in English, and one in Urdu, Polish, Tagalog or Lithuanian.

At first, Mr Taylor is sceptical, but eventually he agrees that the lesson can take place on a 'trial basis'. Following the lesson, when asked by Ms Merrick about how she felt the children were involved in the lesson, Mrs Jeynes shared:

> I have never seen them as engaged as this, there was such a buzz in the room. Some of the kids who were normally very quiet and withdrawn were able to express themselves. What was interesting was seeing how the kids who are usually seen as having nothing to offer in terms of sharing learning are suddenly 'the stars' because they have access to another language. The English speaking kids really liked learning something about other languages, and they were able to compare some of the words and phrases with English ones, so they even learned a little more about how English works too.

Ms Merrick also asked Mr Taylor about his reactions to the lesson and he shared:

> To be honest, I didn't believe that it was possible to have things both ways. That we could be inclusive and feature the diversity of languages in the class while also focusing on meeting the learning outcomes expected of us for exams. You know there are real pressures on us to show progress for SATS examinations, so I don't like to try anything that might compromise on this. But, I have to admit I really liked this approach. I wouldn't try it every day, but it might be good every now and again.

- Why do you think schools may be reluctant to include children's heritage languages as a part of their curriculum?
- Why might there have been such a 'buzz' when Ms Merrick changed the group formation and the nature of their task?
- To what extent do you think that Mr Taylor's observation about the lesson is reasonable?

A review of current policy

There are some anomalies in recent Government policy in England, such as it exists, towards the nature and place of linguistic diversity within schools. As identified below, while the Government recognises that bilingualism is beneficial for the cognitive and social development of individuals and groups, it also suggests that schools should play a minimal role in its promotion, thus:

> The Government recognises the benefits that derive from the maintenance of ethnic minority linguistic and cultural traditions, but believes the main responsibility for maintaining mother tongue rests with the ethnic minority community themselves.
>
> (Department for Education, 2012: 3)

In practical terms, neither resource allocation nor guidance is provided to schools apart from a suggestion that this is the business of outside of school communities. This is significant because schools act as powerful arbiters of socio-cultural creation and continuity (Ball, 2013).

Until relatively recently, local and regional policy implementation addressing minority ethnic experiences and achievement in schools had occurred primarily funded through the Ethnic Minority Achievement Grant, or EMAG. According to Government policy in 2004, the intention was that the grant should be used to 'narrow achievement gaps for pupils from those minority ethnic groups who are at risk of underachieving and to meet particular needs of bilingual pupils' (DfES, 2004: 2).

Over the past few years, however, there have been significant changes to the ways in which EMAG has been funded and how those funds are subsequently accessed and used (NALDIC, 2013). Previously, the grant went to local authorities to improve their capacity in meeting learning requirements of pupils for whom English was an additional language and to address learning of pupils from minority ethnic backgrounds within schools. However, these funds are now provided directly to schools and only made available on the basis that there are EAL learners who have arrived from overseas within three years or less. Additionally, schools should contribute part of these funds back into their local authority (LA) if they wish to avail of professional support from LAs. As funding is no longer specifically protected to assist learners for whom English is an additional language, schools' investment in LA professional development for teachers has been dramatically reduced. Consequentially, professional EAL services within many local authorities have completely disappeared (Jones, 2011; NASUWT, 2012).

Given that official policy reflects an ambivalence regarding the highlighting and incorporation of cultural or linguistic difference, one might assume that there would be a counterbalancing concern for enhancing the English language and literacy skills for EAL pupils. Indeed, because pupils for whom English is an Additional Language now constitute almost 20% of the national school population (Department for Education [DfE], 2014a), in order to promote social cohesion, there would appear to be a national imperative to do so. Yet this cohort of students receives scant attention in terms of a planning for future preparedness of teachers. A recent comprehensive positional review of initial teacher training makes one incidental mention of EAL in the context of a specific school case study which is used to illustrate inclusive practice (DfE, 2015). Neither bilingual inclusion or enhancing English language literacy appear to be priority areas for classroom practice and such ambivalence prompts the question as to what this means for the formation of pupils' educational identities and sensibilities towards the incorporation of their home languages. Because of the official lacuna in providing direction, schools now have to develop their own initiatives to progress learning among students who have English as an additional language. As observed in EAL focused research:

> In light of increased autonomy afforded to individual schools and school networks, it is imperative that schools adopt carefully crafted research informed approaches to supporting effective interventions. These should be designed by teachers who are mindful of the nature of schools' demographic profiles, because the specific nature of student diversities has significant implications for the language and literacy requirements.
>
> (Bracken et al., 2017: 179)

An insight into how this might be achieved is provided in the section below. It outlines the ways in which one school-based research approach was designed and implemented to reveal current practices and to provide suggestions for pedagogical approaches for enhancing multilingualism.

Framing a school-based research approach to inclusive linguistic diversity

To inform a greater understanding of how best schools might facilitate the positive development of linguistic identities among immigrant children, it is important to construct relevant and impactful research. This suggestion is in keeping with recent recommendations that those who are training to become teachers should be provided with the capacity to engage in relevant research and should become aware as to 'how to interpret educational theory and research in a critical way, so that they are able to deal with contested issues' (Carter, 2015: 8). The vignette featured at the start of this chapter, and extended in the first case study, draws on strands of learning emerging from research conducted in Camborne, a large town in a relatively rural setting in the English Midlands (Bracken, 2014). The research was conducted in two maintained primary schools using a critical ethnographic case study methodological approach. It is important to note here what is meant by an ethnographic study and why a critical dimension added to the nature of the study.

An ethnographic approach to research involves immersing oneself into a particular socio-cultural setting such as a school over a long period of time so that one can observe the ways in which lived realities are constructed. The methodology comes from

> an awareness and research orientation towards actively attending to the activities, language, meanings and perspectives of members in the setting. (*It involves* . . .) Immersion, flexibility and openness to the relevant communication and symbolic representations that are congruent with the time place and manner of the subject matter.
>
> (Altheide et al., 2008: 127)

While case studies are individual and specific to particular time frames and geographic areas, they also have the potential to reveal overarching tendencies within a wider social edifice (Bassey, 1999: 23). Case studies have the potential to illustrate how national orientations are interpreted more locally. A further possible role of 'critical ethnographic' research is to identify larger inequalities within social practices and to suggest ways in which these practices might be reoriented to become more inclusive (Howard, 2008; Youdell, 2003).

This approach to research also involves reflecting on one's own socio-cultural positioning. For example, as a researcher, I was aware that my views and values were informed by being part of a dominant cultural, linguistic and racial background while conducting research with a group of children whose cultures, languages and values were 'minoritised', meaning that their power positioning within the school was potentially less influential than those of a normed majority (Connolly, 2003).

In this context, an ethically informed research approach involves processes and outcomes that are closely bound up with reflexive (educationally self-reflective and mindful of power relations) and values-developing practices that incorporate 'the need to constantly interrupt oneself, to make ethico-political decisions to remain alert to the dangers which lurk in the everyday' (Ball, 2013: 149). As educators, how we include or elide linguistic heritage is indeed associated with our own ethical, political and educational values and experiences. Along with other factors, such as resource availability, the values we have inform our actions of ignoring or incorporating the prior language and literacy learning of young people.

Data was gathered and interpreted using non-reductive narrative approaches that enabled the voices of pupils to come to the fore (Clandinin and Connelly, 2000). I was more interested in finding out and sharing what teachers' and children's stories revealed about the culture of schooling rather than seeing whether these stories fit neatly into defined themes or categories. This approach was supplemented by using a Deleuzian philosophical approach that sought to offer creative opportunities for minoritised languages and identities to become other, or different, than how they might be 'normally' experienced in educational settings (Deleuze, 1994; Cole, 2013).

The following section draws on learning from the research data from one of the two case study schools where, to some degree and from my perspective, school leaders and teachers sought to incorporate a diversity of languages and their speakers as creative contributors to curriculum authorship. I consider curriculum here in its broadest sense, and its attributes are made up of dynamic and changing interactions between:

- Subject matter content, for example schemes of work and lesson plans for teaching history in Year 5 and the extent to which these reflect the diversity of students within a setting;
- Resources that are used to support learning and teaching, the books, posters, site visits and wider community involvement and contributions to learning. A question here might be whether and to what extent there is scope for learners to develop bilingual or multilingual resources;
- The teaching and learning environment within classrooms and schools and how these enable interaction between and among groups through the language of English as well as through additional languages;
- The professional capacities and values of the teaching staff, how well disposed teachers and teaching assistants are towards incorporating the lived experiences and languages of a diversity of children; and
- The dispositions of individuals and groups of learners and their views toward multilingualism, their self efficacy and desire (or lack of desire) to maintain language and literacy skills in the languages of the wider communities served by schools.

Pause for thought

Consider:

- In what ways have changes in support and provision for schools and teachers made it more important to engage in school and network-based research projects?
- Do you think public opinion would be favourably disposed towards increasing all learners' knowledge of other languages and language learning? Why might this be?
- Is it desirable to alter public opinions about language use in other wider communities? If so, why? If not, why not?
- What might be missing from the considerations for a linguistically inclusive curriculum such as the one discussed above?

Case study

Facilitating multilingual inclusion

This case study is a composite of findings taken from my doctoral research (Bracken, 2014).

Camborne Community School served a large Polish community. Each weekend, its classrooms were made available for 'Szkoła Sobotnia' or Saturday School. Young Polish language speakers from the wider community were invited to Polish language and literacy classes designed to ensure that children could maintain their literacy in their first language. Mrs Zalewska managed Szkoła Sobotnia, as a teaching assistant with qualified teacher status and a background in applied linguistics; during the week, she acted as the Community School's EAL coordinator. Her role was viewed as being very important within the school because of her knowledge of linguistics and her enthusiasm for promoting respect for linguistic diversity within the school. She was highly regarded by Mr Williams, the school's deputy head teacher, who expressed a sense of pride about being associated with Szkoła Sobotnia:

> We have the Polish school on site which we're incredibly proud of, I think we've got 70 children up to year 7 year 8, the fact that it's celebrating their culture as well, and the fact that the children are learning Polish as well as English, so that the language remains is very, very important. A lot of our Polish children are either very young or have been here for some time, or have been born in the surrounding area and so there's a danger of them, losing their own culture.

> (interview)

Providing access to the Polish school has had a noteworthy positive effect on the intercultural experiences of the Polish EAL learners. It has done so by facilitating a supportive transition to becoming included in a wider, more diverse setting. This is exemplified in how Peta experiences schooling. She is a student in Year 6 who is well regarded by her class peers; she was elected as one of the class representatives and conveys a sense of well measured self-confidence recognised by peers and commented upon by teachers. When interviewed, she spoke admiringly of Szkoła Sobotnia:

> I like it 'cos I can be with people from me, that are like me, that are from the same country as me, and I like, don't have to pretend who I really am, 'cos I'm not scared about what people think about me in Polish school. 'Cos like here, I'm not really in my own country, so I really care about what English people think about me. I just don't know why, but I feel comfortable in Polish school more than English school, I'm not scared, but I feel more uncomfortable in English school rather than in Polish school.
>
> (photo interview Peta)

Having a space to practice one's own cultural understandings and to use one's language would appear to strengthen the sense of self; this encourages learners to better accommodate new learning and new cultural and linguistic practices. Camborne Community School also encourages families to create links with the school by adopting some of the cultural practices of newly arrived communities; this is further explained by Mr. Williams:

> We've just had our second year of our grandparents' day, which is a Polish tradition, a year ago we actually did it the day of our Ofsted inspection, which of course we didn't know this, but it just happened to be the same time, we invited the grandparents of our year one and two children into school. At one point we did have grandparents down the corridor, out the door, across the car park and down, down the road queuing to come in, we were slightly having kittens at that point.
>
> (interview, Mr Williams 26th February 2013)

Interestingly, the event was not recorded in the school's Ofsted report. What is deemed to be important within the school in terms of its own desire to reach out and better serve its wider, more diverse linguistic and cultural communities may not be viewed as important using standardised evaluative measures. However, the school's approach is contentious, and not all parents may welcome a focus on diversity. Mrs Zalewska explained that whilst she had been teaching the Polish children Christmas carols, some of the other children in the class had picked up the words and tunes and had been singing them at home. This prompted a few parents to raise concerns about what their children were learning in school. There was an air of tension between Mrs Zalewska and some of these parents, and so she went to discuss the matter with Mr Williams. As she shared:

> I talked to Stephen [the deputy head teacher, Mr Williams] to make sure nobody is going to end up upset and he was very clear he just said, 'look that is how we do things here, that is how things should be done, even if parents can't recognise the value of that, we

do, and if they don't like it they can always take the children somewhere else'. It was very clear that whatever I do, they know that it is a good thing and bilingualism is valued and that's it.

(interview Mrs Zalewska)

In a follow up interview with Mr Williams, he explained how and why linguistic and cultural inclusion was supported by Camborne Community School. He recognised the role of leadership in formulating an inclusive culture and that this was intentionally cultivated, stating:

It's not a case of well, we've got all these Polish children we need to do something about it, it's more a case of this is our school population this is who we've got and what we do in school is to reflect that and I think if we were a school that was all white middle class children, I think we'd be a poorer school . . . what we do reflects our community, it's what makes this school really special and I'm really proud of it.

(interview Mr Williams)

The incorporation of linguistic diversity within the school has enabled immigrant children to feel at ease with their own multilingualism, as reflected in the way that another Year 5 student speaks about her experiences. Having a mixed heritage family who emigrated from Lithuania some five years ago, Annessa speaks Russian, Lithuanian and English. During an interview, she explained that:

Sometimes we have like a language of the week and in the morning and afternoon we'd have to say like 'good morning' or 'good afternoon' in that language and it was Russian once, but we haven't done Lithuanian, and at the time I had to teach everyone how to say 'hello' and 'good afternoon' in Russian, so if it was morning you'd have to say 'dobre utra' and if it was the afternoon you'd have to say 'dobre dien'.

(interview)

As with elements of the classroom curriculum, the use of the school space and environment is also designed to be inclusive of linguistic diversity. My research field notes identified that the EAL office space in which children engage on a one-to-one level with language support staff within the school acts as an internal nexus with that which is the linguistic other:

The office is quite small and in the centre sits a round table which was surrounded by small child sized chairs, in this way adults using the chairs are metaphorically 'brought down to size' and the sense of physical difference between adults and children is reduced. To the back of the room are book stands on which are stacked books in a diversity of languages pertaining to culture, folklore, history and fiction. This is a space which takes cognisance of pupils' prior linguistic, and cultural heritage, it is a space with potential for the familiar to create continuity from past experiences and thence to create avenues for new learning.

(field notes, Camborne Community Primary)

Teachers and pupils also use this office space to facilitate the taking of SATS through bilingual papers. The tests are translated so that the children are enabled to access the testing regime. Thus, what might be an otherwise exclusionary process is opened up for cultural and linguistic reinterpretation.

The relative ease with which pupils at Camborne Community Primary School share their home languages and how they perceived these as being an integral dimension of their educational experience was a noteworthy feature of this school. Facets of leadership and teacher preparedness interconnect with teaching spaces and resources in order to develop a culture of linguistic diversity and inclusivity. The school has enabled an innovative interpretation as to how languages and learning can be incorporated into the fabric of learning, teaching and assessment.

Reflect on the following:

> Taking risks within schools by promoting multilingualism may prompt resistance from some teachers and parents. How might this be addressed effectively?
>
> What do you think are some of the 'enabling factors' that allow for successful inclusion of diversity of languages meaningfully within schools?
>
> What are the similarities between the school-based inclusive practices in this case study and the classroom practices shared in the vignette at the opening of the chapter (and extended in the first case study)?

Changing minds and changing practices

The research revealed that the role of teacher leadership within a supporting school was an important feature in supporting the inclusion of pupils' languages and cultural identities. Webb and Gulson (2013: 66) identify scope for 'deterritorialisation', or the positive shifting of accepted and normalised practices, through the artistic and creative nature of leadership. There is latitude then for teachers to counter strong social currents towards prejudice and the elision of others' linguistic identities.

In terms of language pedagogy, whether this is oriented towards the teaching and learning of English as an additional language, or towards the inclusion of linguistic diversity in class, a philosophy of learning that incorporates a Deleuzian approach may constructively inform practice. Johnson notes that 'Deleuze's ideas offer rich insights into what language and learning have the potential to be. For Deleuze, learning always emerges from experimentation with the real, rather than from generalised instruction' (2014: 62). This means that there are creative ways in which educators can engage with unexpected and unexplored avenues for learning offered by children's linguistic heritage. This approach contrasts dramatically with an unquestioned delivery of an external curriculum framework that fails to recognise where children come from.

Interestingly, some attributes of the decentralisation of educational policy enable schools to creatively reinterpret the external curriculum. For example, the new languages curriculum for primary schools (DfE, 2014b) identifies that 'learning a foreign language is a liberation from insularity and provides an opening to other cultures' (DfE, 2014b: 226). This curriculum also provides openness of choice regarding what languages might be taught and is non-directive regarding outcomes. This makes it possible for schools to think and act beyond prior limiting readings of what should constitute a 'modern foreign language'. So there is real scope to better include the languages and identities of a diversity of pupils, thus making the educational experience more meaningful for all learners and better reflecting the diversity of the wider school community. By positioning a previously marginalised language at the fore of learning, one allows for a multiplicity of (unpredictable) learning opportunities. These better provide all pupils with capacities, not to name the other, but rather to learn from and perhaps even fleetingly embody the other through, for example, the singing of a Christmas song in Polish, or through the writing of a mathematics problem about fractions in Urdu.

Placing linguistic difference at the heart of learning exemplifies an appreciation for the intellectual potential inherent in language learning and provides educators with scope to adopt what is termed in Deleuzian philosophy a 'pedagogy of difference' (Cole, 2011; Masny, 2006). Through a growing awareness about pupils' cognitive engagement with their own languages, teachers will also become learners, coming to a growing realisation of the grammatical and syntactical form differences evident between languages and enabling learners to attain greater fluency and literacy in the target language of English. It is clear that such a programme of learning will not come about quickly, nor will it be without challenge.

Moving forward

In order to realise the potential for learning from and through a multilingual environment, we need to consider:

- Who should be involved in determining what languages a school might wish to include in its curriculum?
- What knowledge, skills and values will be required by the teaching workforce in order to facilitate the further enhancement of multilingualism within schools?
- How might learning be fostered and assessed in a meaningful way?
- What resources will be required to assist in the enhancement of multilingualism?
- How can communities external to the school be included? This involves consultation with English-only-speaking parents and carers along with those from linguistic minority communities.
- How can the inclusion of diverse languages be incorporated into a cohesive, meaningful school-based policy on language and literacy that considers EAL learning requirements along with those of the English language curriculum?
- How might teachers and learners design research projects to monitor the effects of multilingualism, bilingualism and inclusive cultural and linguistic practices?

Conclusion

When pupils and teachers jointly encounter a shared challenge of learning a second language, conditions are in place to move people along from what they have previously known, and this allows for genuine learning to be attained (Marble, 2012). At a time when there is such ambivalence, if not hostility, towards linguistic difference within schools, and when there are strong narratives towards uniformity and conformity, educators require strength and ethical courage to offer learning through positive engagements with learners perceived as other.

The curriculum can be extended beyond its constraining normed interpretations of what constitutes the nature of language learning. One can move away from a prescription or delivery mode of curriculum (as exemplified in the directive for students to 'learn this list of prescribed words') to a more engaging curriculum that is jointly created with children who know an additional language. In this way, there is a true capacity to learn because the teacher is also positioned in the role of master learner and facilitator; as Deleuze has suggested, 'We learn nothing from those who say: "Do as I do". Our only teachers are those who tell us to "do with me"' (1994: 23).

Collaborative and supportive classrooms and schools will enable all children to realise their learning potentials by creatively including the prior language and literacy learning into the fabric of a relevant and meaningful curriculum. Such a curriculum bodes well for a world in which recognition of difference inspires a movement beyond mere 'acceptance' or 'tolerance' of otherness, but rather seeks an embracing of 'the other' to create something culturally new and jointly shared through a process of reciprocal language learning.

Further reading

Conteh, J. (2015). *The EAL teaching book: Promoting success for multilingual learners*. Exeter: Learning Matters.
Leung, C., & Creese, A. (2010). *English as an additional language: Approaches to teaching linguistic minority students*. London: Sage Publications.

References

Altheide, D., Coyle, M., DeVriese, K., & Schneider, C. (2008). Emergent Qualitative Data Analysis. In S. Hesse-Biber and P. Leavy (eds.), *Handbook of emergent methods*. New York: Guilford Press, 127–151.
Ball, S. (2013). *Foucault, power and education*. (London: Routledge).
Bassey, M. (1999). *Case study research in educational settings*. Buckingham, PA: Open University Press.
Bracken, S., Driver, C., & Kadi-Hanifi, K. (2017). *Teaching English as an additional language in secondary schools: Theory and practice*. Abingdon, Oxon: Routledge.
Bracken, S. A. (2014). Becoming other (ed.): A study of minority ethnic identities in two non-urban primary schools (Doctoral dissertation, School of Education) Leicester: University of Leicester. Available online at: [https://lra.le.ac.uk/handle/2381/31601] (Accessed 20/12/2016).
Bracken, S. A., Clerkin, Á., Mc Donnell, B., & Regan, N. (2008). Teaching and Learning in Plurilingual Schools: Lessons from Classrooms in Dublin 15. In M. Fiedler and A. V. Pérez Piñán (eds), *Challenging perspectives: Teaching globalisation and diversity in the knowledge society*. Dublin: DICE, 51–65.
Carter, A. (2015). *Carter review of initial teacher training*. Department for Education, Crown Publishing. Available online at: [www.gov.uk/government/uploads/system/uploads/attachment_data/file/399957/Carter_Review.pdf] (Accessed 20/12/2016).
Clandinin, D., & Connelly, F. (2000). *Narrative inquiry: Experience and story in qualitative research*. (San Francisco: Jossey-Bass).
Cole, D. (2008). Deleuze and the Narrative Forms of Educational Otherness. In Semetsky, I. (ed.), *Nomadic education: Variations on a theme by Deleuze and Guattari*. Rotterdam: Sense, 17–34.
Cole, D. (2011). The actions of affect in Deleuze: Others using language and the language that we make. *Educational Philosophy and Theory*, 43(6), 549–561.
Cole, D. (2013). Deleuze and narrative investigation: The multiple literacies of Sudanese families in Australia. *Literacy*, 47(1), 35–41.
Connolly, P. (2003). Ethical principles for researching vulnerable groups. *OFM/DFM*. Available online at: [www.ofmdfmni.gov.uk/ethicalprinciples.pdf] (Accessed 08/09/2014).

Cummins, J. (2014). Mainstreaming Pluralingualism: Restructuring Heritage Language Provision in Schools. In P. Trifonas and T. Aravossitas (eds), *Rethinking heritage language education*. Cambridge: Cambridge University Press 1–19.

Deleuze, G. (1994). *Difference and repetition*. Patton, P., Trans. New York: Columbia University Press.

Department for Education. (2012). *A brief summary of government policy in relation to EAL*. Available online at: [www.naldic.org.uk/eal-advocacy/eal-news-summary/240212a] (Accessed 30/01/2013).

Department for Education (DfE). (2014a). *Schools, pupils, and their characteristics: January 2014*. (London: Department for Education). Available online at: [www.gov.uk/government/statistics/schools-pupils-and-their-characteristics-january-2014] (Accessed 02/02/2015).

Department for Education. (2014b). *The national curriculum in England, framework document: For teaching 1 September 2014 to 31 August 2015*. Available online at: [www.gov.uk/government/uploads/system/uploads/attachment_data/file/339805/MASTER_final_national_curriculum_until_sept_2015_11_9_13.pdf] (Accessed 04/08/2014).

Department for Education. (2015). *Carter review of initial teacher training*. Available online at: [www.gov.uk/government/uploads/system/uploads/attachment_data/file/399957/Carter_Review.pdf] (Accessed 20/02/2015).

Department for Education and Skills. (2004). *Aiming high: Supporting effective use of EMAG*. Available online at: [www.naldic.org.uk/Resources/NALDIC/Teaching%20and%20Learning/Efctv_Use_EMAG.pdf] (Accessed 20/03/2012).

Howard, T. (2008). Who really cares? The disenfranchisement of African American males in PreK-12 schools: A critical race theory perspective. *Teachers College Record*, 110(5), 954–985.

Hyltenstam, K. (2015). *Principles of second/additional language acquisition from a psycholinguistic perspective*. Presentation at NALDIC Conference, University of Leicester, Leicester, February 2015.

Johnson, S. (2014). Deleuze's philosophy of difference and its implications for ALL practice. *Journal of Academic Language and Learning*, 8(1), 62–69.

Jones, E. (2011). *Cuts bite in neediest areas of education*. *Guardian*. Available online at: [www.guardian.co.uk/education/2011/oct/14/education-cuts-emag] (Accessed 30/01/2013).

Marble, S. (2012). Becoming-teacher: Encounters with the other in teacher education. *Discourse: Studies in the Cultural Politics of Education*, 33(1), 21–31.

Masny, D. (2006). Learning and creative processes: A poststructural perspective on language and multiple literacies. *International Journal of Learning*, 12(5), 149–156.

NALDIC. (2013). *EAL funding: How the needs of Bilingual learners in schools are funded*. Available online at: [www.naldic.org.uk/research-and-information/eal-funding] (Accessed 20/06/2013).

NASUWT. (2012). *Ethnic minority achievement*. A report on the EMAG research. Available online at: [www.nasuwt.org.uk/TrainingEventsandPublications/NASUWTPublications/Publications/order/summary/index.htm?ContentID=NASUWT_009865] (Accessed 30/01/2013).

Semetsky, I. (2006). *Deleuze, education, and becoming*. Available online at: [www.sensepublishers.com/media/233-deleuze-education-and-becominga.pdf] (Accessed 26/06/2013).

Semetsky, I. (2012). Living, learning, loving: Constructing a new ethics of integration in education. *Discourse: Studies in the Cultural Politics of Education*, 33(1), 47–59.

Stille, S., & Cummins, J. (2013). Foundation for learning: Engaging plurilingual students' linguistic repertoires in the elementary classroom. *TESOL Quarterly*, 47(3), 630–638.

Webb, P., & Gulson, K. (2013). Policy Intensions and the folds of the self. *Educational Theory*, 63(1), 51–68.

Youdell, D. (2003). Identity traps, or how black students fail: The interactions between biographical, sub-cultural and learner identities. *British Journal of Sociology of Education*, 24, 3–20.

Youdell, D. (2011). *School trouble: Identity, power and politics in education foundations and futures of education*. London: Routledge.

6 Religion and belief

Ellie Hill

Morgan is on a semester's exchange at a university in England from her home in the United States. She has joined an undergraduate module on Religion in Education. Her peers are discussing being an inclusive society, based on religious tolerance and respect. They speak openly about their experiences at home and university. Morgan tells the group that this open dialogue is new to her as, at home, religion is not discussed outside of the home. Her fellow students then explain that this is how they can be inclusive, through talking, sharing experiences and listening to each other.

Introduction

Religion and belief, ethnicity, prejudice, fundamental British values, stereotyping: these are all terms that are relevant in the life and education of young people in the education system in Britain. Some conversations can be political, some moral, but always individuals have opinions on these topics. A strongly held opinion, a family value, a changeable position: how do young people manage their experiences around these areas? For some there are positive experiences and shared positions, for others, the experience of exclusion, misrepresentation or unfair labelling.

This chapter reports the experiences of recent education graduates in the area of religion and belief, ethnicity, prejudice, British values and stereotyping. It considers how inclusive they consider their life so far in this area. As future educators and potentially parents, their experience and perspectives are enlightening in terms of the current debate. These areas are facets of everyone's lives, both on a personal level and through lived day to day experience. The media is flooded with stories about ethnicity and faith. Celebrities talk about spirituality and politicians debate their views on immigration and exclusion. We are living in a digital world with access to global news available on our numerous electronic communication devices. Presidential debates for the most powerful political head of state have included critical commentary about position and stance in relation to inclusivity of faith, ethnicity and belief.

Religion in education

We know some views of parents, teachers and secondary school pupils from RE for REal (Dinham and Shaw, 2015). The project sought the views of parents, teachers and students aged 14–15 years about the future of Religious Education (RE) in schools. Despite RE's confused position in the curriculum (one could simply look to Michael Gove, the then Secretary of State for Education, when he omitted RE from the review of school subjects in 2013), it is a statutory requirement for all state schools in England to deliver. But the changing types of schools, including academies and free schools, alongside schools with religious character ('faith schools'), have confused the role. That and a murky past of poor quality teaching identified by the statutory inspection body for schools (Ofsted, 2013) and often inadequate teacher training (APPG, 2013).

Dinham and Shaw (2015) acknowledge the widely held view that learning about religion and belief is critical, with issues necessarily addressed to support our children and young people to become positive and accepting adults. This stands against the risks of a lack of cohesion and inclusion: extremism. There needs to be 'engagement with the rich variety of religion and belief encountered in ordinary, everyday life' (Dinham and Shaw, 2015: 3). Within the context of this chapter, it is important to consider what opportunities there are for learning in this particular field to continue when the school leaver chooses to continue into higher education. How inclusive is the university campus and how open is the dialogue?

This chapter seeks to demonstrate the position and perspectives of university leavers: those who have recently been involved in full-time undergraduate degree study and who are now able to undertake either teacher training or work in another educational setting. Their reflections enable us to have a topical, contemporary overview of the field to inform and engage with educational practice. As will become evident as the chapter unfolds, this group in society is critical in the development of the current political agenda.

Pause for thought

- What was your experience of RE at school if it was part of the curriculum? Did it enable you to learn broadly about other religions and beliefs or none?
- Did university enable you to develop your understanding of other's religion and beliefs?
- Has your experience of university supported your personal growth?
- Does being at university support growth, understanding and respect for others? If so, how?
- What experiences are there at university to engage with the big questions of life and how does it enable the broadening of minds and the notion of inclusion?

Religion and belief

There is a real and a perceived religious landscape extrapolated by the statistics of the UK Census 2011 and then contributed to by the Report of the Commission on Religion and Belief in British Public Life (Butler-Sloss, 2015). The last 50 years have seen a critical change in how members of society define themselves in terms of their religion and belief. The description of oneself as non-religious is currently attributed to around one quarter of people in England and Wales (Office for National Statistics, 2013). This is one in four people recording their own religion or belief as 'none'. In the previous 2001 census, 12.5% of people in England considered themselves non-religious. This timescale spans much of the educational career of the education students that currently attend university. This changing identification and the increased secularisation of Britain could potentially bring a more harmonious coexistence, as the issues that sometimes divide people become less prevalent. It is possible that in modern society, religion and belief could potentially become a non-issue. The Commission on Religion and Belief in Public Life (2015) refers particularly to the reduction in Christian identification: two-thirds of the population would have stated they were Christians only 30 years ago. However, data shows us that today that figure is only 40% of the population. Within the Christian faith practised, evangelical and Pentecostal churches are growing in number.

Research

As an academic team providing university-level courses in Education, we are continually seeking to improve the education delivered to our students. When establishing current best practice, it is important to ascertain the perspectives of recent graduates on their experiences in the areas of religion and belief, ethnicity, stereotyping and prejudice. Primary research was undertaken using one-to-one interviews; the participants were recent alumni who volunteered to take part in the study. They all live in the West Midlands of England.

Adam is a part-time Master's in Education student. He describes how he feels society is today, in relation to including everyone's religion and beliefs:

> I don't necessarily think on a grand scale it need be an issue. We live in a much more secular society these days and people are very much these days, on the whole, accepting of multiculturalism. I think they are much more accepting of people's beliefs: obviously providing it doesn't do harm to anyone else.

Using Adam's views stated here, consider the following questions:

- Do you agree with Adam's position?
- What do you think about his last sentence? What does that mean to you?

Ben is a full-time student studying for his Master's in Education. He also considers the issue when asked about religion and belief in society today:

> it is just that you are of that religion or that faith. No one is going to question it; in fact, you would like to think that it is something that doesn't even matter. For example, someone walks in with a headscarf on and ten years ago you would have said 'oh they are of a faith' but now . . . someone has a head scarf on and you think 'I don't care' or you may not even notice. That is the dream, but I think that it is becoming more of a reality.

- Do you agree with Ben that this is becoming more of a reality?
- Can you see a change from ten years ago in your context?
- What does Ben mean by 'not caring'? Is this a positive development?

When considering these perspectives, we can take a positive reading from them. Those recent graduates saw difference but not as an issue. It is simply part of life. For them, this broad-mindedness and inclusive attitude to all religions, ethnicities and cultures is part of university life. But interestingly, even on campus, there is an awareness of when and where one can talk openly about religion and belief: in the safe space of the lecture or seminar room; in a tutor's office. However, there is a consciousness of the need to be contextual. Words heard out of context can be deemed potentially inflammatory. Shared workspaces, the canteen, the smoking area – these are all, according to the recent graduates in the study, contexts where one should consider carefully one's discussion points. Religion and belief are not always for open and free expression. This is countered by the participants' views that they have learned to be tolerant and respectful of others' positions. They do not assume that theirs is the correct and only viewpoint: they will listen and try to understand the views of others.

Developing an inclusive environment

How does an educational institution ensure it is inclusive when considering religion and belief, ethnicity and culture? What efforts are made to enable all members of a united educational establishment such as a university to feel included? As a university lecturer I believe that we need to ensure there are safe places for individuals and groups to be themselves; we need to ensure that every member of the organisation feels part of it; there is no room for exclusion. The ground rules need to be set and the bar high. There should be no tolerance of stereotyping or prejudice. Through imagery and activity, we need to present ourselves as truly inclusive: truly supportive.

The question is, amongst this changing picture, where do our future educators and teachers develop their values and positions? Dinham and Shaw (2015: 4) talk about the 'vigorous and pervasive debates about religion and belief in contemporary society'. Learning about and from religion and belief should surely help young people be more inclusive. When we gain knowledge about others, we learn to understand that difference is positive. Poorly taught religious educa-tion, whether in the school or the home, has the potential to be divisive. Evidence of this shows that in six out of ten schools in England, the provision of Religious Education is not good enough (Ofsted, 2013). Here lies the challenge: to improve (or remove) such education in schools and hope that the home surrounds the child with positive values. One's home experience, it is clear, is of critical influence.

Ethnicity

Ethnicity can be considered a social construct, with the term seeking to classify according to physical appearance (Cole, 2012). It can endorse distinctions and differences. It is definitely a contested term. When considering inclusion, ethnicity needs to be discussed whilst taking account of the current political climate in the UK and Europe and in the USA. Media reports illustrate that white supremacy has taken a visual position (Ferguson, 2016; Peniel, 2016). Do our curricula across phases of education and across the globe enable positive racial integration and a good knowledge base?

Pause for thought

Cole (2012) talks about the curriculum of the early part of the last century in England and its blatant racism. Consider:

- Has enough changed?
- Are we seeking to integrate different ethnic groups in our schools and communities, or is diversity changing the geography and society to become a different place?
- How do we understand the academic performance of ethnic groups?
- Is nationality an issue?

All these issues need to be considered when thinking about inclusive education.

Over the last 40 years in the UK, there have been several pieces of legislation regarding race, ethnicity and religious belief. The Swann Report (1985) considered the achievement of children from minority ethnic groups. It was reported that concern centred around what was regarded as the Anglocentric bias of the subject matter and the literature studied (1985: 763), and thus curriculum provision was expected to change and be more reflective of the changing society. This was over 30 years ago and was followed by more legislation, notably the Racial and Religious Hatred Act (2006). This established that it is a crime to stir up religious or racial hatred. But the Tell MAMA (Measuring anti-Muslim Attacks) Annual Report 2015 documents 1,128 reports of anti-Muslim incidents from 1 January to 31 December 2015. A significant number of incidents are reported as happening in educational institutions (11%). Of the 46 incidents reported, 76% involved abusive behaviour or physical attack (2015: 39).

The schools' inspection body Ofsted (2015) expects schools to prepare children for life in modern Britain. Schools are expected to evidence that they are teaching children to live in a diverse society with explicit teaching of the protected characteristics, enshrined in the Equality Act (2010). All children should have the right to be safe in a school where they can thrive and learn. During school inspections, Ofsted asks children questions to ascertain their perspective, and expects school leaders to show they are enabling this through the curriculum and personal development opportunities given.

However, universities (with the exception of teacher training programmes) are not scrutinised by the Ofsted inspection framework. They are places of freedom of speech, independent learning, choice and open dialogue. The question is: what is socially acceptable speech in a diverse society? Are schools, teachers and students comfortable with discussing ethnicity and issues related to ethnicity? Universities are still responsible to the law and the Equality Act (2010).

Case study

Kate is a trainee teacher in a West Midlands school. She is discussing safe spaces at university, and reflecting on her recent experience as an undergraduate at a UK university:

> I think you have got to be careful we are all aware of what we are talking about (ethnicity and religion) and we all know and respect that fact that we are discussing it in this nature but other people may think 'why are they discussing that'?
>
> It depends on what is heard or what context it is being spoken about. Perhaps you wouldn't go into the canteen or perhaps in to [the Study Centre] and talk in depth as perhaps you would in a lecture or seminar room. Maybe it is . . . not unsafe, but there are better and worse places to talk about religion and ethnicity. If someone was in here now, they may say 'why are you talking about ethnicity and religion?' and they have perhaps heard a word I have said. So I think there are unsafe places to talk about it: it all depends on what context it is taken in.

Kate, along with many other students, is conscious of being 'PC' (politically correct). When involved in a debate within a seminar, students are able to speak freely and rules are co-constructed to ensure every member of the seminar (students and staff) can express views if they wish to.

Consider:

- What might make appropriate ground rules to promote a 'safe space'?
- What issues or elements might undermine such an approach or make it difficult?

Modood and Acland (1998) explored ethnicity and higher education. For them, education is seen as a way of increasing social mobility and an effective way of combating racism in future employment. Almost 20 years on, the Casey Review (2016: 86) reported that:

> White graduates achieve significantly higher degree classifications than graduates from other ethnicities, with a 15% difference between Black and other minority ethnic groups and their White counterparts in attainment of first or upper second class degrees – even allowing for prior qualifications and other influencing factors.

The report also presents statistics showing that the number of unemployed white men and women is disproportionate to the unemployed men and women from other ethnic groups. However, it is over 50 years since the Race Relations Act (1965). Education should be providing the vehicle for understanding of cultural diversity and mutual tolerance. Three generations after this, there is still a gap in the educational and employment success of some minority groups.

Pause for thought

Reflecting on the discussion outlined above, consider:

- Is your university course/school curriculum developing a positive and inclusive position on ethnicity? Is it racially impartial? Should it be?
- Is there a variety of representation via images in your educational setting showing different ethnicities positively?
- Are library resources varied in their imagery? Do book covers represent the diversity of ethnicities in your locality and beyond?
- If your setting lacks a diverse mix of students and staff, is there an effort to respond to this with education?

The European Union referendum in Britain (2016) centred on the issue of immigration. The latest statistics for Britain (2011 Census) show that there is a growing change in community makeup. Some areas in London, Birmingham and other cities are shifting from predominantly white to predominantly ethnic minority populations. London can be seen as unique; currently its ethnic and racial diversity is reflected in its trade identity. However, according to Judah (2016), we can expect more than half of Britain's districts to become more like London by 2050. In 2013, 1 in 13 (7.8%) of the usual resident population of the UK were from black, Asian and minority ethnic backgrounds. This compares to 1 in 20 (5.0%) in 2004 (Office for National Statistics, 2011). There are rising numbers of ethnic minority children starting at schools in England, with distinctions *within* their racial or ethnic groups as well as *from* their white British national classmates; some will be third generation residents in the UK or more. So are current migrants going to be able to integrate? Alternatively, is it a future of racial and ethnic groups living alongside each other? Many new faith schools are being established and they enable different groups to be educated separately. This is unlikely to change with the government's encouragement of the Free School programme. Parents choose the school for their children. Free schools are opening, which is expanding the number of schools with religious character. Johnston et al. (2006) explored school preference and found that parents want to send their child to a school that has children who are similar to them. This data is from minority groups and the dominant majority; but essentially this is about parental choice. Anecdotal data (Hopwood, 2007) indicates that the number of pupils home educated is increasing, with religious reasons being a factor of the choice. Schools plan trips to visit places of worship, including mosques, and many parents refuse to let their children attend. Phillips calls this 'the effect of ethnicity on school choice' (2016: 46). As educators, we need to consider whether we are prepared to understand the complexities and particular cultural and religious needs of the children and families with which we work, and to consider how we prepare student teachers and others on university courses in the field of Education Studies to consider the issues.

Case study

In a US middle school, the student population is diverse and reflective of the local community. On a visit there, the students are undertaking a project, making sports bags from textiles. They are invited to choose their fabric and use the sewing machines to sew their bag.

The class teacher is a white male. I asked him how he creates such a positive classroom atmosphere when his life is so different from the lives of these 12- and 13-year-olds. He tells me the school staff are invited to attend 'Cultural Conversations'. They receive a stipend and Professional Development points for doing so. Some examples from the series are:

- embracing the linguistic and cultural assets of your classroom;
- understanding gang involved youth, with a focus on how best to serve this population;
- unconscious bias;
- the needs of refugees;
- Polynesian culture; and
- Latino culture.

This enables the staff (who generally do not have similar backgrounds) to understand further the lived experience of their students and enable them to support the students better. One teacher commented that it was an enriching opportunity and lent insight into some of the challenges facing his students on a daily basis. He felt a little more credible and understanding of their lives.

It is important to consider whether education is, or can be, the conduit for equal opportunities or equity. To explore this further it is necessary to start with an analysis of stereotyping and prejudice in education settings.

Stereotyping and prejudice

Allport (1954: 434) stated that: 'We cannot agree with those enthusiasts who claim that "the whole problem of prejudice is a matter of education"'. It has been many decades since this was written, and it still is important today to discuss this concept. Behaviours and attitudes are developed through family life and influenced by peers and the media. Allport reported on research undertaken with higher education students in South Africa. White people with different levels of education were asked questions about 'natives', and the university-trained respondents were more positive and less prejudiced in their responses. Allport concluded that education lessens anxiety and insecurity, and enables a more holistic view of society, thereby summarising that university-educated students know that their wellbeing is linked to others.

But what of this in today's widening participation university population? If every other young person (i.e. approaching 50%) is attending university, shouldn't we be living in a prejudice-free world?

Since the 1950s, the change in society has been immense. Many students that attend university now are mixing with new friends and fellow scholars from a wider range of backgrounds – including their religious beliefs and cultural traditions. In addition, anxiety is rife: students are increasingly reporting mental health issues and have more insecurities as general awareness increases. This increase has been reported to the Higher Education Funding Council for England (HEFCE) (2015: 3) as being a result of developments in awareness of mental health; earlier diagnoses; the reputation of student services; and financial pressures.

Case study

During an interview Adam, a student mentioned earlier in the chapter, was keen to explain that he remembered a teacher in his childhood being prejudiced against anyone in the class who was not of the Christian faith:

> I went to a Church of England School and I didn't enjoy my time there, I really didn't and I felt there was some stereotyping towards some of the students who went there who weren't from a Christian background. I felt it was more socially acceptable then – it was more seen as, not just a stereotype but more seen as 'it's just the way'. In retrospect I have realised that those types of students were discriminated against.

Adam continued, putting forward the view that his recent undergraduate years, twenty years later, have been experienced differently:

> I can say I have never experienced any form of prejudice at this institution at all. It is brilliant and very, very inclusive and I think that is the nature of universities. They are institutions of forward thinking, they are institutions of enlightenment, it is effectively the nature of the university. I don't think any institutes these days can afford to be stereotypical towards anyone or afford to be bothered with any form of prejudice, I just don't think they can. I think they would shoot themselves in the foot.

Consider:

* Is Adam's assertion that an organisation would 'shoot itself in the foot' by showing prejudice or by stereotyping people a good reason for that approach?
* What values do you think should motivate inclusive practices and policies?

Many students have shared with me their childhood experiences of stereotyping and prejudice, often when judged for being Christian or not. Experiences vary from those who attended schools with a religious character ('faith schools'), to those who attended a community school (not sponsored or endorsed by religious groups). What about Adam's perspective from his recent undergraduate experience? It is positive. Does that reflect the university experience today for all? Adam is a white male. Does that protect him from being the recipient of prejudice and stereotyping?

> Reflecting on your own experience, consider:
>
> - Whether you have memories of stereotypical behaviour or prejudice from your own child-hood or schooling?
> - If you had such experiences, were they related to your faith or the faith position of the perpetrator?
> - Have you encountered any religious or racial prejudice at university? If so, how did you react? Are there procedures to support you or others? Would you know what to do if you encountered such prejudice?

As educators, we may still make assumptions about the learners in our classrooms. We may hold stereotypes without intent but they are there, for example: a lecture room filled with white students – all Christian; a student in a veil – Muslim.

Those of us fortunate enough to teach modules in the field of religion can open the questions and labelling up to the floor. I have found students very happy to speak in this environment about their own faith, or their choice to have no religion. Students will explain their home lives and the belief systems of their families. Grandparents' views are often very different from the students' perspectives. Nevertheless, this openness and willingness to talk about one's own position is very different from the experiences these students tell of in the work place, or outside of university.

Case study

A class of postgraduate trainee teachers are asked to create group presentations on the main world faiths to develop their subject knowledge. Daryl asks if he can research and present on atheism. The tutor agrees and the following week the presentations take place. Within the safe environment of the seminar room, where rules of conduct are pre-agreed, the students present their scholarly research. Daryl talks about what being an atheist means to him. The group listens and asks him questions about his belief system. He is quite defensive, anticipating certain awkward questions. The group, guided by the tutor, listen respectfully and share their preconceptions and stereotypical thoughts, addressing them through the process.

A group of society that receive considerable prejudice is Muslims. The Tell MAMA Annual Report (2015) on *The Geography of Anti-Muslim Hatred* illustrates, with statistics, the rising scale of attacks on Muslims, particularly women. A confusion about the beliefs and lived experiences is presented, and distorted, by the media, politicians and other voices. It is imperative that the students that graduate from our universities have been able to challenge these misrepresentations. Both the Tell MAMA Annual Report (Faith Matters, 2015) and Butler-Sloss (2015) call for the media to be held account-able for its reporting, and acknowledged for effective presentation of religion. Social media is a very prevalent part of society; it can have both positive and negative roles, and the individual consumer has to be discerning when reading it. This exemplifies the need for encounters and dialogue in higher education – thus developing the young person's capacity to choose to be involved or to rebuke messages that perpetuate stereotyping and prejudice.

Research

Kate, a trainee teacher in a primary school, comments on social media:

> I just completely disagreed with everything they said and it was awful really because you think 'why do you think that way?' . . . there are people I have known that are very, very open about how they feel on social media but when it comes to having a conversation . . . soften how they feel a little bit.

She continues, sharing an item on social media:

> about a lady, she has got a black husband and she said it was the first time after Brexit that he was racially abused on the train in his life in public and it almost made it that it was ok to be that way around somebody and I think it's oh well everyone voted for it, the majority voted for it, so it's fine to be, not a racist but to be unaccepting of others, of others beliefs and religions.

Consider:

- What are the implications for us as educators of the political changes that occur?
- How would you respond to a pupil or student in your care who reflected this position, whether it was their own values or those of their parents?
- What should be done to educate students about the role of social media as a means of sharing stories about prejudice and stereotyping?

The United States presidential election campaign of 2016 included commentary on different groups of people: Muslim, black, white and Christian. There were so many identifiers and then opportunities to stereotype and label. The curriculum we teach can and should enable a positive understanding and respect for diverse groups of society.

Schaffner et al. (2017) wrote an analytical paper for a conference presented in January 2017 entitled 'Explaining White Polarization in the 2016 Vote for President: The Sobering Role of Racism and Sexism'. They note that the 2016 US presidential candidates included ethnicity and gender in their campaign. The fact that the vote also showed the largest gap between votes of college and non-college educated white people in over 40 years relates to the study earlier mentioned by Allport. This divide became the most significant factor in the final result. This correlates with Adam, whose perspective, as a graduate, is that there is no prejudice or stereotyping in his university. This develops the view of university as a safe and inclusive place: an open and liberal environment, but which is not reflective of wider society and behaviour outside of it. However, data is not available to illustrate whether this is, in fact, an accurate picture of university life per se, and therefore is limited to the experience of the participants in this study.

There seems to be a realistic premise that schools will also be environments that are free of stereotyping and prejudice. However, when prospective trainee teachers are asked in my Education lectures to list all the stereotypical terms they know, the list is exhaustive. There is a tension, there-fore, between the ideal of an inclusive and prejudice-free experience of education, and the reality faced by many students.

Research

Kate is reflecting on an instance when she was in a lecture with a visiting speaker:

> A woman came in and spoke from the council who worked with families from the traveller community and she said there was a lot of stereotyping from schools and just from the community itself. I have seen it first-hand. I think we can all relate to that from media reports and in fact, I feel that the travelling community is the only one that it is still allowed to be racist towards. That is my opinion, that is not fact, that is what I believe. People will make comments about it and if you change the word 'traveller' for 'Asian' or 'black' then what they are being is effectively racist. It is almost saying it is allowed to happen. I am not sure why that is, in my opinion it is the community that is under-represented in the media as well; often slated. After that lecture it made me realise that the stereotypical view is that the traveller community don't value education – but I think they do. It is a different type of education – so we can sit here and say 'this is how you educate a child', but they may educate in a different way and for us to sit back and say that they don't value education, I think that alone is bad and that was something that was discussed as well.

Consider:

- Do you think Kate is right?
- Have you experienced negative stereotyping in school of any groups?
- What would you do?

For further discussion about Gypsy, Roma and Traveller children, see Chapter 4 on Learners and Learning.

In my own experience as a teacher, I recall a Teaching Assistant commenting about a traveller child who had arrived at school late with: 'what do you expect from them?' It is not only the curricu-lum that needs to establish positive values and challenge stereotypes, but the ethos of the school and the behaviour of the staff. Schools are actively engaged in the logging of racist incidents, and most promote a positive emphasis on the social, moral, spiritual and cultural development (DfES, 2014) of pupils. These are all aspects of an effective school with a good moral stance. But the personal belief system and attitudes of the role models around children are the hardest to change.

British values

> What we value is sometimes reflected in the things that we do, but it can also be evident from what we do not do.
>
> (Woolley, 2013: 190)

In the discussion above, it is clear that for pupils and students that an inclusive educational journey needs to reflect a curriculum and ethos that has considered and includes religion and belief, ethnicity, stereotyping and prejudice. This comes from the attitudes and behaviours of leaders and educators. What they value will build this experience for the young people educated within the setting.

Over the course of our lifetime, we develop our values, change our values and reflect on our values. Young children are influenced mostly by their family, but this changes through the teenage years to be one's peers. Another huge impact on schools is the requirement for schools to promote fundamental British values (DfE, 2014).

These are identified as being:

- democracy;
- the rule of law;
- individual liberty; and
- mutual respect for and tolerance of those with different faiths and beliefs and for those without faith.

Schools are required to promote these values through their SMSC (Spiritual, Moral, Social and Cultural Development) programme. In addition, Ofsted requires evidence that children in schools are well-prepared for life in modern Britain.

Case study

Mark is sharing his experience of seeing British values at a placement in a primary school:

> I would argue that a lot of them are generic values of perhaps Western culture more so than other cultures, but I would say with respect it is probably the value in most cultures, so it is not particularly British, but it is just the fact that the school is in Britain.

Whilst Kate's view is:

> I think that to label values as British, I think it disregards others a little bit, I think it's because there are really, really broad values of democracy and respect that should be

cross cultural. I don't understand the whole labelling of 'British' to be honest. I think that is wrong and they should be universal really.

Consider:

- Are British values any different from universal values?
- Is there a distinct 'Britishness' in the fundamental British values list and should we be embracing the patriotic nature of them or admonishing the title and living the values, regardless of our home country?
- Is it inclusive?

When considering how inclusive we are as a society, we need to bear in mind the increased diversity amongst people in terms of cultural and religious backgrounds. The picture of Britain's main faiths has changed significantly in the last half-decade. The media portrayal can contort the reality and lead us to raise the profile of Islam higher than the size warrants. In fact, there is still less than 10% of the population identifying as Muslims, Hindus and Sikhs (Butler-Sloss, 2015), with the 2011 Census (Office for National Statistics, 2013) detailing that 4.8% of the population are Muslim.

Phillips (2016) calls the range of ethnicity and faith in Britain 'superdiversity'. In a super-diverse society, how do we include all religions and beliefs, and how do we include those who profess to have no religious belief?

Religion and belief can be experienced in a range of ways. For Trevor Phillips (2016), the former chair of the Equality and Human Rights Commission, the discussion is one of complacency – complacency about the diverse nature of Britain and complacency over inclusion. He speaks of the British value of democracy, but questions whether Britain is really upholding democratic practices. We know that, statistically, different groups of children perform at different standards throughout their schooling. Ethnicity is a factor here, with African Caribbean boys underachieving compared to their peers (see also Chapter 4 on Learning and Learners). From Swann (1985) onwards, research has demonstrated this disparity. The Lambert Research Project Brief (2015) states that DfE data from 2014 shows that only 16% of Black Caribbean men go to university. They cite factors such as stereotyping, teachers' low expectations, exclusions and head teachers' poor leadership on equality issues as reasons for the difference in standards. This is a concerning set of data that illustrates great differences, with Black Caribbean students experiencing a combination of negative factors to prevent their equal achievement in society and education.

Butler-Sloss (2015: 6) states:

> Furthermore, intra- and inter-faith disputes are inextricably linked to today's geopolitical crises across the Middle East, and in many parts of Africa and Asia. Many of these disputes are reflected back into UK society, creating or exacerbating tensions between different communities.

It is important to encourage more open discussion about issues like this in order to consider how we can start to change attitudes so groupings do not become aggressive or hostile to one another. A key aspect of this discussion is the consideration of how we can make social groups more inclusive.

Moving forward

In order to develop inclusive practice we need to consider:

- how recent graduates view their experiences positively in the area of religion and belief, ethnicity, stereotyping and prejudice, and what we can learn from their experience;
- how there needs to be engagement with these issues across education settings, including in the university sector;
- how inclusive the university campus is and whether open dialogue is encouraged and enabled, and how;
- that there is still a need for understanding of safe spaces and how to develop them;
- that the religious landscape is changing and we need to reflect this in curriculum;
- that university alumni are open to diversity;
- that we need to educate young people to be critical consumers of media and social media;
- whether different ethnic groups achieve differently at university; and
- whether our policies and practice enable reporting of prejudice and stereotyping.

Conclusion

This chapter has explored religion and belief, ethnicity, stereotyping and prejudice. Using the perspectives of recent graduates, there is the sense that progress is being made towards inclusive attitudes. However, the wider political position across Europe and the USA has identified a misalignment with this positively accepting position. We need to enable university students to recognise these issues and to feel empowered to embrace different identities and belief systems. Preventing the exclusion of individuals or groups is of key importance.

If you ask any university its mission, it will be to be inclusive; any school will be the same. This is a challenge but one to which we need to aspire.

Further reading

Butler-Sloss, E. (2015) Report on the Commission on Religion and Belief in Public Life. *Living with difference: Community, diversity and the common good*. Available at: www.woolf.cam.ac.uk/uploads/Living%20 with%20Difference.pdf (Accessed 21 February 2017).
Phillips, T. (2016) Race and Faith. *The deafening silence*. Available at: www.civitas.org.uk/content/files/Race-and-Faith.pdf (Accessed 21 March 2017).

References

All-Party Parliamentary Group on RE (2013) Re: The Truth Unmasked *The supply of and support for Religious Education teachers*. Available at: http://religiouseducationcouncil.org.uk/media/file/APPG_RE_-_The_Truth_ Unmasked.pdf (Accessed 21 February 2017).
Allport, G. W. (1954) *The Nature of Prejudice*. Boston: MA: Addison-Wesley.
Butler-Sloss, E. (2015) Report on the Commission on Religion and Belief in Public Life. *Living with difference: Community, diversity and the common good*. Available at: www.woolf.cam.ac.uk/uploads/Living%20 with%20Difference.pdf (Accessed 21 February 2017).

Casey, L. (2016) The Casey Review. *A review into opportunity and integration*. Available at: www.gov.uk/ government/uploads/system/uploads/attachment_data/file/575973/The_Casey_Review_Report.pdf (Accessed 21 February 2017).

Cole, M. (2012) 'Racism and education: From empire to ConDem.' in Cole, M. (ed.) *Education, Equality and Human Rights*. Abingdon: Routledge, 79–100.

Department for Education (2014) Promoting Fundamental British Values as Part of SMSC in Schools. *Departmental advice for maintained schools*. Available at: www.gov.uk/government/uploads/system/uploads/ attachment_data/file/380595/SMSC_Guidance_Maintained_Schools.pdf (Accessed 22 March 2017).

Dinham, A. and Shaw, M. (2015) *RE for Real: The future of teaching and learning about religion and belief (full report)*. Available at: www.gold.ac.uk/faithsunit/reforreal (Accessed: 21 February 2017).

Equality Act (2010) UK. Available at: www.legislation.gov.uk/ukpga/2010/15/contents (Accessed 10 March 2017).

Faith Matters (2015) *The geography of anti-Muslim hatred tell MAMA annual report 2015*. London: UK. Available at: www.tellmamauk.org/wpcontent/uploads/pdf/tell_mama_2015_annual_report.pdf (Accessed: 10 March 2017).

Ferguson, J. (2016) UK hate group leader disputes neo-Nazi title: 'I'm a skinhead and a white supremacist'. *The Daily Record*, 31 March. Available at: www.dailyrecord.co.uk/news/scottish-news/uk-hate-group-leader-disputes-7659206 (Accessed 10 March 2017).

HEFCE (2015) *Delivering opportunities for students and maximising their success: Evidence for policy and practice 2015–2020*. Available at: www.hefce.ac.uk/media/HEFCE,2014/Content/Pubs/2015/201514/ HEFCE2015-14.pdf (Accessed 21 March 2017).

Hopwood, V., O'Neill, L., Castro, G. and Hodgson, B. (2007) *The prevalence of home education in England: A feasibility study research report RR827*. Available at: http://dera.ioe.ac.uk/7792/1/RR827%20r.pdf (Accessed 21 March 2017).

Johnston, R., Burgess, S., Wilson, D. and Harris, R. (2006) School and residential ethnic segregation: An analysis of variations across England's local education authorities. *Regional Studies*, 40(9), pp. 973–990.

Judah, B. (2016) *This is London: Life and Death in the World City*. London: Picador.

Modood, T. and Acland, T. (1998) *Race and Higher Education: Experiences, Challenges and Policy Implications*. London: PSI. Vol. 841.

Office for National Statistics (2011) *2011 census*. Available at: www.ons.gov.uk/census/2011census (Accessed 21 March 2017).

Office for National Statistics (2013) *Religion in England and Wales 2011*. Available at: www.ons.gov.uk/ peoplepopulationandcommunity/culturalidentity/religion/articles/religioninenglandandwales2011/2012-12-11 (Accessed 21 February 2017).

Ofsted (2013) *Religious education: Realising the potential*. Available at: www.gov.uk/government/uploads/ system/uploads/attachment_data/file/413157/Religious_education_-_realising_the_potential.pdf (Accessed: 21 February 2017).

Ofsted (2015) *School inspection handbook: Handbook for inspecting schools in England under section 5 of the Education Act 2005*. Available at: www.gov.uk/government/publications/school-inspection-handbook-from-september-2015 (Accessed 10 March 2017).

Peniel, J. E. (2016) 'White Lives Matter', now a hate group, is part of a long arc of white supremacy. *The Daily Record*, 31 August. Available at: www.theguardian.com/commentisfree/2016/aug/31/white-lives-matter-hate-group-white-supremacy

Phillips, T. (2016) Race and Faith. *The deafening silence*. Available at: www.civitas.org.uk/content/files/Race-and-Faith.pdf (Accessed 21 March 2017).

Race Relations Act (1965) Available at: http://nationalarchives.gov.uk/cabinetpapers/themes/race-relations.htm (Accessed 21 March 2017).

Racial and Religious Hatred Act (2006) Available at: www.legislation.gov.uk/ukpga/2006/1/pdfs/ ukpga_20060001_en.pdf (Accessed 21 March 2017).

Schaffner, B. MacWilliams, M. and Nteta, T. (2017) 'Explaining White Polarization in the 2016 Vote for President: The Sobering Role of Racism and Sexism.' *Conference on the U.S. Elections of 2016: Domestic and International Aspects*. IDC Herzliya Campus. January 8–9, 2017. Available at: http://people.umass.edu/schaffne/ schaffner_et_al_IDC_conference.pdf (Accessed 21 March 2017).

Swann, M. (1985) *Education for All Report of the Committee of Enquiry into the Education of Children from Ethnic Minority Groups*. London: Her Majesty's Stationery Office.

Woolley, R. (2013) 'Values.' in Taylor, K. and Woolley, R. (eds.) *Values and Vision in Primary Education*. London: Open University Press, 189–205.

7   Dis/ability

Sharon Smith

We all face barriers in our lives, but problems accessing basic activities can develop into huge barriers for those living with particular needs and requirements. This became a reality for me when I recently planned a well-earned short break away at a luxury hotel with my husband, who has a mobility difficulty. Having made them aware that we would require a room with an accessible shower, preferably close to all the hotel facilities, they assured me that they would book us into one of their disabled suites.

On arrival, we discovered that our room was on the second floor and that the service lift (not the guest lift) was the only access to it through the Spa. The entrance to the Spa building was at the top of the hotel drive. Suitcases in tow, with no help offered by the hotel staff, the next obstacle was to pass through five fire doors. We entered into our room to see the only access to the balcony was over a step.

Introduction

The notion of disability has tended to conjure up a perspective of 'lacking and unable to do something', and this can certainly be seen in the historical view of disability. In more recent years, through greater social awareness and re-framing the notion of disability as the ability *to do something with adaptation* or *by using a different approach*, it has become possible for the barriers of disability to be redefined as 'abilities' for those with particular needs, or as 'accessibility' requirements.

The definition of a person with particular physical requirements such as mobility needs is often developed using the approach of a medical model (Mallet and Runswick-Cole, 2014). This can be seen to be quite negative as it focuses on a deficit model, or the inability to do something. Historically we would have considered most disabilities to be dealt with outside of the normal environment, and consequently many people with disabilities were institutionalised. Changes such as the adoption of the Salamanca Statement (UNESCO, 1994) and the Disability Discrimination Act (DDA, 1995) promoted a social model approach. The DDA, for example, made discrimination in the workplace and public life illegal and ensured that those with particular needs defined as 'impairments' were given the same equal access and opportunities as those deemed 'normal'. The DDA highlighted the needs of individuals and the concept that wherever possible all individuals should have their needs met. The term 'reasonable adjustments' was introduced to cover situations where the needs of an individual could not be fulfilled, resulting in the need for reasonable adjustments to occur. For example, it may not be possible to put a lift in a building due to building regulations or a building being protected because of its historical importance. However, some alternative option could be offered such as a room on the ground floor. In the hotel case outlined in the vignette at the start of this chapter, all legal requirements were clearly being met, but the consideration of the needs of the individual is where the 'reasonable adjustments' fell short; it is recognised that all cases are not the same and it would be difficult to fulfil all individuals' requirements. This highlights the able person's responses to disability as a process and not a social construction of achieving equal status for all. In contrast, we may consider the accessibility of facilities for parents and those with gender requirements; most toilet facilities and in some cases lifts state 'disabled', thus setting apart the individual unseen/invisible needs of others who may wish to access services 'for the disabled'. If we were to construct a more acceptable model of accessibility, then this would be open to a range of needs and begin to define a more open social model approach. (For further discussion about gender accessible toilets, see Chapter 8 on Gender Diversity.) It is for these reasons that at times in this chapter I use the term dis/ability (disjointing the deficit and the ability).

Hodkinson and Vickerman (2016), in exploring definitions of inclusion, highlight that special educational policy uses deficit language, referring to weakness or disability and, as they highlight, 'definitions employing language and categorization shackle an individual's inclusion to entrench societal attitudes' (2016: 8). They explore this notion by using the example of Professor Stephen Hawking and that of a Prime Minister to explore the term 'weakness', and highlight that in such a situation where quantum physics is discussed between the two in a conversation, then without doubt Stephen Hawking would not be displaying a weakness. They confirm a belief held within my own practice and experience that disability is therefore constructed within society's notion, described by Hodkinson and Vickerman as 'hieratical notions of normality' (2016: 9).

Through providing a definition of disability and considering the historical perspectives of disability, an argument is presented that challenges us to consider to what extent have we raised expectations and aspirations for those with 'disabilities'. More importantly, has society taken these expectations seriously or just paid lip service to them?

This chapter explores the changes in policy which have impacted on societal changes in attitudes towards disability, as well as the historical perspectives and definitions of disability which have created barriers in the past. It also examines how those with disability have been empowered through inclusion with reference to social perspectives and, in particular, how media have constructed and influenced society's approaches through image based viewpoints.

In presenting some dialogue around the perceptions of disability and its definition, the intention is to enable the reader to consider their own viewpoint in relation to their current practice and resources, in a context set against a backdrop of political and legal agendas.

Definition

The term disability is a negative one, as the suffix 'dis' highlights a deficit or inability. The notion of disability is often characterised as a physical concept and is defined within the English language as a weakness, or even a sickness (Hodkinson and Vickerman, 2016). Disability in these terms is often reinforced in society through the use of imagery or symbols which emphasise accessibility to services and environments, such as that of using a wheel chair or a hearing aid loop. I would consider the symbol of a wheel chair as one which indicates primarily a mobility and accessibility concern, not necessarily a disability.

A disability can be defined as an individual person's need which may require some adjustment in order to access the world around them. Sometimes these individual needs are obvious, but we are not always as aware of the difficulties some individuals face as their personal needs are 'hidden'. Although these needs may be less obvious, these individuals nonetheless can have barriers placed before them as a result of environmental issues and personal perspectives. This is highlighted within the vignette at the beginning of the chapter, where the physical disability was not necessarily obvious, and in this case the individual's difficulties are adjusted through specialist footwear, and no other mobility aids such as a walking stick are evident. The notion of someone being 'dis/abled' suggests the vision of someone being abled who has somehow become un-abled. How, therefore, can we move away from the deficit model to the idea of someone being 'abled', but requiring additional support or an adjustment? In other words, the idea of them being en-abled.

Wiley (2015: 242) considers that labelling concedes to producing a 'negative and stigmatizing meaning to what are naturally occurring individual differences' and continues to argue through examples of obesity that society 'dehumanises' individuals. His argument offers an additional point to how we might continue to support individuals with particular needs without some identification of those needs. From my own approach to teaching, what is generally good for learners with specific needs suits a range of other learners who may have particular needs which are not identified or disclosed. Many learners do not disclose a specific need such as dyslexia or mental health concerns. It would therefore be considered good practice to ensure notes are available prior to a teaching session for those learners with dyslexia, and providing opportunities for tutorial support or embedding a session to promote 'well-being' would also be considered good practice. Other adjustments can be made in anticipation of personal needs, such as suitable access to a room, or a desk being suitably adjusted (this could be for a person with accessibility needs ranging from a wheel chair user to a student who has restricted growth). By taking such steps, we remove the notion of 'dis/ability', as we are providing a positive environment and promoting inclusion where we develop a culture of acceptance for all needs.

Mallett and Runswick-Cole (2014: 3) regard the Oxford English Dictionary definition as recognising firstly a disability in terms of 'lack' and secondly as a 'condition'. This confirms the definition as being in the realm of the medical and social model approach. Mortimore (2008: 40) highlights the social model as a perspective which removes a 'problem', whereas the medical model highlights barriers both physically and in terms of cultural beliefs. In recognising this, Mortimore goes on to argue that the social model enables the individual to have autonomy and 'focuses upon the dismantling of barriers and grants individuals the power and responsibility to make decisions about their future'.

In contrast, we can view the term 'disability' as a legal requirement which enables the individual then to access systems and requirements as a result of this 'label'. Therefore, the regulations that govern and protect an individual enable them to access society, employment and basic rights on an equal basis with any other human being. We can define this further within the term 'inclusion', which provides for a value, belief or conceptual approach to the acceptance of all to accessing a given situation, such as education. We can certainly see that policy has developed a more inclusive approach through acknowledgement of inclusive agendas, but pivotal to success in this area are the personal perspectives of the individuals delivering or managing budgets and training to ensure inclusion happens.

Pause for thought

Consider the language we use in describing individual needs:

- What do we define as 'normal'?
- How can we ensure the language we use promotes a positive viewpoint for individuals deemed as 'disabled'?
- How can we change the language we use to promote an inclusive ethos and move towards a social model approach?

We can define the social model of disability as a positive viewpoint; however, this can be disputed. Mallett and Runswick-Cole (2014: 11) highlight Watson's (2002) views that not all people with individual needs consider themselves to be disabled, and this is exemplified in the case study of Alison Lapper (outlined later in this chapter). Mallet argues that we can sometimes over-compensate for disability, and in presenting a social model we are identifying the individual with the problem, not a need or requirement; as Mallett and Runswick-Cole indicate, we neglect to see a wider perspective on individual differences in society such as age, gender or ethnicity. This argument considers the approach to inclusion and how far we have really moved to the notion of an inclusive ethos and not just an approach. I argue that we need to move forward in applying an ethos and not an approach, which indicates the need for a more robust legal requirement than that of a personal approach to recognising others' differences. Wiley (2015) writes about modifying our beliefs and adapting our approaches, but with constraints on financial resources, the impact of limited physical resources produces barriers to the notion of a social model, and it is important to consider the impact that the current economic and political climate will have on continuing to develop an inclusive approach or at least maintain it.

Pause for thought

A student who has accessibility needs is part of a group of students who are completing an outdoor activity. Is the approach to change the activity to meet the needs of that individual student or to ensure all activities embrace an accessibility viewpoint in the first place?
   Consider:

- Are we applying an adaptation to a setting or a policy to facilitate a person's needs?
- Are we applying an ethos which naturally embeds the person's needs into our setting and approaches?
- To what extent do we define our values and beliefs in relation to the financial implications?

Historical perspectives

Historically we can see the development towards a more open approach, where we can integrate disability into society. Mallett and Runswick-Cole (2014: 67) document the historical perspective, succinctly highlighting the approaches in ancient Greece and the links to the writing of scholars and the belief that deformities and impairments were 'supernatural', resulting in persecution. We can see through Mallett and Runswick-Cole's account that over time the approaches differed and developed, with aspects of the responsibility for disability falling to the community for 'care'. In the United Kingdom, the development of legal care and reform emerged significantly in the post–Second World War era and with radical social changes in educational policy, developments then focused on education as a right for all, highlighting special educational needs. However, the impact of war time atrocities and the Holocaust highlighted the perception of an 'ideal man', and the extent to which this has impacted on a stronger drive for inclusion, to challenge that notion of the perfect specimen, should be considered. Policy within the UK and international United Nations convention (2006) has driven this recognition of the human rights of all individuals, and the legal implications of such policies have been progressively implemented in many contexts.

Borsay (2005: 102) recognises that these historical developments have impinged on some social attitudes and that some policy has created more barriers to our current day thinking. An example is the opening of special schools in 1880; whilst this altered the exclusion of disabled people from education, we may question the current thinking and its impact on inclusion as a notion. Throughout this period of time the Eugenics Education Society was established (Kellet, 2008) and terminology was negative and provided a deficit notion with the use of demeaning terms such as 'feeble-mindedness', 'idiocy' and 'imbecility', all defining a person as part of a sub group of society.

In Britain before the late eighteenth century, disabled children were considered incapable of education, and as highlighted by Borsay, '"disabled" children were generally regarded as just "lunatics" and were dismissed as irretrievably "mad"; without an unimpaired mind and body, rationality and hence full personhood were impossible'. Mallett and Runswick-Cole (2014) highlight the work of Borsay (2005) and argue that in exploring the historical perspectives we may wish to consider the viewpoints of those documenting the changes, and indeed consider whether those who were pivotal in driving change had some agendas which were driven from government viewpoints or from financial agencies.

Political and legal agendas

Vargas-Baron (2014) identifies that the Salamanca Statement (UNESCO, 1994) provided a framework for action and in doing so created a focus on child's rights, enabling each child to achieve his or her full potential. This pivotal change in the child's rights enabled an education system to develop which promoted an equal approach internationally. We have indeed seen changes within the educational needs of children in the United Kingdom, and demonstrated a shift in society's perspectives towards an inclusive approach through the Warnock Report (1978). It should be noted that at the time the report was written, terms such as 'handicapped' were still used; however, it promoted a move away from this negative terminology.

Ekins (2012) debates some of the changes to the current system in the UK and highlights that we still need to develop policy further; indeed we have seen the full implication of the changes in the Code of Practice for Special Education Needs from 2001 to the present version of the Code of Practice Special Education Needs (DfE, 2015). Initially the Special Education Needs Code of Practice (DfE, 1994) highlighted that the school should meet the needs of the child, and that the parent(s) and children should be consulted in the provision. In the interim years the Code of Practice (DfES, 2001) refined the process required to support the child, moving to a more coherent way to enable identification of needs and for appropriate provision to be put in place through Individual Educational Plans (IEPs).

Significantly we have seen changes in the age covered by the Code of Practice (DfE, 2015) with an inclusion of those up to the age of 25 years old and the inclusion of disability within its provision (Windwood, 2016). In addition, the requirement to apply the Code is statutory and the scope of the Code now extends to a wider range of educational providers, including special or further education and sixth form colleges. The drive is to ensure that the approach within education is more inclusive, whoever the provider is, and that it requires each provider to take responsibility in enabling the needs of the learners it educates. Previously the requirements were seen to be met once the school had provided some intervention. School Action and School Action Plus have been replaced by SEN Support, placing the emphasis on the school. The current code is aimed at making the system more child-centric, bringing all of the agencies involved together to provide a more coherent service. In addition, the new Education, Health and Care Plans (EHC Plans) have replaced Statements of Special Educational Need (DfE, 2015).

Booth and Ainscow (2011) highlight that education is a route towards changing society's viewpoints – the 'Index for Inclusion' (Booth and Ainscow, 2011: 10) provides an approach to supporting and developing educators which they highlight as providing a wider remit as 'it is linked to democratic participation within and beyond education'. Through our education system, we can model expectations and develop viewpoints, and we can see from the legislation and policy that the expectation for a more inclusive society has emerged. Indeed, the Equality Act (Legislation.gov.uk, 2010) and other frameworks such as Article 30 of the *Convention on the Rights of Persons with Disabilities* (UN, 2006) confirm the rights of those with disabilities as being an equal right.

Armstrong et al. (2010: 4) highlight that policy has an impact on society; it has 'a significant role in promoting social cohesion in societies that are increasingly diverse'. In identifying this they concede that agencies have a role to play and that the impact of international agencies 'have been powerful advocates of "inclusion" as a core principle of schooling and education systems'. We can see that since the Salamanca Statement (UNESCO, 1994) policy across Europe and further afield has moved forward; as Calderson-Almendros et al. (2014: 251) discuss, the move forward still needs addressing, as the 'social disability model emphasises something that historically constituted a boundary'. Indeed, research undertaken during the EU-funded GUIDE Project (2013) presented later in this chapter highlights the need to move international and European policy forward; definitions and terminology are major factors in developing this successfully, as seen from the discussion on the use of DSM V4 (World Health Organisation, 1992).

Whilst historical evidence shows the poor attitude toward dis/abilities conveyed in and by society, trends towards inclusive approaches have developed. Culture places high importance on the viewpoint of individuals' needs, as highlighted by Haller's (2010) view that people who have not experienced disabilities (the non-disabled) learn about these through the media and through culture. Mallett and Runswick-Cole (2014: 14) highlights the portrayal of disability through media in fictional characters such as Frankenstein, and we can see through English literature the portrayal of Tiny Tim in Dickens' *A Christmas Carol*. We have currently seen a more positive promotion of dis/ability through sports and the promotion of greater normality is evident in the Paralympics – the inclusion of a range of individual needs within the sporting arena has enhanced society's outlook.

Shakespeare (2016: 1137) reviews the impact of the Paralympics and recognises that the coverage of 'the Paralympic Games showcases what disabled people can do, challenges negative attitudes, and potentially open minds and doors'. The impact of the Paralympics normalises individual needs, rather than highlighting them as 'out of the ordinary' or taking place with adaption for their particular needs by making adjustments. The further portrayal in media and advertising of the growing normalisation of individuals with dis/abilities is transforming society's viewpoint and acknowledging that a person in a wheel chair can also have a sense of humour. The way media views disability and transmits this to society can determine a societal outlook and portray either a positive or negative viewpoint. Recently, within London Fashion Week, the debate emerged in relation to using models who had a disability. If we view how fashion portrays disability, it provides a particular figure for fashion. This viewpoint has a powerful media platform. Within this debate, the press recognised that the very word 'disabled' does not portray that disabled people can in fact be powerful, and it was recognised that the word in itself was dated and disabling. This debate went on to state and echo a social model perspective that makes the point that people with disabilities are not disabled by their impairment or need, but by the barriers created by society.

Pause for thought

Reflecting on the ideas about London Fashion Week and the Paralympics, consider:

- How has the media portrayed disability?
- What impact do the semiotics of disability have on our thinking?

Reflect on the use of a symbol of a wheel chair to identify an accessibility toilet.

- How might this make you view the notion of accessibility?

The GUIDE Project 2013: challenges and perceptions

In examining the debate around inclusion and the perspectives on individual needs or disabilities, I am able to draw upon my own research relating to European perspectives on disability. The aim of the European Union Comenius-funded GUIDE Project (2013) was to inform policy within the European Union and to provide opportunities to develop good practice. The training materials designed as a result of the project are intended to enhance teachers' skills for supporting students with learning difficulties, improving their ability to apply inclusive strategies within their classes. The GUIDE Project contributes to the achievement of the 'Strategic objective 3: Promoting equity, social cohesion and active citizenship', as set out by the Strategic Framework for European Cooperation in Education and Training ('ET 2020'). The framework was set up to ensure that European students with mild learning difficulties were taught with innovative teaching strategies. The project also addressed the objectives of the policy paper of the European Commission (2017) *Rethinking education: Investing in skills for better socio-economic outcomes* by supporting initiatives to train teachers appropriately to support students with a diverse range of needs.

The main outcome of the GUIDE Project (2013) was to address the need for teachers in mainstream schools to be trained to work with students with special educational needs. The project focus was on teachers working in secondary schools with students aged between 12 and 18 years, depending on national education systems. The project research highlighted the main aspect of training required, materials were developed to support training needs and data from initial questionnaires and interviews indicated these needs. From the data the project identified five main areas to develop training packages for the school teachers; these were:

- autism spectrum
- moderate learning difficulty
- Attention Deficit Hyperactivity Disorder (ADHD)
- dyslexia and/or dyscalculia
- speech, language and communication needs

Defining the definitions

The GUIDE Project (2013) consisted of five European partners whose project output was to design a manual for 'Teaching Strategies with Students with medium-light cognitive impairment (MLC)' and provide an online resource. At the onset of the project, the team from the UK recognised the different approaches to inclusion in each country and the varying attitudes and values towards disabilities. It was evident early on in the project that the terminology used was defined from DSM V4 (World Health Organisation, 1992) and was outdated, using such terms as 'mental retardation'. In using DSM V4 for setting requirements within education settings, it implied a 'medical model' approach. Indeed, it was evident from further discussion that the social model of disability was not widely used. However, in using DSM V5 (World Health Organisation, 2001), more acceptable terminology was used, moving the terminology on from 'retarded' to 'impaired'.

Evidence within the research was gathered through questionnaires, interviews and focus groups. The research gathered data from 145 schools and 12 further education colleges were contacted. Participants in the interviews were selected randomly from all those who responded to the questionnaire. The data from the interviews highlighted some main themes:

- The importance of defining the terms and jargon used for identifying needs. There is a need to ensure that the terms medium-light cognitive impairment (MLCI), special educational needs and disability are defined clearly. From the responses, it was found that there was a lack of clarity amongst the respondents in this regard.
- It is important to help young people to take ownership of the strategies that will aid their learning.
- Promoting student self-advocacy is very important.

Conclusions from the project highlighted that it is essential to understand each learner as an individual, rather than as a person with a label or a child with a special educational need. It is also important to help learners to live and learn with independence, building self-esteem, self-advocacy and self-direction. The project also highlighted the different models of approach in providing support with learning in schools. Within the EU, in some areas the main focus of additional support in the classroom was in using the 'specialist' teacher approach; this facilitated more one-to-one interaction, and the students were typically withdrawn or removed for the support. This model can be challenged as it does not necessarily advocate an inclusive approach. Indeed, Balshaw and Farrell (2002) advocate a more inclusive approach. It was particularly highlighted in the data from the GUIDE Project (2013) interviews that teachers did not always see the use of TAs as positive (see also Chapter 11 on Teaching Assistants and Inclusion).

Research

As a part of Work Package 3 for the GUIDE Project, data was initially gathered from the five partner countries through a questionnaire with education professionals, and from this a sample was randomly selected to gather further data through interviews. Significantly, the data from the participants varied across the partnership and the data showed how the impact of support from TAs varied and also how the deployment of TAs varied.

Results from interviews show the views of teachers, that:

- The use of the Teaching Assistant can impair group working in some cases; those TAs supporting just physical needs stay too close to the learner; and this has an effect on group dynamics and learning.
- Boys find the TA less acceptable. It's a gender thing: girls work better with the TAs.
- Some participants highlighted that in using a TA this can segregate the learner, and one participant commented that 'within the gender groups, there appears to be an attitude of treating the learner as a "pet", but this can be determined by the personality of the learner. I don't consider there to be equal interaction'.

In contrast, Blatchford et al. (2012) consider some of the different approaches in using TAs but concluded that TAs with appropriate training are effective resources and their support promotes inclusion through integration in class work.

The findings from the GUIDE Project (2013) highlighted some key themes around the use of Teaching Assistants and their roles, and the training provided for them is a key area that needs to be considered by teachers working with young people with special educational needs (Hewston et al., 2015). The project findings also highlighted that some participants were more inclusive than others, and practice was not consistent within the partner countries. These examples from participants highlighted that they were not as inclusive as examples from the UK and that the involvement of parents and carers within the education was limited; the parents' voice was not always considered to be important and it was evident that the established ethos of the educational system was not to be questioned.

Pause for thought

Reflecting on the findings of the GUIDE Project (2013), and the earlier discussion about the medical and social models of disability, consider:

- how to develop a more inclusive approach which removes labels;
- the use of visual symbols: what signs might depict open access or access friendly facilities, which could be just as accessible for those with children or with mobility concerns; and
- the extent to which policy has been instilled within the hearts and minds of individuals who on a day to day basis are not in contact with disability.

Case study

The following two case studies present contrasting experiences of inclusion and inclusive practices. Both case studies have been taken from open sources (Lapper, 2006; Blackburn, 2013). The first focuses on Alison Lapper and an individual's physical needs, whilst the second focuses on Ros Blackburn highlighting a hidden disability.

Alison Lapper: physical disabilities

Alison Lapper was born in 1965 and was considered at birth as not likely to survive. She was born with a congenital malformation called phocomelia, a birth defect which at the time was associated with Thalidomide. She spent most of her formative years in an institution, and notes in her autobiography that the medical profession viewpoint was that 'disabled children should not live at home with their parents' (Lapper, 2006: 19); she comments that staff tried to normalise her condition with prosthetics. Alison highlights that if only the workshop technicians had asked her what would work for her in the beginning and a more collaborative approach had been applied, 'the results would have been more impressive' (Lapper, 2006: 37). Alison highlights that she 'was considered to be severely disabled and hate that phrase with a passion, but that was a label I lived with for nineteen years of my life' (2006: 18).

Public perceptions are challenged by Alison's approach, who openly states in her autobiography that, with a few a notable exceptions, people are not documented as celebrities if they have disabilities; she notes Heather Mills and Stephen Hawkins amongst a few.

If we view the personal case of Alison, who defines herself not as disabled but 'just different', then we remove the barriers that the term disabled or impaired can place on an individual. Mallett and Runswick-Cole (2014) explores the presence of body as defining disability; however, it is clear from Alison that her viewpoint is subject to a personal perspective that identifies a known ability to do things in a distinct way. This defines her ability to function within a world that has not adapted to her approach of 'we all do things differently'. Her viewpoint expresses that society's approach defines disabled people as a drain on society. Alison's viewpoint is poignant as she was disabled throughout her life, whilst a non-disabled person may look on disability as a deficit rather than as an individual's needs being different.

Reflecting on my husband's mobility needs outlined in the vignette at the beginning of the chapter highlights that a person could be considered disabled after being able, and the notion of no longer being able to do something and having a dis-ability is therefore an acquired condition. Arguing this viewpoint, Alison's definition is clearly acceptable as being 'normal', as her needs have always been the same and she has not adapted her lifestyle but has had the environment adapted for her. Arguably, for an 'able-bodied' person, a term I find debatable in this context, adapting would suggest a dis-ability to do something, but in fact, the ability to do something is decided by the environment rather than the person's ability to function. Alison's story challenges government agendas and public definitions and highlights a conflict in attitudes between policy and practice.

Alison's story considers a personal perspective which highlights barriers which existed and still exist in some areas, in recognising individuals rather than just their disability, often highlighted by the use of terms such as 'a disabled person' and not a person with disability/ individual needs. Such terms create barriers which are in place as a result of personal perspectives created by society. Reclaiming the land for an individual is highlighted by Alison's approach, and requires society to view her as different and not disabled.

Ros Blackburn: hidden disabilities

I had the pleasure of hearing Ros Blackburn speak about herself, and the struggle she has had to function in life. I was aware that she was medically diagnosed with Autism, but her overall presentation seemed confident and controlled. It was during her presentation that she explained the difficulties she had in functioning in everyday life; her stories of going shopping and engaging in sport highlighted an aspect of her Autism that made her daily life problematic.

Her particular needs were hidden yet were significant in that most of the daily tasks many people take for granted were difficult for her, and she could only make sense of the world with support. Considering these particular needs highlights that society is generally not always set up to allow for successful interaction. The abstract language we use and the social behaviour we require from each other all have the potential to create barriers. Ros Blackburn (2013) highlighted in her address that living each day was difficult and 'the outside world is a totally baffling incomprehensible mayhem . . . It is a meaningless mass of sights and sounds, noises and movements coming from nowhere, going nowhere'.

Jordan (2013), in enabling us to understand the characteristics and mindset of Autism, highlights that we have to rely on what those with Autism can understand, and this might be related purely to the characteristics of the world they live in and the people they know. This might be through learnt communication processes such as symbols or gestures through facial expression. Jordan considers the way forward is to develop relationships, both parental and professional, to enable a more meaningful world to exist for those with Autism. She highlights that in teaching children/young adults with Autism we have to try alternative methods, and comments that 'with Autism, we often have to do things "back to front"' (Jordan, 2013: 22); she considers that the way forward is to find things they are interested in.

I noted from the GUIDE Project (2013) research that a teacher shared an interesting story relating to one of her pupils, which echoes this abstract view. The teacher had asked her pupils to write a story about a picture which showed a man holding a suitcase which had opened and the contents strewn onto the floor. As a result, many children wrote about the man being a spy and the suitcase falling open. However, one learner was quite imaginative and explained that the suitcase had exploded and the contents had been projected violently from the box. This imaginative approach showed an abstract thinking process, which we may consider to be 'outside the box'.

Understanding the world we function in is important and knowing and making sense of it allows us to function successfully. However, for many people with Autism the ability to function successfully in everyday life is impaired. This hidden disability creates barriers. Research during the GUIDE Project (2013) highlighted some aspects of Autism, and the GUIDE Manual discussed some of the symptoms of Autism. It highlighted the need to present a social model approach to Autism in preference to a medical model which creates a negative response. Historically we would have seen people with Autism misunderstood and institutionalised, and we can see elements of this within the Alison Lapper case study outlined earlier, viewed from the perspective of a person with a physical disability. In examining the research from the GUIDE Project, the terminology in relation to particular needs can be challenged and indeed can cause some areas for discussion.

These 'hidden' factors create a disability to function, which we can see in Ros Blackburn's case, but many individuals have hidden disabilities which could range from dyslexia and other learning needs, to degrees of visual impairment, and well-being needs such as emotional difficulties or mental health concerns. How we manage this diverse range of needs is determined by the value base we have and the mindset we use in approaching these diverse needs. If we could consider approaching a wide range of needs as the 'norm', then the need to identify dis/ability to make adjustments would not be required. Indeed, in moving to a social model we meet a wider range of needs in a more effective manner. If we consider this as a requirement of practice in education, developing an acceptance of others rather than identifying and setting precedents to meet individual needs, we would see a more inclusive approach. Whether the ability to move forward is down to policy, or mindsets or values, is up for debate, but I believe that we have to move away from a deficit model if we are to move towards achieving true inclusion.

Having considered the approaches to how we view disability within our society, we can now see how our approach to individual needs has developed through policy and changes in our mindset and beliefs. We can see through the personal perspectives within the case studies how we can adapt our approach and environment to promote a more inclusive society.

Moving forward

In order to develop inclusive practice in the areas of ability and disability, we need to consider:

- How we maintain a consistent approach to inclusion with changing governments and variations in policy;
- How we develop a proportionate, balanced and effective approach to inclusion; and
- How thinking can be shared and developed internationally, with increasing globalisation and the contrasting rise in nationalism.

Conclusion

The rights of an individual are at the heart of this chapter, as is the aspiration to enable those with individual needs. The definitions and social constructs have evolved through historical changes in society, through medical advancements and from changes in legislation. We have seen the gradual development of a more positive approach that promotes an inclusive attitude. However, the true evaluation of our approach is how we manage this and develop our commitment to *enabling* rather than *adjusting* the environment, curriculum and social attitudes. As Alison Lapper highlights, we should consider the 'norm' as accepting that some people do things differently.

Further reading

Boyle, C. & Topping, K. (eds.) (2012). *What Works in Inclusion?* Maidenhead: Open University Press. Bristol: CSIE.

Glazzard, J., Stokoe, J., Hughes, A., Netherwood, A. & Neve, L. (2010). *Teaching Primary Special Educational Needs*. Exeter: Learning Matters.

Haddon. M. (2003). *The Curious Incident of the Dog in the Night-Time*. London: Vintage Books.

Hodkinson, A. & Vickerman, P. (2009). *Key Issues in Special Educational Needs and Inclusion*. London: Sage.

References

Armstrong, A.C., Armstrong, D. & Spandagou, I. (2010). *Inclusive Education: International Policy and Practice*. London: Sage.

Balshaw, M. & Farrell, P. (2002). *Teaching Assistants: Practical Strategies for Effective Classroom Support*. London: David Fulton.

Blackburn, R. (2013). *Understanding Impairments in Sports Training*. Worcester: University of Worcester. Unpublished.

Blatchford, P., Russell, A. & Webster, R. (2012). *Reassessing the Impact of Teaching Assistants*. Abingdon: Routledge.

Booth, T. & Ainscow, M. (2011). *Index for Inclusion: Developing Learning and Participation in Schools*. 3rd edn. Bristol: CSIE.

Borsay, A. (2005). *Disability and Social Policy in Britain Since 1750*. Basingstoke: Palgrave Macmillan.

Calderson-Almendros, I., Ruiz-Roman, C., Kiuppis, F. & Hausstatter, R. (2014). *Inclusive Education Twenty Years after Salamanca*. New York: Peter Lang Publishing.

Department for Education (DfE) (1994). *Special Education Needs Code of Practice*. Nottingham: DfE.

Department for Education (DfE) (2015). *Special Education Needs and Disability Code of Practice: 0 to 25*. London: DfE.

Department for Education and Science (DfES) (2001). *Special Education Needs Code of Practice*. Nottingham: DfE.

Disability Discrimination Act (DDA) (1995). London: HMSO. Available at: www.legislation.gov.uk/ukpga/1995/50/contents (Accessed: 22 March 2017).

Ekins, A. (2012). *The Changing Face of Special Educational Needs – Impact and Implications for SENCO and Their Schools*. London: Routledge.

European Commission (2017). *Strategic Framework – Education & Training 2020*. Available at: http://ec.europa.eu/education/policy/strategic-framework_en (Accessed: 22 March 2017).

GUIDE (2013). *Guidelines for Teachers Working with Students with Medium-Light Cognitive Impairment*. Available at: www.project-guide.eu/

Haller, B. A. (2010) *Representing Disability in an Ableist World: Essays on Mass Media*. Louisville, KY: Advocado Press.

Hewston, R., Smith, S. & Woolley, R. (2015). *Experiences of Education Professionals Supporting Learners with Additional Needs in European Union Partner Countries*. Birmingham: Aston University, TEAN.

Hodkinson, A. & Vickerman, P. (2016). Inclusion: Defining definitions. In Brown, Z. (Ed.), *Inclusive Education Perspectives on Pedagogy, Policy and Practice*. Oxford: Routledge, 7–13.

Jordan, R. (2013). *Autism with Severe Learning Difficulties*. Souvenir Press. Available at: https://ebookcentral. proquest.com/lib/worcester/reader.action?docID=1648823 (Accessed: 22 March 2017).

Kellet, M. (2008). Special educational needs in context: A historical overview. In Matheson, D. (2015) (Ed.), *An Introduction to the Study of Education*. 4th edn. London: Routledge, 321–333.

Lapper, A. (2006). *My Life in My Hands*. London: Pocket Books.

Legislation.gov.uk (2010). *Equality Act 2010*. Available at: www.legislation.gov.uk/ukpga/2010/15/contents (Accessed: 20 March 2017).

Mallett, R. & Runswick-Cole, K. (2014). *Approaching Disability*. London. Routledge.

Mortimore, T. (2008). Social and educational inclusion. In Ward, S. (Ed.), *A Student's Guide to Education Studies*. Abingdon, Oxon: Routledge.

Shakespeare, T. (2016). The Paralympics: Superhumans and mere mortals. *The Lancet*. Volume 388, No. 10050, pp. 1137–1139, 17 September. DOI: http://dx.doi.org/10.1016/S0140-6736(16)31600-2 (Accessed: 19 February 2017).

UNESCO (1994). *The Salamanca Statement and Framework for Action on Special Needs Education*. Paris: UNESCO.

United Nations Assembly Convention (2006). *Convention of the Right of Persons with Disability*. New York, NY: United Nation.

Vargas-Baron, E., Kiuppis, F. & Hausstatter, R. (2014). *Inclusive Education Twenty Years after Salamanca*. New York: Peter Lang Publishing.

Watson, N. (2002) 'Well, I know this is going to sound very strange to you, but I don't see myself as a disabled person: Identity and disability', *Disability and Society*, Volume 17, No. 5, pp. 509–527.

Wiley, L.A. (2015). Place values: What moral psychology can tell us about full inclusion debate in special education. In Bateman, B., Wills Lloyd, J. & Tankerskley, M. (Eds.), *Enduring Issues In Special Education-Personal Perspectives*. London: Routledge, 232–250.

Windwood, J. (2016). Leading and managing for inclusion. In Z. Brown (Ed.), *Inclusive Education Perspectives on Pedagogy, Policy and Practice*. Oxford: Routledge, 23–33.

World Health Organisation (1992). *The ICD-10 Classification of Mental and Behavioural Disorders: Clinical Descriptions and Diagnostic Guidelines*. Geneva: World Health Organization.

World Health Organisation (2001). *International Classification of Functioning, Disability and Health (ICIDH-2)*. Geneva: World Health Organization.

8 Gender diversity

Ruth Hewston

Girls . . . were allowed to play in the house . . . and boys were sent outdoors . . . Boys were noisy and rough, and girls were nice, so they got to stay and we had to go. Boys ran around in the yard with toy guns going *kksshh-kksshh*, fighting wars for made-up reasons and arguing about who was dead, while girls stayed inside and played with dolls, creating complex family groups and learning how to solve problems through negotiation and roleplaying. Which gender is better equipped, on the whole, to live an adult life, would you guess?

Keillor (1994: 12)

Introduction

Educational practitioners are aware of numerous factors which have a direct impact on children's educational experience and journey. For many learners, their gender may have a significant influence on their engagement and achievement in education. This includes both their biological gender and the gender they identify themselves as being. Much of the research on the impact of gender on education has focussed on these factors of engagement and achievement. However, a growing body of research also explores gender diversity, the notion that gender is non-binary and its implications for an individual learner's educational journey. Both foci have important implications for inclusion, exploring how each child can be supported to achieve their full potential and how addressing the protected characteristic of gender can support a more inclusive and equality driven educational experience for all.

This chapter seeks to discuss gender identity, issues of equality and perceptions of gender disparity in educational achievement and attainment. The discussion also explores the challenges of creating a gender inclusive education setting, including the development of a culture and ethos which recognises the needs of gender diverse learners. Recommendations are also made for moving the gender equality agenda forward within education settings.

Gender identity

Before opening the discussion on the impact of gender on learning and education, it is important to identify what we mean by the term gender. Gender refers to the social and cultural differences that may identify an individual as being male or female. It contrasts with the term sex, which refers to the biological characteristics of an individual. Consequently, gender refers to the socially constructed masculinities and femininities (Bartlett and Burton, 2016) created within society. Bartlett and Burton (2016) also highlight that gender contributes to ideas that males and females should engage in certain behaviours, beliefs, tasks and attitudes congruent with their gender. Furthermore, while there are distinct male and female biological differences, it is 'society and the culture we live in that creates the notion of masculinity and femininity' (Bartlett and Burton, 2016: 43).

Pause for thought

Reflection on the quotation from Keillor (1994) presented as a vignette at the start of this chapter:

- Are the differences in play a result of sex or gender differences?
- Are the gender stereotypes we form based on play behaviours observed in young children?
- Where do these behaviours originate?
- Are the differences in play discussed by Keillor a response to biological differences or socially constructed behaviours?
- How are gender identified and behaviours constructed (i.e., male, female and gender diverse)?
- What social and cultural factors could have affected the gender stereotypes seen?

In light of this definition, education provides an essential tool in the social construction of gender identities. Inclusive teaching has a significant role to play in addressing the social perceptions of what it means to be male or female. Westwood (2013) supports this idea by suggesting that traditional gender stereotypes and gender-specific role expectations can be dispelled by adopting inclusive approaches to teaching and learning. The social context of schools, colleges, universities and education settings provide an opportunity for gender to be constructed independent of biological sex, and assumptions based on both sex and gender to be challenged. Inclusive educational practices can be extremely positive for those that may be marginalised by their gender, but are also good practice for all in the classroom, enabling them to recognise the diversity of gender within wider society. Inclusive practices which support and promote equality of opportunity irrespective of gender also have important implications for children's wider understanding of gender diversity. Developing children and young people's awareness of what it means to be male, female and gender diverse can also lead to a shift in future society's socio-cultural thinking.

Gender equality

Forde (2008) suggests that although the significant advances made by girls and women, both as learners and educational professionals, may lead some to believe that gender is no longer a concern, this viewpoint is misguided and further efforts are needed. Forde (2008) suggests there are still groups of girls and women who do underachieve, or are at risk of underachieving, in education. The historical emphasis on tackling underachievement and attainment among boys has further compounded this issue. Furthermore, they argue that the emphasis on tackling performance among one gender only serves to highlight and disadvantage the opposite gender, creating competition between the two. Evidence suggests that the distinction between females and males in learning starts from an early age.

Francis (2010) discusses various viewpoints and historical research that suggests children within the early years do not initially understand toys to be gendered; however, they rapidly learn and perceive that some toys are 'for boys' and some 'for girls'. Explanations for this suggest that young children may be directed towards specific toys congruent with their gender, or that they actively use specific toys to delineate their gender stereotypes. Nevertheless, evidence from early years education and from contemporary marketing by toy companies promotes that, from a very early age, the nature of children's learning may be influenced by their gender. Eggen and Kauchak (2010) suggest that these gender differences continue and become more apparent in later school years and that additional evidence shows some teachers continue to treat male and female learners differently at all ages and phases of education.

Historically, the perception is that gender differences in education have been maintained by the adoption of a gender-biased curriculum, school uniforms and expectations of behaviour. This suggests that girls and boys have very different experiences of education. Over the years, several educational policies have specifically aimed to address this perceived difference. Notably, the Education Reform Act (1988) had a significant impact on gender equality and established a core curriculum to GCSE (General Certificate of Secondary Education) for both male and female learners. However, by gender there are still some discrepancies in pupils' achievement and decisions to study specific subjects. These differences have been frequently discussed around the decision to study STEM subjects (science, technology, engineering and maths) beyond GCSE by female learners. However, these are not the only differences, and this will be explored later in this chapter.

Issues of gender equality are particularly relevant within specific ethnic and community groups. Traveller communities are recognised as one of the most disadvantaged minority ethnic groups in the UK (DfES, 2003). Lloyd and McCluskey (2008) highlight the key contradictions concerning Gypsy and Traveller communities' marginalisation in education, suggesting that where perceived cultural characteristics exist, these have often been seen as problematic barriers toward the education system or as an excuse for those communities to exclude themselves from educational provision. In relation to gender inclusion, adapting education to meet the needs of Traveller communities creates significant dilemmas (Bloom et al., 2014). Bloom et al. (2014) suggest differing opinions for these concerns. Some participants they interviewed suggested that the education system should provide for children to assume traditional roles seen in Traveller society, which may involve stereotypical perceptions of labour in relation to gender, for example, males managing a business and females being primarily responsible for the home and family. However, other interviewees suggested it was important for education that aspirations not to conform to assumed engendered roles were considered.

Bloom et al. (2014) highlight that this presents a dilemma as to whether the provision of education should include 'stereotypical notions of what is perceived as being culturally relevant' or 'more universal values of gender equality in favour of a relativist approach to Traveller children' (2014: 8). Nevertheless, the challenges presented within gender equality also need to be considered as part of a broader inclusive agenda and must consider ethnicity and socio-cultural values and beliefs in order to be successful. It is an inappropriate assumption that beliefs about what it means to be female and male are the same within all communities and that these value systems are not influenced by broader ethnic and cultural beliefs and values.

Looking beyond the UK, the PISA (2012) study (Programme for International Student Assessment) shows some differences between male and female achievement among OECD countries (Organisation for Economic Co-operation and Development). Girls tended to have significantly better scores than boys in reading. For maths, boys were significantly ahead of girls in half the participating countries; however, the difference was much smaller than for reading. In the other participating countries, there was no difference in maths achievement of boys or girls (PISA, 2012). Harber (2014) highlights that internationally there are some 'dominant or hegemonic forms of male identity internationally which have traditionally preserved patriarchal power and privilege' (2014: 162). Bartlett and Burton (2016) point out that these forms promote perceptions of male dominance and female subservience in global communities. Thus, international evidence suggests that a significant number of countries still have gender disparity in relation to educational achievement and attainment. UNESCO (2015) highlighted that although between 2000 and 2015 significant progress had been made in relation to gender parity, almost a third of countries with data available showed gender disparity remained. This suggests the wider societal concern about gender equality is not an exclusively euro-centric issue and needs to be addressed at a global level.

Research

UNESCO (2015) makes the following statements:

- 'Attempts to increase access to school for girls will be thwarted if social institutions, norms and practices continue to be discriminatory.'

  (2015: 24)

- 'The recruitment of female teachers at all levels of education, textbook and curriculum reform, and training in gender-sensitive teaching are critical to improving gender equality in schools.'

  (2015: 153)

- 'Boys experience disparities in secondary education. Although gaps have narrowed or closed in many rich countries, they have widened in others, and the problem is emerging in some poorer countries.'

  (2015: 153)

Consider:

- At a school level, what strategies can be adopted to address these challenges?
- At a policy level, what changes should be made to address these challenges strategically?
- How do these key issues reflect your own experiences of education?

Impact on learning

Attainment and achievement

The clear majority of research, which has focussed on the attainment and achievement of male and female students, has examined performance in mathematics, verbal skills and cognitive abilities (Bramley et al., 2015). Although evidence suggests that performance of both boys and girls has significantly improved over the last 20 years, this rate of improvement appears to be higher among female students. Within the UK, Department for Education figures for GCSE performance show girls tend to outperform boys in most subjects. In 2016, mathematics was the only subject where boys outperformed girls (DfE, 2017). The gap between boys' and girls' achievement is particularly significant in English Language. Moving away from grade attainment, evidence also suggests there is a disparity between the STEM subjects; in most cases the proportion of boys being entered for these courses is greater than that of girls (Bramley et al., 2015). However, this has not always been a stable pattern. In 2014, the number of boys and girls taking the three single science courses (biology, physics and chemistry) was comparable. This disparity in subject choices raises some important questions, particularly in relation to the STEM subjects. Notably, discussions have focussed on the reasons why fewer female students have been entered for the single science subjects, and the attractiveness and relevance of the curriculum towards female interests and career aspirations. Readers will want to consider whether gender affects access to science subjects in their own context.

Continuing in to further education, at A Level, overall female students achieve higher average point scores than their male counterparts, a pattern which has remained stable in recent years. In relation to participation in maths and science subjects, except for biology, a higher number of male students are entered for these subjects. The gender gaps in maths, physics and computing achievement has also widened since 2015 (DfE, 2017). In relation to subject choices at A Level, a significantly larger percentage of male students are opting to study mathematics and physics; however, a significantly large percentage of female students are opting to study psychology, art and design and sociology (see www.cambridgeassessment.org.uk for further information). From an inclusive perspective, gender appears to be having an impact on achievement, as well as behaviour, subject and career choices (for a discussion about support for career choices see Chapter 9). Francis et al. (2014) explained this by suggesting that many students, both male and female, refer to stereotypical gender differences even whilst rejecting the idea that gender and other structural differences impact on their experience. For this reason, their subject and career choices are informed by subconscious and stereotypically held beliefs about their gender, and the decisions they make may, in part, conform to these firmly held views.

These trends continue into higher education (HE). Hillman and Robinson (2016) highlighted that male underachievement continues into the university sector in recruitment, retention and degree classification statistics. Furthermore, in relation to wider inclusion agendas for students from disadvantaged backgrounds and some ethnic monitories, Hillman and Robinson (2016) argue that these differences will only be addressed by focussing on male and female achievement. Resolving disparity in recruitment, retention and achievement data for ethnic minorities and disadvantaged groups will not be achieved if gender is ignored. They also argue that, although the financial gains for women HE graduates are not as significant as those for their male counterparts, HE remains attractive for women, particularly as non-graduating women achieve significantly less than non-graduating males.

In addition, there are also gender disparities in students' choices of subject at degree level. Hillman and Robinson (2016) point out that in 2014/15 only 17% of undergraduate Education Studies students were male and 15% of computer science undergraduates female. Male students also appear to outnumber female students at postgraduate (PG) research levels (53% to 47%), a number attributed to a significant difference in STEM subjects at PG level. In contrast, female students significantly outnumber males in PG taught degrees (59% to 41%) (Hillman and Robinson, 2016). The reasons for these differences are not fully clear; however, disparity between the genders appears to occur in several key areas and across all phases of education.

From an educational professional perspective, this raises some interesting points. Bartlett and Burton (2016) highlight that it is inappropriate to make generalisations about the underperformance of both male and female students. Aside from gender, some students of both genders do well and outperform their counterparts. However, there are also significant issues relating to additional factors, such as ethnicity and socio-economic background, which have an impact on gender achievement, particularly for working-class girls (Richards and Posnett, 2012, cited in Bartlett and Burton, 2016) which need consideration (see also Chapter 2 on Social Inclusion and Social Class). Oates (2015) also highlights that the issue is very complex and to make the assumption that the underperformance of boys is a result of gender stereotyped behaviours, which include lower engagement with learning among boys, is misguided (Younger et al., 2005). Oates (2015) more broadly suggests that these differences could also be explained by pupil grouping, approaches to assessment, teacher styles and expectations, role models, teacher approaches to praise and reward, and the curriculum itself. It is also important to note that although there is evidence of difference between the genders in areas of achievement and attainment, the differences are not always large and there is greater evidence of variation within the genders than between them (Bartlett and Burton, 2016).

Pause for thought

Consider:

- How a teacher's beliefs about gender stereotypes may influence their approach to teaching boys and girls.
- How the curriculum may be biased towards the gender of a particular group of students.
- Other than gender, what other factors could contribute to differences in attainment and achievement?
- How do the achievement and attainment statistics compare with your own experiences of education?

Additional needs

Evidence suggests that boys are more likely to be identified as having special educational needs (SEN) when compared to girls. Seventy percent of learners identified with SEN are boys, and they are much more likely to attend specialist school provision (DfE, 2007). Evidence also shows that boys are nine times as likely as girls to be identified with autistic spectrum disorder and four times as likely to be identified as having behavioural, emotional and social difficulties (BESD) (DfE, 2007). Furthermore, evidence suggests that gender is a better predictor of being identified with BESD than social class and ethnicity (DfE, 2007). Evidence from the DfE (2016) suggests that, although there has been some reduction, this pattern has continued and there is a higher number of boys with a statement or Education, Health and Care (EHC) plan. These findings raise important questions: whether specific learning needs are biologically more prevalent among males than females, whether educational professions are more likely to identify needs within a specific gender or, as discussed earlier, whether gender stereotypes of behaviour and engagement with learning influence professional perspectives. (For further discussion of issues relating to special educational needs and disability, see Chapter 7.)

In relation to gifted and talented learners, findings relating to gender have been mixed. Much of the research surrounding highly able learners has focussed on general achievement and attainment in specific STEM subjects. Freeman (2004) found that gifted girls in Britain surpass achievement of gifted boys in almost all subject areas. However, this difference could be explained by variations in the learner's confidence in their abilities or differences in the curriculum itself. In a geo-demographic analysis of the social origins of students identified as gifted and talented in England, over 37,000 gifted and talented students admitted to the National Academy for Gifted and Talented Youth (NAGTY) were analysed in relation to social background, gender, ethnicity and school type (Campbell et al., 2007). Evidence suggested gender distribution closely followed national distribution patterns and a relatively equal proportion of male and female students were identified as gifted (i.e., NAGTY 49% male, 51% female; national picture 51% male, 49% female). This suggests that within secondary schools, male and female students are equally as likely to be identified as gifted and talented. Contrastingly, Callahan and Hébert (2014) found evidence to show differences between male and female learners in general attributions of success and specific discipline attribution. Highly able male learners are more likely to attribute success to ability and failure to a lack of effort. In contrast, able female learners appear to attribute failure to not working hard enough rather than lack of knowledge or skills (Freeman, 2004).

From an inclusive perspective, the experience of male and female learners with specific needs (i.e., SEN or highly able) may be influenced by gender. However, evidence consistently suggests that social background and ethnicity play a significant role. Educational professionals should take all these factors into consideration if they wish to create an inclusive setting that meets the needs of all these individuals.

School culture and ethos

In the recent decade, significant forward steps have been made in education with respect of gender diversity and its impact on educational experience. However, education is embedded within a larger social context, which predominantly discusses gender in alignment with birth sex. It often fails to recognise the wider gender diversity within our schools, colleges, universities and education settings. Journals, such as *Gender and Education*, have emerged that focus on the social injustice of such concepts and seek to further understanding of the place of gender in relation to other key differences which also may marginalise a learner or impact on their inclusion. In response to this issue, in order to develop an inclusive ethos, education settings should be supported to move away from this binary view of gender (i.e., male or female) to a more gender diverse perspective. Furthermore, Guasp

(2012) found evidence to suggest that over half (55%) of lesbian, gay and bisexual young people have experienced homophobic bullying in school. This evidence clearly demonstrates that a diverse range of genders may be 'othered' by the education system (i.e., male, female and 'other' learners). This wider educational context suggests that, both academically and socially, children and young people may be treated differently by virtue of their gender.

Within the context of education, this perspective highlights several challenges to address. This discussion will focus on five of these primary concerns: the adoption of gender specific uniform and dress codes, the provision of gender inclusive facilities (e.g., bathrooms), curriculum concerns, the representation of gender within the teaching profession and gender interaction.

Gender specific dress codes

Most schools within the United Kingdom require students to wear a school uniform or adhere to a specific dress code. The suggestion is that a school uniform improves pupil behaviour both in and out of school, contributes to school ethos and gives pupils a sense of identity with their school. However, there is very limited research evidence to support these ideas. From a gender inclusive perspective, there has been significant discussion that expectations on male and female students to conform to specific dress codes (i.e., boys unable to wear skirts) do not support the creation of an inclusive setting. The assumption is that prescribed dress codes based on biological sex expect a particular type of gender performance. This requirement to conform to specific dress codes also frequently means gender is seen as a binary construct. Furthermore, feminist discussion also considers whether enforced wearing of skirts expects girls to embody certain gender traits (Happel, 2013). Aapoia et al. (2005) argue that skirt wearing consciously and unconscious modifies behaviour to conform to certain expectations:

> Young women must monitor and control what can and cannot be seen, and be responsible for the effects of the sexual meaning of their body parts in social relations . . . restrict their move-ment so as to preserve 'modesty' . . . in order to allow them to do everyday activities without the ascription of sexual meaning.
>
> Aapoia et al. (2005: 140–1)

For learners whose gender identity does not align with their biological sex, this expectation can create a challenging, and potentially upsetting, situation. In relation to inclusion, schools must consider and provide flexibility in their school uniform requirement which recognises gender diversity. Given the socially constructed nature of gender, the suggestion would be for education settings to consider the gender the learner identifies with as a means of identifying the appropriate dress code to be worn. Some inclusive schools do take this approach; however, this is not universal and is often at the dis-cretion of the school leadership team.

Gender inclusive facilities

The availability of facilities within education institutions may discriminate against learners who are non-gender-normative. Rasmussen (2008) argues that bathroom facilities are a daily aspect of gen-der identity, presenting daily challenges for gender diverse individuals. She suggests that 'toilets don't just tell us where to go; they also tell us who we are, where we belong, and where we don't belong' (2008: 440). Bathroom facilities are frequently labelled as male or female, either using language (i.e., women, girls, men, boys) or a symbol. Hence, bathroom facilities within education settings are often seen as gender binary. Gender binary facilities force individuals to misgender themselves or feel invalidated as they are forced to use facilities that do not align with their gender identity. For gender diverse learners, this may present a source of confusion, apprehension and discomfort. Consequently, this has a wider impact on the learner's educational experience. Rasmussen (2008) argues that within a school, bathroom facilities can become a site of persistent discrimination, harassment and violence.

Following an inclusive agenda, addressing this issue presents various challenges. Increasingly university and higher education institutions are adopting more all gender or gender neutral inclusive bathroom facilities. For learners who identify outside the gender binary, these facilities provide a more inclusive environment that avoids specific gender identities and are adapted to meet a gender diverse community. In addition, research has argued that all gender inclusive facilities are also supportive of individuals with disabilities and specialist needs. Within schools, the introduction of gender neutral facilities has raised concern, particularly from parents, that unisex facilities may leave children vulnerable to abuse or early sexualisation. Some of the discussion also argues that both male and female young people should be provided with a safe space, both physically and emotionally.

Ingrey (2012) argues that more knowledge and research evidence is needed, through policy and practice, to explore educational institutions' normalisation of gender as binary. Settings wishing to develop their inclusive provision need to consider the availability of inclusive facilities. Similar to meeting the needs of those with disabilities, education settings need to identify daily activities that place gender diverse learners as equals. Consideration should also be given to the division of facilities based on gender (social constructed identities) rather than sex (biological differences).

Curriculum concerns

In relation to equality and the achievement of specific genders, the content and nature of the curriculum is often discussed. Evidence suggests that the nature of the education system, particularly in schools, is very female oriented. Bartlett and Burton (2016) highlight that the nature of assessments, shifting towards coursework and away from examinations, may also favour female students. This may in part contribute to differences in achievement and attainment previously discussed. DCSF (2009) suggest there is no specific bias in the school curriculum and that there are aspects of the curriculum content which have specifically been chosen to engage male and female learners. They also argue that the idea that the content of secondary education curriculum reflects particularly gendered interests and that these interests equate to achievement is a myth (DCSF, 2009). However, it is important to recognise that a balanced curriculum for gender diversity should seek to represent all genders equally, particularly in fields which stereotypically may hold gender-biased perceptions: for example, the representation of successful female scientists within the science curriculum. This balanced curriculum should also seek to recognise and include gender diverse topics within its subjects, supporting learners' awareness and acceptance of the non-binary spectrum of gender.

Pause for thought

Consider:

*   To what extent are notable male and female figures discussed and studied within the curriculum (i.e., historical figures, theorists, scientists and authors)?
*   What steps could schools take to develop a gender inclusive approach to dress codes?

Representation of gender

DfE (2015) evidence suggests that in 2014, 80% of full-time equivalent staff working in schools were female. Furthermore, 74% of all teachers across education were female. In relation to other school roles, 79% of all support staff and 91% of learning support staff are female (for a further discussion of the role of Teaching Assistants in schools, see Chapter 11). To address this, there has been an increasing priority in teacher training recruitment to increase the number of male teachers entering the profession, particularly in primary schools (Francis et al., 2008). The perception has been that by increasing the proportion of male teachers who also could be seen as role models by learners, this would also address underachievement among boys. However, little research evidence supports this proposition (Carrington and Skelton, 2003). Seeing boys as a homogenous group suggests all other factors are also similar (e.g., ethnicity, social class). However, research suggests that this is not the case and that the gender of the teacher is not important to learners. Furthermore, Lahelma (2000) found evidence to suggest that individual teacher ability was far more important to learners than their gender. Numerous studies have also supported this, suggesting that there is no correlation between gender and pupil achievement. There is also no robust research evidence to suggest that the gender of the teacher has an impact on the teaching attitudes or approaches used (DfE, 2015). In conclusion, the notion that classroom inclusion could be supported by a greater representation of male teachers should be dismissed. A greater emphasis should be placed on the diverse ways gender may be represented in the classroom, rather than a focus on biological sex of the teacher and staff within the setting (Francis et al., 2008).

Gender interaction

Research into teachers' perceptions of gender differences, associated interactions and teacher gender expectations in the classroom have all been shown to have a significant impact on both engagement and learners' self-perception (Francis, 2002). Evidence also suggests that teachers tend to spend a larger proportion of their time with boys rather than girls within the classroom. However, Bartlett and Burton (2016) raise the important point that beliefs about identity and teacher's perceptions relating to gender achievement, behaviour and engagement with learning may contribute to the issue, creating a self-fulfilling prophecy regarding children's education. Consequently, an inclusive setting welcoming of gender diversity should adopt whole-school strategies and challenge gender assumptions in to order to achieve a fully inclusive ethos and school culture.

Pause for thought

Consider an educational setting you engage with or that is familiar to you:

- How does the setting ensure everyone is included?
- How does the setting promote gender equality and equity?
- How does the setting respond in an inclusive way to issues relating to gender?
- What further steps could the setting take to ensure gender diversity is supported?
- Which policies, legislation and guidance support practitioners within the setting to work inclusively in relation to perceptions of gender roles, gender assumptions and gender stereotypes? (Consider national, local and setting-specific policies.)

Moving forward

In order to work towards inclusive practice in relation to gender we need to consider:

- The interaction of gender with learners' social backgrounds and ethnicities;
- The individual needs of the learner, irrespective of their gender identity;
- The setting's culture and ethos in supporting gender equality and diversity;
- The representation of gender equality and diversity within the curriculum content, teaching and assessment patterns;
- The accessibility of facilities to learners of all genders; and
- The expectations on learners that are non-gender specific or stereotyped.

Conclusion

Returning to the quotation that opened this chapter, it is clear from the discussion that assumptions cannot be made about gender and the impact it has on a learner's educational journey. Evidence suggests that differences do exist between male and female learners' educational achievement and attainment, and this may influence learners' aspirations and career choices. More importantly, inclusive education should not seek to define gender as a binary construct, but recognise, respect and value a more fluid and diverse gender definition. Only this approach may address gender disparity and create a more gender inclusive culture, ethos and setting.

Further reading

Arnot, M. and Mac an Ghail, M. (2006) *The Routledge reader in gender and education*. New York: Routledge.

References

Aapoia, S., Gonick, M., and Harris, A. (2005) *Young femininity: Girlhood, power and social change*. New York: Palgrave Macmillan.

Bartlett, S. and Burton, D. (2016) 'Influence of gender on achievement', in Richards, G. and Armstrong, F. (eds.) *Key issues for teaching assistants: Working in diverse and inclusive classrooms*. 2nd edn. Abingdon: Routledge, pp. 42–51.

Bloom, F., Hamilton, J., and Potter, M. (2014) 'Challenges and barriers in primary school education: The experience of Traveller children and young people in Northern Ireland'. *Education, Citizenship and Social Justice*, 9(1), 3–18.

Bramley, T., Vidal Rodeiro, C. L., and Vitello, S. (2015) Gender differences in GCSE. Cambridge Assessment Research Report. Cambridge, UK: Cambridge Assessment. Available at: www.cambridgeassessment.org.uk/Images/gender-differences-at-gcse-report.pdf (Accessed: 12 December 2016).

Callahan, C. M. and Hébert, T. P. (2014) 'A critical analysis of research on gender issues in gifted education', in Plucker, J. A. and Callahan, C. M. (eds.) *Critical issues and practices in gifted education: What the research says* (2nd ed.). Waco, TX: Prufrock Press, pp. 267–280.

Campbell, J., Muijs, D., Neelands, J. G. A., Robinson, W., Eyre, D., and Hewston, R. (2007) 'The social origins of students identified as gifted and talented in England: A geo-demographic analysis'. *Oxford Review of Education*, 33(1), 103–120.

Carrington, B. and Skelton, C. (2003) 'Re-thinking "role models": Equal opportunities in teacher recruitment in England and Wales'. *Journal of Educational Policy*, 18(3), 1–13.

Department for Children, Schools and Families (DCSF) (2009) *Gender and education – mythbusters: Addressing gender and achievement: Myths and realities*. Available at: http://webarchive.nationalarchives.gov.uk/20130401151715/www.education.gov.uk/publications/eOrderingDownload/00599-2009BKT-EN.pdf (Accessed: 3 March 2017).

Department for Education (DfE) (2007) *Gender and education: The evidence on pupils in England*. Available at: http://webarchive.nationalarchives.gov.uk/20130401151715/www.education.gov.uk/publications/eOrderingDownload/00389-2007BKT-EN.pdf (Accessed: 15 January 2017).

Department for Education (DfE) (2015) *School workforce in England: November 2014*. Available at: www.gov.uk/government/uploads/system/uploads/attachment_data/file/440577/Text_SFR21-2015.pdf (Accessed: 3 March 2017).

Department for Education (DfE) (2016) *Special educational needs in England: January 2016*. Available at: www.gov.uk/government/uploads/system/uploads/attachment_data/file/539158/SFR29_2016_Main_Text.pdf (Accessed: 1 December 2016).

Department for Education (DfE) (2017) *Revised GCSE and equivalent results in England: 2015 to 2016)*. Available at: www.gov.uk/government/statistics/revised-gcse-and-equivalent-results-in-england-2015-to-2016 (Accessed: 28 March 2017).

Department for Education and Skills (DfES) (2003) *Aiming high; raising the attainment of Gypsy Traveller pupils*. London: DfES.

Eggen, P. and Kauchak, D. P. (2010) *Educational psychology: Windows on classrooms*. (8th ed.). Upper Saddle River, NJ: Pearson-Prentice Hall.

Forde, C. (ed.). (2008) *Tackling gender inequality: Raising pupil achievement*. Edinburgh: Dunedin Academic Press Ltd.

Francis, B. (2002) *Boys, girls and achievement: Addressing the classroom issues*. London: Routledge.

Francis, B. (2010) 'Gender, toys and learning'. *Oxford Review of Education*, 36(3), 325–344.

Francis, B., Burke, P., and Read, B. (2014) 'The submerge and re-emergence of gender in undergraduate accounts of university experience'. *Gender and Education*, 26(1), 1–17.

Francis, B., Skelton, C., Carrington, B., Hutchings, M., Read, B., and Hall, I. (2008) 'A perfect match? Pupils' and teachers' views of the impact of matching educators and learners by gender'. *Research Papers in Education*, 23(1), 21–36.

Freeman, J. (2004) 'Cultural influences on gifted gender achievement'. *High Ability Studies*, 15, 7–23.

Guasp, A. (2012) *The school report: The experiences of gay young people in Britain's schools in 2012*. Stonewall: University of Cambridge. Available at: www.stonewall.org.uk/sites/default/files/The_School_Report__2012_.pdf (Accessed: 8 November 2016).

Happel, A. (2013) 'Ritualized girls: School uniforms and the compulsory performance of gender'. *Journal of Gender Studies*, 22(1), 92–96.

Harber, C. (2014) *Education and international education: Theory, practice and issues*. Oxford: Symposium Books.

Hillman, N. and Robinson, N. (2016) *Boys to men: The underachievement of young men in higher education – and how to start tackling it*. Available at: www.hepi.ac.uk/wp-content/uploads/2016/05/Boys-to-Men.pdf (Accessed: 21 January 2017).

Ingrey, J. C. (2012) 'The public school washroom an analytic space for gender: Investigating the spatiality of gender through students' self-knowledge'. *Gender and Education*, 24(7), 799–817.

Keillor, G. (1994) *The book of guys*. London: Faber and Faber.

Lahelma, E. (2000) 'Lack of male teachers: A problems for students or teachers?' *Pedagogy, Culture and Society*, 8(2), 173–185.

Lloyd, G. and McCluskey, G. (2008) 'Education and Gypsies/Travellers: "Contradictions and significant silences"'. *International Journal of Inclusive Education*, 12(4), 331–345.

Oates, T. (2015) An analysis of the gender divide – from primary school to the workforce, paper presented to Gender differences – the impact on secondary schooling – boys or girls, who's winning? London, October 2015. Available at: www.cambridgeassessment.org.uk/Images/gender-differences-tim-oates.pdf (Accessed: 15 August 2016).

Programme for International Student Assessment (PISA) (2012) *PISA 2012 results: The ABC of gender equality in education: Aptitude, behaviour and confidence*. Available at: www.oecd.org/pisa/keyfindings/pisa-2012-results-gender.htm (Accessed: 5 March 2017).

Rasmussen, M. L. (2008) 'Beyond gender identity'. *Gender and Education*, 21(4), 431–447.

Richards, G. and Posnett, C. (2012) 'Aspiring girls: great expectations or impossible dreams?', *Educational Studies*, 38(3), 249–259.

UNESCO (2015) *Education for all 2000–2015: Achievements and challenges (EFA Global Monitoring Report)*. Available at: http://unesdoc.unesco.org/images/0023/002322/232205e.pdf (Accessed: 12 November 2016).

Westwood, P. (2013) *Inclusive and adaptive teaching: Meeting the challenge of diversity in the classroom*. Oxon: Routledge.

Younger, M., Warrington, M., and McLellan, R. (2005) *Raising boys' achievements in secondary schools: Issues, dilemmas and opportunities*. Maidenhead: Open University Press/McGraw Hill.

9   Aspirations and social mobility

Jane Owens

When Kate was 15, she wanted to be a hairdresser – her mother was a hairdresser, and Kate helped her to cut family and friends' hair. A few years later, Kate accompanied a friend who was seeking legal advice from a solicitor. She had never met a solicitor before, and thought their work sounded interesting – she also liked the young woman who advised her friend. She now wants to find out more about training to be a solicitor, and thinks it must be a great way to meet and help people.

Introduction

As we progress through life, we make decisions about what we want to learn and what jobs we want to do. These decisions are influenced, consciously and unconsciously, by a range of factors: whilst some of these factors will help us to progress in life, others can restrict our aspirations and our social mobility:

> The transition from school to work is vital because choices made at this point will have lifelong effects. Making a good transition into work can overcome earlier disadvantage. Making a bad transition can mean a lifetime of poverty.
>
> (House of Lords 2016: 15)

Those of us working in education can help our students to make informed decisions about their next steps by providing effective careers education, information, advice and guidance (known as CEIAG in England) and, as part of that, assisting them to identify and explore the factors influencing their aspirations. We can also aid them in their development of social and cultural capital: whilst some young people can draw upon a wealth of capital (social, cultural and economic) to smooth their transition to adulthood and economic independence, others cannot (see also Chapter 2 on Social Inclusion and Social Class). This leads to a very unequal playing field – whilst we will never completely equalise the chances of every young person, we can play a role in helping those who need our assistance.

This chapter starts by discussing Bourdieu's concept of capital and its links to social mobility. It then considers the role that careers education, information, advice and guidance (CEIAG) and work experience can play in helping to address some of the inequities that exist between our students and the impact that government policy has had upon its provision within schools, in England, over the past twenty years. It then explores some career decision-making theories and links them to the concepts of capital and of social mobility. The chapter concludes with some benchmarks that those involved in education can use to evaluate current practice within their institution(s).

Capital: Pierre Bourdieu

In order to establish an understanding of key concepts relating to aspiration and mobility, it is first important to consider the concepts of capital, particularly focusing on social capital and cultural capital, as conceptualised by Bourdieu (1930–2002), and relate this to social mobility and to CEIAG.

As noted in Chapter 2, Bourdieu was a French sociologist and philosopher who expressed the view that our 'capital' will dictate our position in society. In addition to the already established concept of economic capital, he considered other forms of capital that we can possess and which can be of benefit to us. He was interested in exploring inequity in power and inequity in access to resources, and how these influence the development of social class and elites.

Whilst economic capital refers to the financial resources we possess, and cultural capital refers to our knowledge of, or familiarity with, 'how things work' along with, for example, our skills, qualifications, possessions, accent and clothing, social capital is about our relationships with others. People can be very supportive of those in possession of the same forms of cultural capital as themselves ('you are one of us'), but exclude others without it.

If we consider school students, their social capital will enable them to access resources through the groups and networks that they (and those they know) are part of. For example, by helping them to find work experience placements and jobs.

Pause for thought

Think about your students, or the people with whom you were educated:

- Can you identify those with the most and least valuable assets in terms of their social capital? How does/did their social capital help or hinder their access and progression to their desired opportunities?
- How could those of us working within education help our students to develop their social capital?

In his paper on developing social capital in schools, Comer (2015: 226) suggests that education systems are based on an 'outdated science' which views our genes as the primary factor in influencing our brain development and ability to learn, leading 'to a notion that school performance capacities are predetermined; that some can learn well and some can't'. He regards this as having created an education system with a focus on academic learning and where too few schools consider how they can develop their students' capital and prepare them for adult life. However, he identifies an exception to this – schools whose student population comes from 'better educated families' – and regards them as paying more detailed attention to their students' non-academic development.

Pause for thought

- Do you agree with Comer's view as outlined in the preceding paragraph? Is it relevant to the education system in the country you grew up in and/or are now living in?
- Has the importance given to students' non-academic development changed in your lifetime?

If you are interested in this particular area, you could explore the issues by comparing and contrasting the provision detailed on a sample of school websites. For example:

- What extra-curricular activities are available to their students?
- What opportunities exist for contact with employers, both on and off school premises?
- Who is responsible for finding the work experience placements? Is it the school, or are students expected to find their own placement(s)?
- Are these activities/experiences optional, are they targeted at particular cohorts or do all students take part?

The Economic and Social Research Council (ESRC) is currently funding ASPIRES2, a ten-year longitudinal research project (2009–2019) to explore young people's career aspirations and the influences upon them. Whilst the focus is on science careers, its findings are of wider relevance.

In February 2016, the project reported its analysis of survey data on 13,421 fifteen- to sixteen-year-old students from 340 secondary schools in England (296 state schools and 44 independent schools). It found that 62.5% of these students had received careers education and 44.8% had been on work experience.

The findings of particular relevance to our exploration of capital include:

- Students with very high cultural capital were 1.49 times more likely to have received careers education than students with very low cultural capital.
- Those in the lowest ability grouped classes were significantly less likely to report that they had received careers education and/or work experience.
- There are social inequalities when you consider who has and who has not received careers support: 'Girls, minority ethnic, working-class, lower-attaining and students who are unsure of their aspirations or who plan to leave education post-16 are all significantly less likely to report receiving careers education'.

(Archer and Moote 2016: 2)

- Students who had been on work experience placed a value on these placements. However, it was more often the case that they had been found by their parents/families rather than by their school: 'meaning that students from socially advantaged families were more likely to be able to arrange "quality" work experiences and placements'.

(Archer and Moote 2016: 5)

The project findings reflect my own experiences. As a generalisation, having undertaken careers-related work in a range of state schools and in fee-paying independent schools, the latter group appears to provide a wider range of extra-curricular activities and more employer contact for their students.

The issue of inequalities in individual capital also become very apparent when I provide careers guidance in schools. When a young person is considering a specific job, we discuss what they already know about it and how they can find out more – for example, through work experience or work shadowing – before they commit themselves to that path. The young people described in the case study below are students I met during such interviews, and who were both considering a career in journalism.

Case study

Mark attends a state school. He wants to be a sports journalist – he has been writing for the school magazine and has also started a football blog. None of his family are involved with journalism, nor do they have any friends who can help him find a placement, so he is planning to write to newspapers, magazines and online sites asking for work experience.

Fatima attends an independent school. She wants to be a journalist, but does not have any relevant experience. However, her uncle is the editor of a national daily newspaper and he has told her that she can spend part of her summer holidays in London where she can live with him and his family, and gain work experience on his newspaper.

Clearly, each student's social and cultural capital will vary irrespective of whether they are in a state or independent school. However, families with the funding to pay for their child to be privately educated may be more likely to have social capital that will help them to gain access to professional workplaces.

Consider:

- What are your own experiences of seeking work experience, whether that is for yourself, a family member or students in a school that you work in?
- What role did/do family members or contacts play in finding the work experience placement(s)?

If chance networks play an important role in career choice and career development, what does this mean for the young people we work with? Before considering some ways in which schools can help their learners, we will briefly look at some recent research into social mobility.

Social mobility

When people talk about social mobility, they are often referring to the extent to which individuals are able to move upwards in society: 'It is about a person's chances of success compared to people with different backgrounds. It shows how fair a society is and whether opportunities for people to succeed are equal' (House of Lords 2016: 18).

Our social mobility is inextricably linked to our possession of capital. The National Equality Panel (2010) found, through their research, that children from a higher social class, and with a relatively low assessment of cognitive ability, ended up overtaking those from a lower social class who had been initially assessed as having high cognitive ability. They also noted that 'it is clear that we live in a far from perfectly mobile society. People's occupational and economic destinations in early adulthood depend to an important degree on their origins' (2010: 393).

The RSA (2011: 9) found the Panel's findings to be interesting, and in line with their own research into capital and social mobility; however, they also provided the caveat:

> We do not wish to imply that the young people concerned in this research do not have social capital, or are in deficit in some way. Rather, we are arguing that they lack specific kinds of cultural, financial and institutional capital that facilitate progress in education and prestigious (especially professional) careers.

They go on to describe young people from high-income groups as 'fish in water' in relation to higher education and professional careers, and those from low-income groups like 'fish out of water'. They reach this conclusion as the former group are more likely to have experience and knowledge of how higher education works, how applications are made, the courses that lead to specific professional roles, plus the social networks and contacts that can help a child to gain a work experience placement and other useful things to put on their curriculum vitae (CV).

Let us consider the educational background of some of the highest echelons of UK society as stated within the Sutton Trust's 2016 report entitled 'Leading People 2016: The educational backgrounds of the UK professional elite' (Kirby, 2016):

- Members of Parliament (MPs): 32% were privately educated.
- Cabinet ministers: 50% were privately educated.
- Shadow cabinet ministers: 13% were privately educated.
- Senior judges: 74% were privately educated.
- Permanent secretaries, who are the most senior of civil servants: 55% were privately educated.

The report also stated that, in 2015–16, around 7% of UK school children were privately educated (Kirby, 2016).

Pause for thought

Consider:

- Are privately educated people represented in such proportions (see bullet points listed above) because they are the best candidates for those roles?
- What role might social capital have played, throughout their lives, to enable them to reach these positions?

Now look at the short vignette that started this chapter, and the case study about journalism in the previous sub-section:

- What do these experiences tell us about social capital and social mobility?
- What could their schools have done to help these young people to develop their social capital?

Whilst effective CEIAG and work experience will never create an even playing field between young people, they can play a significant role in addressing the inequities: 'career guidance is a valuable part of the public-policy tool-kit to enhance social mobility' (Hooley, Matheson and Watts 2014: 32). For example, by helping students to learn about jobs and careers that they may not previously have heard about or considered, and understand what they need to do to gain access to them.

Careers provision

Careers education, information, advice and guidance (CEIAG)

Those who work in education can help their students to make informed decisions about their next steps by providing effective CEIAG and, as part of that, assisting them to identify and explore the factors influencing their aspirations. They can also aid them in their development of social and cultural capital: whilst some young people can draw upon a wealth of capital (social, cultural and economic) to smooth their transition to adulthood and economic independence, others cannot. This leads to a very unequal playing field – whilst we will never completely equalise the chances of every young person, we can play a role in helping those who need our assistance.

Before going any further, it is worth defining what is involved in each aspect of CEIAG:

- Careers education involves learning, through the school curriculum, about careers, the opportunities available and what work involves. It can also include work experience and enterprise education. Schools are responsible for its delivery.
- Careers information is what it says: information about different careers, about the routes into them and about the labour market.
- Careers advice helps people to explore and use careers information. The person providing the advice will give their ideas and suggestions.
- Careers guidance is one-to-one support which helps individuals to consider their skills, strengths and interests and relate these to the opportunities available. It will be more non-directive than careers advice, with more time spent asking questions to help the person explore their own thoughts and interests. It will also (at its best) help people to consider the factors that influence their thinking.

To offer an effective programme, schools need to make sure that all four aspects of CEIAG – education, information, advice and guidance – are available to their learners.

Pause for thought

Using the definitions given above, think about the CEIAG you experienced whilst in education:

- On a scale of 0 (not available) to 10 (excellent), how would you rate each of the four CEIAG elements: careers education; careers information; careers advice; careers guidance?
- What are your reasons for giving each rating?
- How could the CEIAG provision have been improved?

- What opportunities did you have for gaining work experience whilst in education?
- If you went on work experience, who made the arrangements?

If you are working in education, now think about the setting you work in and ask yourself the same questions. You could consider those you place on work experience programmes and/or those who come to work on placement with you.

Work experience

An important contributor to young people's understanding of the realities of working life is work experience. It can be transformational. Within the Education and Employers Taskforce's (2012) report 'Work Experience: impact and delivery – insights from the evidence', Brian Lightman – the then General Secretary of the Association of School and College Leaders (ASCL) – expressed his view that:

> work experience can make a significant difference to the motivation, attainment and progression of students. As a headteacher I have seen attitudes to school of many young people completely transformed as a result of their highly positive experience on a placement. Those who lacked the necessary motivation or maturity to work to their full potential have often returned from placements fuelled up as a result of an experience which can genuinely be life changing.
>
> (Education and Employers Taskforce 2012: 4)

This report's main findings included:

- Young people's horizons could be broadened through the greater use of work experience placements. Currently, around 50% of such placements are sourced by young people and their families through their current social networks.
- Placements can challenge young people's views of various occupations, and of the people who hold those roles, helping to challenge stereotypes.
- Privately educated students have greater access to high quality placements when compared to students who attend state schools, and more should be done to provide them with more equal access.

Unfortunately, in the same year, the government removed the statutory duty on secondary schools in England to provide work-related learning at Key Stage 4 (for those aged 14–16 years). What impact might the ending of this statutory duty have had upon young people? Which groups of young people might this removal have had the most negative effect upon?

Government policy

This section focuses, in the main, on the policy and practice relating to CEIAG in England, providing an example of how a system can be changed to the detriment of the majority. Whilst reading this section, reflect upon your own experiences (whether they are from your time as a student, or when working in an education setting). We start with a consideration of CEIAG, and then focus on work experience.

A brief history

In July 2016, a House of Commons Business, Innovation & Skills and Education Committee, brought together to focus upon CEIAG, published its findings:

> We are very disappointed that careers advice and guidance is still poor in so many schools: the system has failed too many young people for far too long.
>
> (House of Commons 2016: 8)

This was not always the case in the UK. Starting in the late 1940s, local authorities employed Youth Employment Officers to help young people in their transition from school to work. In 1973, the Employment and Training Act created the Careers Service, which focused most of its support on young people in schools. Schools were responsible for delivering careers education and used the Careers Service as a resource for delivering careers advice and guidance and developing links with employers. Legislation was further strengthened by the 1997 Education Act, which required schools to provide careers education and gave the Careers Service a statutory right of access to pupils.

In 2000, CEIAG was dealt a major blow when the government announced its creation of the Connexions Service, an attempt to develop an integrated youth support service but solely funded by the Careers Service budget. Forty-seven localised Connexions Partnerships were created between 2001 and 2003, each with the flexibility to decide how to deploy resources to meet the needs of the 13–19 age group (and up to 25 years of age for young people with learning difficulties and/or disabilities (LDD)). As the Connexions Service's main target was to reduce, by 10%, the proportion of 16–18 year olds not in education, employment and training (NEET), many partnerships prioritised those who were NEET, or at risk of becoming NEET, leading to a reduction in careers support for other young people.

In its report 'Unleashing Aspiration', the Panel on Fair Access to the Professions described Britain as a 'closed shop society' (DCSF 2009: 6). It criticised the Connexions Service for having 'focussed on the disadvantaged minority to the detriment of the aspirational majority. Across the board too many able children from average income and middle class families are losing out in the race for professional jobs' (DCSF 2009: 6).

In the same year, the Department for Children, Schools and Families (DCSF) strategy document 'Quality, Choice and Aspiration' (2009) included a key theme of raising aspirations and driving social mobility:

> Now more than ever young people need access to good IAG. This strategy . . . puts in place the building blocks for an IAG system which gives every young person the high-quality support they need to release their talents, thus setting them on the path to success.
>
> (DCSF 2009: 6)

However, the plans did not come to fruition as a Coalition Government replaced the Labour Government after the 2010 General Election.

In line with the Coalition Government's commitment to increasing school autonomy – as exemplified by increasing academisation and encouraging the development of free schools and university technical colleges (UTCs) – schools, in 2010, were given responsibility for providing all aspects of

CEIAG, albeit with no additional funding. They could then decide, within the rather vague limitations of some statutory and non-statutory guidance, what they would provide and what support (if any) they would purchase.

At the same time, local authorities no longer had to provide universally available careers support. Many chose to cut their provision, and focus resources on those regarded as the most disadvantaged or at greatest risk. The failures of this approach swiftly became apparent. Whilst some schools procured the external impartial one-to-one support for their learners, others did not, resulting in a postcode lottery that has been highlighted by Hooley, Matheson and Watts (2014).

In November 2014, in an attempt to address this inequality in provision, the then Education Secretary Nicky Morgan announced the creation of an employer-led body called the Careers & Enterprise Company:

> The careers and enterprise company will focus on young people aged 12 to 18, helping them access the best advice and inspiration about the world of work by encouraging greater collaboration between schools and colleges and employers . . . This will ensure employers are supporting young people with decision-making and career development at every stage of school life. The brokerage arrangement will enable employers to talk directly to pupils about the opportunities available and ensure they are able to consider all the options as they move through school.
>
> (Morgan 2014: online)

Then, in March 2015, the government published 'Careers guidance and inspiration in schools: Statutory guidance for governing bodies, school leaders and school staff', which stated that employers can 'help to boost young people's attitudes and employability skills, inform pupils about the range of roles and opportunities available and help them understand how to make this a reality' (DfE 2015: 5). One may wish to question what had happened to the provision of impartial one-to-one careers advice and guidance, delivered by a qualified careers adviser? Hooley, Matheson and Watts (2014) saw a similarity between the way that careers guidance professionals and teachers were regarded by the government, with little esteem being held for professional qualifications.

Problems were still evident in November 2015 when the Chief Inspector of Schools, Sir Michael Wilshaw, stated:

> Too often . . . inspectors . . . go into secondary schools and because headteachers are so concerned about filling their sixth forms to ensure that their budgets are strong, they will give the wrong advice to youngsters and be selfish in their careers advice . . . . Most successful heads . . . understand that good careers education is not a bolt-on, it's an integral part of raising achievement.
>
> (TES 2015: online)

In December 2015, the Education and Childcare Minister Sam Gyimah – during a talk on the government's vision for careers education at the Westminster Employment Forum – announced that the Department for Education would publish a careers strategy 'in the coming weeks' and that 'by 2020 we want a system where young people (and their parents/carers) have timely access to the information and data they need to make informed decisions on their education, training and employment options' (GOV.UK 2015: online). However, in December 2016, it was announced that there would be no careers strategy after all.

Pause for thought

Consider the importance that the UK government places on the role that employers can play in terms of CEIAG support in schools, as outlined in previous paragraphs:

- What do you see as the advantages and disadvantages of using employers to 'boost young people's attitudes and employability skills, inform pupils about the range of roles and opportunities available and help them understand how to make this a reality'?

  (DfE 2015: 5)

- Bearing Sir Michael Wilshaw's comments in mind, what can be done to ensure that young people receive 'unselfish' careers advice?

Before moving on to consider how people make decisions about their future careers, it is worth pausing and focusing upon CEIAG provision in a broader range of contexts.

Case study

The Transition Year

At ages 16–17, between their Junior and Senior cycles of education in Ireland, students in the majority of schools can opt for a Transition Year (TY) instead of the usual curriculum. In a minority of schools, the TY is mandatory.

Students spend their TY undertaking activities that prepare them for life after school – these can include work experience, employer and university visits, enterprise education, international visits and the development of personal skills.

Guidance counsellors

Some countries, including Finland and Ireland, have guidance counsellors who are based in schools. They are often qualified teachers who have undertaken substantial training to fulfil a guidance role. Their remit can be broad, encompassing careers guidance along with personal counselling.

The schooldekaan (careers coordinator)

In some schools in the Netherlands, the careers guidance programme is planned by the schooldekaan. The role is evolving from one that solely delivers, to a role that also coordinates provision from other staff across the school. The schooldekaan role includes providing information and one-to-one advice for students; coordinating careers activities delivery by a team of tutors; and developing links between the school and local businesses.

Consider:

- What might be the strengths and the drawbacks of the above approaches?

Career decision-making theories

When discussing how a school's CEIAG programme can contribute towards greater equality between its students in terms of their aspirations and social mobility, it is essential to include some consideration of how people make their learning and career decisions:

> Theories of decision-making can be divided into two categories: normative theories are those that describe how people should make decisions, whilst descriptive theories provide accounts of how people actually make decisions.
>
> (Diamond et al. 2014: 50)

Too much of the provision in the UK has been based on some old, and very influential, normative theories with little consideration given to descriptive theories. By neglecting these descriptive theories, we could be hindering young people's ability to develop their capital and take full advantage of the opportunities available to them. Some examples of normative and descriptive theories are briefly outlined in the following pages.

Pause for thought

Consider how you decided which subjects to study and what job(s)/career(s) to pursue. For example:

- How did you decide which subject(s) to study in the later stages of your schooling?
- What factors did you take into account when deciding on your career aim?
- How did you hear about each of the jobs you have held?

We will now use your reflections to consider the career decision-making theories that have often informed CEIAG in schools – these 'normative' theories are linked to how we think people make decisions rather than how they may actually make them. Normative decision-making theories could also be described as 'rational' in that they describe a logical, step-by-step and information-driven process. Two examples are the Theory of Vocational Choice (Holland 1959) and the D.O.T.S. model (Law and Watts 1977), both of which are briefly outlined below.

Holland's Theory of Vocational Choice (1959) emphasises the importance of identifying individual differences, and also work differences, then considering how they match. Several career inventories have been based on this theory – they ask the user various questions about their interests, and then match them to work contexts which reflect their chosen characteristics. These inventories are often used to help learners reflect upon their interests prior to making a learning or career choice.

Another example of a normative/rational career decision-making approach is the D.O.T.S. model (Law and Watts 1977). It suggests key elements of a CEIAG programme as:

Step 1: Start with the development of self-awareness. (What do I like/dislike doing? What are my skills/abilities/values?)

Step 2: Raise opportunity awareness. (What courses/jobs can I access? What are the entry requirements? What are the labour market trends?)

Step 3: Use this information to inform decision-making about next step(s). (How can I use the
data I've gathered in the above stages to help me reach a decision about my next step(s)? Am
I going to be able to do what I would like to do? What should I consider as my 'plan B' if I
don't get my first choice?)

Step 4: Develop transition learning to help learners gain knowledge of application procedures,
and 'how things are done' in that field of work. (What should I put in my personal statement?
What do I need to include in my CV/resume?)

Pause for thought

Reflect on your own learning and career journey – does the D.O.T.S. model reflect your
decision-making process at each transition point? Were there any factors that influenced you
that are not evident within it?

When I started my degree in English Literature, I planned to progress onto a postgraduate librari-
anship course. However, during my second year – while sitting in the students' union – I listened in
on a conversation between a friend and her friend who had just arrived back from an interview for a
place on a postgraduate diploma in careers guidance offered in Manchester. Having heard about the
college and the course, I decided to be a careers adviser rather than a librarian – I thought the job
sounded interesting, and also thought that I would get extended school holidays. Whilst the job was
interesting, I was wrong about the holidays!

When reflecting upon my own career path, I realised that chance meetings and discussions – an
important part of 'descriptive' career decision-making theories – have significantly influenced my
own decisions and that I have not always followed the normative decision-making path exemplified
by the D.O.T.S. model.

Two descriptive career decision-making theories that have emerged over the past few decades
both highlight the importance of chance, and of maximising your likelihood of hearing about opportunities through expanding your network of contacts. These theories are the Happenstance Learning
Theory (Krumboltz 1996) and the Chaos Theory of Careers (Pryor and Bright 2003).

The Happenstance Learning Theory (Krumboltz 1996) emphasises the lack of control we have
on many aspects of our lives, including our career path, and the importance of viewing unplanned
events in a positive manner. It encourages those providing careers support to help their clients to take
actions that may result in the development of new contacts and opportunities.

The Chaos Theory of Careers (Pryor and Bright 2003) suggests that we are each influenced by a myriad of different people and things – such as our family, friends, teachers,
gender, location and health – and that these influences are constantly changing. Similar to
Krumboltz, they identify chance events as playing a key role within career development and
recommend that we keep an open mind when these events occur, considering how we can
put them to best use.

Pause for thought

As mentioned earlier, I can recognise the role that unplanned events and chance have played in my own life and have heard similar stories from many of my career coaching clients.

- What role, if any, have unplanned events and chance played in your career path or in that of those around you?
- Have you heard about, or been able to access, any learning or work opportunities through your network of contacts, or the contacts of those around you?

My interest in this topic started when I was delivering a career coaching workshop and asked participants to reflect upon their own learning and career journey. Whilst some reported a rational sequential structure (see Holland 1959; Law and Watts 1977) – particularly those who were planning to go into a 'profession' such as teaching – most mentioned the role that chance had played. For example, one had heard through a friend about a job that was available, and another was referred by a family contact for an internship in the company they worked for. Both led to full-time jobs within those organisations.

This type of chance can disadvantage those who do not have many connections:

> Small and medium-sized businesses in particular rely on informal means of recruitment, such as word-of-mouth. Using this sort of recruitment means that applicants' existing social connections and networks are important and lead to their success. Not all young people will have these connections.
>
> (House of Lords 2016: 6)

I chose to explore the relevance of some of the above-mentioned career decision-making theories by conducting a small research study whilst working in the Netherlands.

Research

Whilst a guest lecturer at a Netherlands university, I ran a workshop on career coaching and career decision-making. The twelve students who took part were from a range of countries in the European Union and were spending a semester at the university as part of a teacher training course.

During the workshop, I asked them to reflect upon the ways in which they had made their learning/career-related decisions and which, if any, of the theories we discussed were relevant to those processes. Seven students selected one theory/model and two selected two theories/models:

- four recognised aspects of the Chaos Theory of Careers

(Pryor and Bright 2003)

- three recognised aspects of the Theory of Vocational Choice

(Holland 1959)

- three recognised aspects of the Happenstance Learning Theory

(Krumboltz 1996)

- one recognised aspects of the D.O.T.S. Model

(Law and Watts 1977)

Three students did not select any theories/models. This may have been due to one or more factors, including my insufficient explanation of the questionnaire and/or the theories/models, their understanding of the terminology (as English was not their first language) or that none were relevant to their decision-making processes.

Whilst a range of theories/models were recognised by the students, a closer look at their reasons for their selection indicates that the 'rational' theories/models – as represented by Holland's Theory of Vocational Choice (1959) and Law and Watts' D.O.T.S. Model (1977) – were familiar to the students as means by which they had sought to identify their future career path, not their reasons for actually deciding upon a route to follow.

In contrast, some of the comments made in relation to the 'descriptive' theories/models – as represented by Krumboltz's Happenstance Learning Theory (1996) and Pryor and Bright's Chaos Theory of Careers (2003) – were either about how the student found out about a career pathway that interested them, such as outdoor education or applied psychology, or about being open to new opportunities.

Moving forward

In order to develop inclusive practice in the areas of aspiration and motivation, it is important to consider some key factors:

- Social capital and cultural capital
- Young people's career aspirations
- Social mobility
- Careers education, information, advice and guidance (CEIAG)
- Work experience
- Government policy
- Career decision-making theories

and how they link together to influence young people's career progression.

In order to work towards inclusive practice in supporting young people's aspirations and social mobility, and particularly the roles that CEIAG and work experience can play in helping young people to develop their capital, we could usefully consider the eight benchmarks that Sir John Holman and his team developed as a result of research they carried out for the Gatsby Foundation, resulting in a report entitled 'Good Career Guidance'.

They reached a judgement on what 'good' CEIAG could look like, and used this to create eight benchmarks for good career guidance which they encouraged UK secondary schools to audit their current practice against. The benchmarks are:

- A stable careers programme.
- Learning from career and labour market information.
- Addressing the needs of each student.
- Linking curriculum learning to careers.
- Encounters with employers and employees.
- Experiences of workplaces.
- Encounters with further and higher education.
- Personal guidance.

(The Gatsby Charitable Foundation 2014: 7)

Further details, and an explanation of each benchmark, can be found in the full report: www.gatsby.org.uk/uploads/education/reports/pdf/gatsby-sir-john-holman-good-career-guidance-2014.pdf

Those working in education, or who have a teenage child or children who are studying, might wish to use the above benchmarks to reflect upon the current provision that they are familiar with.

Conclusion

Inequality is embedded in the transition from education to work in the UK, with young people's aspirations and ability to progress often relying upon their family's economic, social and cultural capital. Whilst social mobility has been a key focus of recent UK governments, their actions have often led to a reduction in the support available to help young people address this inequality.

Schools can, and in some cases do, play a key role in helping young people to make informed choices about their next steps, raise their aspirations, and take actions that will assist their progression. Rather than relying on employers to provide the careers advice and guidance support to young people in schools, governments should encourage schools to audit their current CEIAG provision and take steps to fill any gaps, drawing upon the expertise of professionally qualified career guidance practitioners where appropriate.

Finally, whilst writing this chapter a new UK Prime Minister was appointed. In her inaugural speech, on 13th July 2016, Theresa May stated:

When it comes to opportunity we won't entrench the advantages of the fortunate few, we will do everything we can to help anybody, whatever your background, to go as far as your talents will take you.

(May 2016: online)

The link with social capital and social mobility is clear, and it will be interesting to see what actions (if any) result from this statement and what role (if any) schools will be asked to play. Or will government policy continue to militate against its stated aim of increasing upward social mobility, and continue to maintain the status quo?

An early indicator is that, on 1st November 2016, Neil Carmichael MP and Iain Wright MP – Co-Chairs of the UK Parliament's Education, Skills and the Economy Committee – said that:

> The Government's lack of action to address failings in careers provision is unacceptable . . . Ministers appear to be burying their heads in the sand while careers guidance fails young people, especially those from disadvantaged backgrounds . . . Impartial advice and guidance and high quality careers education is vital if we are to achieve the social mobility and aspiration that the Prime Minister has talked about.
>
> (Parliament.UK 2016: online)

Further reading

The Gatsby Charitable Foundation (2014). *Good career guidance*. Available at: www.gatsby.org.uk/uploads/education/reports/pdf/gatsby-sir-john-holman-good-career-guidance-2014.pdf

Hooley, T., Matheson, J., & Watts, A.G. (2014) *Advancing Ambitions: The Role of Career Guidance in Supporting Social Mobility*. London: Sutton Trust.

Hooley, T., Neary, S., Morris, M., & Mackay, S. (2015) *Effective Policy Frameworks for the Organisation of Career Guidance Services: A Review of the Literature*. London and Derby: SQW and the International Centre for Guidance Studies, University of Derby.

Social Mobility Commission (2016) *State of the Nation 2016: Social Mobility in Great Britain*. London: Her Majesty's Stationery Office.

References

Archer, L. and Moote, J. (2016) *ASPIRES2 project spotlight: Year 11 students' views of careers education and work experience*. Available at: www.educationandemployers.org/research/aspires-2-project-spotlight-year-11-students-views-of-careers-education-and-work-experience/ (Accessed: 29 December 2016).

Comer, J. (2015) Developing social capital in schools. *Society*, 52(3), 225–231.

Department for Children, Schools and Families (DCSF) (2009) *Quality, choice and aspiration*. London: DCSF.

Department for Education (2015) *Careers guidance and inspiration in schools: Statutory guidance for governing bodies, school leaders and school staff*. Available at: www.gov.uk/government/uploads/system/uploads/attachment_data/file/440795/Careers_Guidance_Schools_Guidance.pdf (Accessed: 29 December 2016).

Diamond, A., Roberts, J., Vorley, T., Birkin, G., Evans, J., Sheen, J. and Nathwani, T. (2014) *UK Review of the provision of information about higher education*. Leicester: HEFCE.

Education and Employers Taskforce (2012) *Work Experience: Impact and delivery – insights from the evidence*. Available at: www.educationandemployers.org/research/work-experience-impact-and-delivery-insights-from-the-evidence/ (Accessed: 29 December 2016).

The Gatsby Charitable Foundation (2014) *Good career guidance*. Available at: www.gatsby.org.uk/uploads/education/reports/pdf/gatsby-sir-john-holman-good-career-guidance-2014.pdf (Accessed: 29 December 2016).

GOV.UK (2015) *The government's vision for careers education* [Speech by Sam Gyimah to the Westminster Employment Forum]. Glaziers Hall, London. 3 December 2015. Available at: www.gov.uk/government/speeches/sam-gyimah-where-next-for-careers-education-and-guidance (Accessed: 14 March 2017).

Holland, J. (1959) A theory of vocational choice. *Journal of Counseling Psychology*, 6, 35–45.

Hooley, T., Matheson, J. and Watts, A.G. (2014) *Advancing ambitions: The role of career guidance in supporting social mobility*. London: Sutton Trust.

House of Commons (2016) *Careers education, information, advice and guidance*. First Joint Report of the Business, Innovation and Skills and Education Committees of Session 2016–17. London. The Stationery Office.

House of Lords (2016) *Overlooked and left behind: Improving the transition from school to work for the majority of young people*. London: The Stationery Office.

Kirby, P. (2016) *Leading people 2016: The educational backgrounds of the UK professional elite*. London: Sutton Trust.

Krumboltz, J.D. (1996) A learning theory of career counseling. In M. L. Savickas and W. Bruce Walsh (Eds.), *Handbook of career counseling theory and practice* (pp. 55–80). Palo Alto, CA: Davies-Black.

Law, B. and Watts, A.G. (1977) *Schools, careers and community: A study of some approaches to careers education in schools*. London: Church Information Office.

May, T. (2016) *Statement from the new prime minister Theresa May*, 13 July 2016. Available at: www.gov.uk/government/speeches/statement-from-the-new-prime-minister-theresa-may (Accessed: 29 December 2016).

Morgan, N. (2014) *New careers and enterprise company for schools*, 10 December 2014. Available at: www.gov.uk/government/news/new-careers-and-enterprise-company-for-schools (Accessed: 29 December 2016).

National Equality Panel (2010) *An anatomy of economic inequality in the UK: Report of the national equality panel*. London: Centre for Analysis of Social Exclusion.

The Panel on Fair Access to the Professions (2009) *Unleashing aspiration, the final report of the panel on fair access to the professions*. Available at: http://webarchive.nationalarchives.gov.uk/+/:www.cabinetoffice.gov.uk/media/227102/fair-access.pdf (Accessed: 29 December 2016).

Parliament.UK (2016) *Government inaction on careers provision failings is unacceptable*. Available at: www.parliament.uk/business/committees/committees-a-z/commons-select/education-skills-and-economy/news-parliament-2015/careers-advice-government-response-16-17/ (Accessed: 29 December 2016).

Pryor, R.G.L. and Bright, J.E.H. (2003) The chaos theory of careers. *Australian Journal of Career Development*, 12(2), 12–20.

RSA (2011) *Not enough capital: Exploring education and employment progression in further education*. London: RSA.

TES (2015) *Ofsted chief: 'Selfish' schools are failing pupils over careers advice*. Available at: www.tes.com/news/school-news/breaking-news/ofsted-chief-selfish-schools-are-failing-pupils-over-careers-advice (Accessed: 29 December 2016).

10 Sexual behaviours and development

Sophie King-Hill and Richard Woolley

Lucy is sixteen years of age and has been seeing a boy of the same age for six months. They have been sexually active for a while. She has just discovered that she is pregnant. They had been using condoms during sex on most occasions, but not always. Lucy has just completed her GCSEs and is expecting good grades. Her ambition is to continue her education and to go to university to study engineering, hopefully in her home city. Her parents have gone from an initial reaction of shock and anger to being supportive, but her boyfriend has made it clear that he does not want any further contact with her.

Introduction

Sexuality, sexual behaviours and sexual development have, historically, been viewed as controversial topics within education. This appears to stem from the stigma that surrounds these topics and a cultural context in which discussions about sex are still often taboo. Over recent years, there has been a move towards addressing these topics within schools, which appears to be linked to various influencing factors such as high teenage pregnancy rates, media influences and increased aware-ness of risks and how to prevent them. The UK government has regularly returned to discussions about making sex and relationships education mandatory in schools, but Parliament has failed to bring this into law on numerous occasions. At the time of writing, Relationships and Sex Education will become mandatory in secondary schools, and Relationships Education in primary schools in England. However, the scope and content of these subjects is to be a matter for consultation. Further, there is a growing debate about inclusive relationships and sex education, which includes the breadth of sexual orientation. Traditionally, where sex education has taken place in England it has focussed on heterosexual activity (with mandatory teaching on reproduction in the science curriculum).

This chapter explores a range of factors that affect the sexual behaviours and development of young people, seeking to consider how the education system might develop inclusive approaches to the provision of support and guidance.

Media influence

There are many facets to the influence and impact of the media on the sexual behaviours of children and young people. The term media covers a broad range of products from social media sites to televi-sion and the internet. Daguerre and Nativel (2006) propose that teenagers are living in a sexualised environment, yet much of the information that is portrayed is often from a skewed perspective. Brook

(2010), a free sexual health and contraception service for under 25s, highlights that females are frequently portrayed as sex objects in the media, putting pressure on young girls to conform to such perceived norms of sexuality. They point out that pregnancy and the consequences of unprotected sex are rarely shown by the media and if they are such consequences are normally misconstrued. Brook (2010) also highlights that pornography is now readily accessible on the internet and no longer a top shelf product only for adults, giving an unrealistic version of sexuality and providing young people with false expectations.

Media products can also have a positive impact, particularly where television programmes or advertisements show a representative cross-section of the diversity of society. Over past decades, the number of characters in soap operas who are lesbian, gay, bisexual or transgender has increased significantly, and the degree of sensationalism has diminished, but not disappeared altogether. There is still a tension when the inclusion of such characters is deemed to be tokenistic, and this is a debate which no doubt will continue. Readers may wish to consider how a breadth of diversity across issues relating to identity, including sexual orientation, gender, disability, ethnicity, age and marital status is portrayed within the broadcast media that they access. Furthermore:

> An early introduction to education about sex and relationships is sometimes believed to 'destroy children's innocence'. However, children and young people are exposed to sexual imagery in the media and advertising, which can give them a distorted view of sex, relationships and sexuality without any consideration of possible outcomes such as sexually transmitted infections and unwanted pregnancy. A trained and confident teacher will work with parents to give children and young people appropriate and accurate information to help them make sense of the imagery that surrounds them.
>
> (NICE, undated: 28–29, cited in Mason and Woolley 2011: 45)

Sexual identities

Children are aware of a range of sexual or sexualised identities from a young age, although this does not mean that they are aware of any associated sexual behaviours. They may play mummies and daddies with their friends, without any biological knowledge of how a baby is made. Even an inquisitive child who asks where babies come from is not expecting a graphic account of the reproductive process, and will happily accept an answer explaining that an egg grows and develops inside mum. Concerns are sometimes expressed that early relationships and sex education will encourage children to experiment and to try out sexual activity. However, research indicates that the opposite is the case, with the age of sexual debut delayed amongst those receiving early education.

Key to this is the provision of high quality, age appropriate relationships and sex education within the school system.

Research

A key element of supporting the development of children and young people is ensuring that the adults working with them are enabled to give appropriate support.

Research undertaken during 2016 with student teachers in their final year of training identified a range of concerns and apprehensions, including those relating to children's sexual identities and development. Of 105 responses from student teachers on courses in England, the overall levels of concern showed that 91% of respondents identified one or more issues relating to relationships and the ways in which relationship issues impact on well-being (e.g. sexual orientation, growing up, families and homophobia). Participants stated that:

> I wouldn't have a problem teaching [about homophobia] but I feel that it is an issue that many parents may have strong feelings about towards the teaching of it and I think this is where the main difficulties would lie.
>
> Female undergraduate student (teaching children
> aged 3–7 years), East Midlands of England

Similarly:

> I do not think some issues which are becoming of increasing importance such as trans-gender children and homophobic bullying are dealt with in teacher training as it is pre-sumed that students will know how to deal with these when they arise. I think that more should be done to address how to deal with such issues identified and how it can be integrated into the curriculum.
>
> Female undergraduate student (training to teach children
> aged 5–11 years), North West of England

This corresponds with findings from a similar study (Woolley 2010) in which 64.3% of 160 respondents identified sex and relationships issues as being in their top three areas of concern. These studies suggest that student teachers are aware of the complexities in addressing issues relating to sexual orientation and sexuality, and some of the contrasting viewpoints that they will encounter. These can include the view of parents and carers, those of colleagues working in the school or setting, and the views of children (whether personally held or repeated from adults). Furthermore, there is a need to have the confidence to address bullying when it relates to sexual identity, or perceived identity:

> Throw away comments such as 'you're gay' need to be tackled and understood that this is homophobic language, however the children might not realise they have done anything wrong.
>
> Female undergraduate student (training to teach children
> aged 3–11 years), East Midlands of England

Consider:

- Why student teachers may be particularly apprehensive about addressing issues relating to relationships and sex education;
- The extent to which you think children and young people are aware of issues relating to sexual identity and sexual orientation, drawing on your own memories of schooling or more recent experience;
- How school policies relating to relationships and sex education address issues in an inclusive manner (you may wish to access examples of policies through an internet search of local schools).

In 2009 DePalma and Atkinson argued that sexualities equality 'remains the one area of inclusion still largely unaddressed within the field of primary education' (2009: 838). In England at the present time, every school is required to have an anti-bullying policy and a policy addressing sex and relationship education. The extent to which these deal with a fully inclusive approach to how individual members of staff and students identify varies considerably, even though the National Curriculum for England (DfE, 2014) and the Equality Act (Legislation.gov.uk, 2010) identify specific characteristics that are protected under law, including sexual orientation. This is particularly pertinent when more than half of gay young people are never taught anything about lesbian, gay and bisexual issues at school, and only half of them say that their schools identify homophobic bullying as being wrong (Guasp 2012: 4).

Stonewall identifies that 96% of gay pupils hear homophobic remarks such as 'poof' or 'lezza' used in school (Guasp 2012: 2). When addressing the final point made by the student teacher, above, whilst the child may not realise the meaning of the word 'gay' they have used, they will know that they have used the word with unpleasant intent. Thus, a classroom rule 'We use words in kind ways' provides the opportunity to speak about respect for others, focussing on motivation and intention.

Sexual behaviours

When considering sexual behaviours in an educational setting it is useful to explore how the parameters are set for what is perceived to be healthy and unhealthy. It is useful to note, at this point, that very little empirical data exists on sexual behaviours in children and young people in a UK context (for well-known studies outside the UK context, see Ryan et al. 1996; Finkelhor 1995; Finkelhor, Ormrod and Chaffin 2009). An example of this lack of empirical evidence is demonstrated in a recent systematic review of harmful sexual behaviours and children and young people that was completed by the NICE Public Health Advisory Committee (Hackett 2016), in which only nine studies were present, in a UK context, that met the inclusion criteria and showed that lesser harmful sexual behaviours are the least researched. This lack of evidence may be due to the difficulty in carrying out this research from an ethical standpoint due to the mutual exclusivity of childhood and sexuality that exists in UK culture.

There appears to be a wealth of subjectivities when trying to define sexual behaviours, both healthy and harmful, in a UK context. This is reflected by Hackett (2014), who asserts that there is a lack of clarity in the terminology that surrounds sexual behaviour in children and young people which has led to incorrect classification of behaviours, and in terms of the educational context, the ambiguities that exist in this area may be further exacerbated due to the wealth of subjectivities that exist in this area, especially when sexual behaviours is not a specialism of a professional, which is the case for many educators. Harmful and healthy sexual behaviours, therefore, appear to be difficult concepts to pin down due to the multi-layered nature of the contexts that exist around them in an educational setting. Another important facet is highlighted by Ryan and Lane (1997), who note that perspectives on sexual behaviours that are harmful tend to be limited in Western cultures as a phase or a normal part of growing up. This is a point for consideration bearing in mind the target-driven agenda of most educational settings and the lack of focus and obligation for being trained, teaching and approaching this area. When considering definitions that are applicable to an educational set-ting, Ryan and Lane (1997) point out that coercion, exploitation and aggression in sexual behaviour should always be considered harmful, yet subjectivities still exist of what constitutes these elements and how they may be assessed differently by diverse educators. Hackett (2014: 1) puts forward a definition of what constitutes harmful sexual behaviour:

> Sexual behaviours expressed by children and young people under the age of 18 years old that are developmentally inappropriate, may be harmful towards self or others, or be abusive towards another child, young person or adult.

Yet again, however, the definition still has subjective elements, which appears to be a reflection of the contested and varied area of sexual behaviours in children and young people.

Pause for thought

In a report published by Stonewall (Guasp 2012), it was identified that the presence of homo-phobic language is closely linked to the prevalence of bullying. In schools where homophobic language is prevalent, 68% of gay young people were bullied, compared to 37% in schools where such language was rarely or never heard.

Consider:

- Whether the use of homophobic language is, in itself, a form of sexualised behaviour.
- Why pupils say that only 10% of teachers challenge homophobic language every time they hear it.
- How you respond to the finding that: 'Three in five lesbian, gay and bisexual pupils who experience homophobic bullying say that teachers who witness the bullying never intervene'.

(Guasp 2012: 4)

Whilst assessing sexual behaviours may not be deemed as an educator's role, it is important to note that from a safeguarding point of view sexual behaviours cannot be ignored and that there does appear to be a level of harmful sexual behaviours amongst the under 18s. A summary of sexual offending in England and Wales (ONS, 2011) stated that in 2011, out of 5977 sexual offenders

8.2% were under the age of 18. In a similar vein, Radford et al. (2011) produced a report on child neglect which found that of 6000 participants, 65.9% of reported sexual abuse was carried out by under 18s. In addition to this, Hackett (2014) highlights that children and young people who display harmful sexual behaviours are a heterogeneous group and that a vast diversity exists, indicating that over the career of an educator very varied sexual behaviours of children and young people may be encountered (for further reading, see studies by McCrory et al. 2008; Smith et al., 2014; Smith et al. 2013; Hackett, Phillips, Masson and Balfe 2013, 2012; Taylor 2003).

One way around these inconsistencies may be through professional training for educators in the area of sexual behaviours and children and young people. However, it is useful to note at this point that, as Hackett (2016) implies, there have been no major studies that assess the long-term impact of professional training in sexual behaviours on the outcomes for children and young people and that training in this area is sporadic.

Research

King-Hill (2016) carried out an evaluation of the Brook Traffic Light Tool training (TLT) (2013) that had been rolled out by Cornwall Local Authority, in the south-west of England, to all professionals working with children and young people in the locality.

The TLT is an age specific traffic light system that can be used by professionals to assess and respond to sexual behaviour that is displayed by children and young people. The study found that overall the tool appeared to be working within the context into which it was embedded in terms of raising professionals' confidence in the area of sexual behaviours and in turn impacting upon the actions taken when sexual behaviours were apparent in children and young people. The study also highlighted the relatively high numbers of sexual behaviours (in all three categories: red, amber and green) that non-specialist professionals were encountering with children and young people, which again appears to highlight the need for raised awareness in this area for educators. The results from the study also indicate that developing a shared language between professionals also supported cross-agency working when dealing with sexual behaviours, providing clarity to risk assessments that were being carried out. The evaluation concludes by pointing out that the profile of sexual behaviours in children and young people has been raised as a result of the training, indicating that this may be the way forward when considering a consistent approach to sexual behaviours in children and young people in an educational setting.

Consider:

- Should all education professionals receive training in how to identify harmful sexual behaviours, in order to protect children and young people?
- Are some sexual behaviours a normal part of development, and thus not a cause for concern?
- How can a range of professionals (for example, teachers, nurses and social workers) be enabled to develop a shared understanding of issues relating to child development?

This section has stressed the difficulty in defining harmful sexual behaviours in children and young people and has highlighted the multi-faceted contextual elements that surround such behaviours in children and young people. It has also highlighted that there is relatively little empirical evidence in the area of sexual behaviours in children and young people in the UK educational context, which adds to the subjectivities and complexity that surround this area. The available evidence indicates that the numbers of children and young people who display harmful sexual behaviours are not insignificant in number; the evidence also highlights that they are a very diverse and varied group. With this in mind therefore, it is likely that educators may come across sexual behaviours in children and young people and that training and self-education may be an avenue to increase confidence and clarity in this sensitive and subjective area.

Teenage pregnancy and education

There seems to be an apparent lack of awareness in contemporary culture of the complexities that surround the relationship between teenage parents and education. Arai (2009) states that there appears to be a blame culture surrounding this particular group of learners and that many assumptions for the causes of teenage parenthood are based in populist views (King-Hill 2013). That said, the perception of the teenage parent does appear to stem from the ideological perceptions of childhood in the West and their mutual exclusivity with sexuality.

Arai (2009) points out that teenage pregnancy evokes emotive responses and has been previously portrayed as an epidemic in the media (see for example MailOnline 2010). Quotes often in the media refer to the UK as topping the [European] league of teenage pregnancy and the teen pregnancy disaster (MailOnline 2010; SunOnline 2010). Duncan, Edwards and Alexander (2008) refer to the myth of the teenage pregnancy epidemic and the assumption of rapidly increasing teenage birth rates and the reaction of the government to this perception, stating:

> All these [assumptions] are unfounded, but all serve to bolster the negative evaluation of subsequent teenage parenting, and hence the nature of the policy response.
>
> (Duncan, Edwards and Alexander 2008: 9)

Duncan (2010) builds upon this, commenting on the perceived issues with teenage pregnancy and its impacts upon national concerns that the morality of the UK is decreasing. Duncan (2010) also points out that there is a national concern for associated health risks of teenage pregnancy; however, on further exploration of this it does appear that poor health outcomes are related to socio-economic status rather than early parenthood (see Alldred and David 2007). Upon deeper exploration of empirical evidence, the assumptions that surround teenage parents (and in particular teenage mothers) – that of a wasted life, poor motivations and immorality – appear unfounded. The reasons for teenage parenthood are wide and varied, are not bound by policy discourse and societal beliefs and appear to be a contested issue within policy discourse, public opinion and research findings.

Research

Studies by Daguerre and Nativel (2006); Alldred and David (2007); and Duncan, Edwards and Alexander (2008) on teenage parents appear to conflict with policy discourse perspectives. As Daguerre and Nativel (2006) state, the number of teenage conceptions to young women from low socio-economic backgrounds are disproportionately high; therefore, there are links with working-class stereotypes and assumptions that teenage parents are a drain on society and a deviant group within Western culture. Yet upon exploration of empirical evidence, these assumptions appear unfounded, with many studies finding that becoming a parent can be the stabilising influence in already chaotic lifestyles. Duncan (2010) points out that the pregnancy can enhance future aspirations and educational goals rather than becoming the catalyst for deprivation and educational failure, making what can be offered to the teenage parent, in terms of education, a key component in their future success.

Alldred and David (2007) completed an ethnographic qualitative study on the impact that parenting had on ten teenage girls, with poor behavioural histories, in a local community. This study found that nine out of ten of the young parents in the study had a renewed positivity towards education, with the education system letting them down, instead of harnessing the potential window for change. The study concludes by discussing the recognition that these young mothers had, as a direct result of parenthood, for the importance of education and its link to paid employment, with a goal of providing for their children.

Similarly, a small-scale study by King-Hill (2013) analysed the accounts of four teenage parents, aged 15–19 years old, focussing upon the reasons for their pregnancies, their behaviour traits and their link to education in the context of their transition to parenthood by attempting to gain a view of the lived experiences of the participants. Three main themes emerged as part of the analysis:

1   Emotional and social disadvantage
2   Parenthood as a catalyst for positive change
3   Education as a means for social acceptance

This study concluded that all of the participants in the study had emotional events that appeared to trigger risky sexual behaviours, resulting in pregnancy. All suffered negative educational experiences prior to pregnancy and all had low socio-economic status. Transition to parenthood appeared to provide structure, routine and a renewed vigour towards education. For all of the participants in this study, rather than a symptom of exclusion, parenthood in teenage years became an act of inclusion through the means of education.

In a qualitative study conducted by MacVarish and Billings (2008), thirty-five pregnant teenagers were interviewed, with seventeen being followed up a year later. Within this study, their behaviours were examined through in-depth interviews. A strong theme within this study was that motherhood was viewed as a positive transition from 'bad girl' to 'good mum', creating optimistic feelings towards education and the 'new beginning' that it provided for both the mothers and their children. However, it was also found that the mothers in the study were also protective of their time with their infants, highlighting that family values were a crucial aspect of parenting for them.

Pause for thought

Consider the example of Lucy, outlined in the vignette at the start of this chapter:

- What factors may affect Lucy's future life chances and opportunities?
- How does Lucy's situation compare with the research studies outlined in the previous sections of this chapter?
- Did you make any assumptions or presumptions about Lucy and her situation that you may now question?
- Might your responses have been different if Lucy was 15 years of age?

Reflecting further on the issues raised in the research outlined above, consider what factors might affect Lucy's ability to continue with her education and to realise her ambition to become an engineer.

Categorise the factors that you have identified. How many of them are:

- Social (founded in relationships, including the family and wider community)
- Economic (based around finance)
- Systemic (affected by the systems of society, including the education system)
- Personal (relating to Lucy's individual circumstances)
- Other

Explore what provision is made in your own context for teenage parents. Are support and advice services available? Is childcare accessible in order to support continuing education for the parent? Does the system support the inclusion of both parent and child within the education system?

Part of the Millennium Cohort study (Hawkes 2008) used quantitative data to examine three areas of influence for teenage mothers, these being life course experiences, differences in the early life circumstances of their children and the cognitive, behavioural and health outcomes for their children at ages three and five. Statistical data were gained using the survey-based data of 2831 teenage parents. The study found that 60% of the young parents already came from disadvantaged backgrounds, with the pregnancy having no major impact upon the disadvantage already experienced. The study concludes that it was the level of disadvantage, rather than the age of the parent, that impacted upon the cognitive abilities, behaviour and health outcomes of the children of the teenage parents, and that social inequality and lack of employment and educational opportunities are the major influencing factors within these fields.

A small-scale qualitative study conducted by Duncan, Edwards and Alexander (2008) explored the experiences of teenage parents, examining their support needs and attitude towards education and employment. The study found that young parents found a new sense of responsibility in parenting which gave them a pathway into education and employment that they did not have prior to the pregnancy, viewing participation in education and the labour market as an integral part of their parental responsibilities.

The studies above suggest that becoming a teenage parent has no effect on future employment and health prospects due to the teenager most likely coming from a low socio-economic background. Duncan (2010) suggests that teenage pregnancy can become a stabilising influence in a person's life, with parenthood becoming a potential way out of social disadvantage rather than a cause of it.

With all of this in mind, therefore, it is surprising that avenues for teenage parents through the education system are few and far between, with many sources of specific ring-fenced funding being discontinued at the end of the teenage pregnancy strategy in 2010, as the UK teenage pregnancy rates had been reduced. Despite this reduction, teenage parents are still an element of Western society and, if the evidence is correct, becoming a teenage parent can become a stabilising influence, with education providing the means for acceptance.

Consent

An understanding of consent is an essential aspect of sexual development and appropriate behaviours. In 2015 the PSHE Association published guidance on teaching about consent, with a focus on Key Stages 3 and 4 (young people aged 11–16).

The guidance identified that young people should learn about consent before they become sexually active; otherwise it is too late. It highlights that consent:

- is the responsibility of the person seeking consent; they need to be sure that the other person has the freedom and capacity to give it;
- must be clearly given, and if this is not the case, or consent is retracted, then consent has not been given;
- is mutual within healthy relationships, and the choice to give consent or not must be respected.

It is interesting that almost a third of pupils in secondary schools felt that they had not been taught about consent, according to a survey undertaken by the Sex Education Forum which consulted almost 900 children and young people aged between 14 and 25 years (Sex Education Forum 2014). However, 96% of respondents were aware of the age of consent. The PSHE Association guidance (2015) provides clear definitions of both consent and sexual consent, which are worth quoting here in full:

> Consent is agreement which is given willingly and freely without exploitation, threat or fear, and by a person who has the capacity to give their agreement.
>
> Sexual consent refers to a positive choice to take part in a sexual activity by people who understand the nature and implications of the activity they are agreeing to. Both parties take part not because they have to, but because they want to. Consent must be free – an active, personal choice; it must not be inferred, assumed, coerced or gained by exploitation. In addition, the person giving consent must have the capacity to do so: they should be old enough, have all the information they need to make the decision, and be in a fit state to give consent (and not, for example, with their judgement impaired by alcohol or drugs). It is the person seeking consent who is legally and ethically responsible for ensuring that consent is given and meets these criteria, and because people may change their minds or consent to one activity but not another, the

seeker of consent should not see seeking consent as a 'one-off' but rather a continuing process of making sure the other person is consenting.

(PSHE Association 2015: 6)

The definitions are drawn from the Crown Prosecution Service's guidance on consent, and are thus rooted in law. Further, the guidance notes that a variety of facets can impact on a person's ability to give or understand consent:

The sexual orientation, gender identity, and socio-economic, family and cultural background of pupils – and whether they have special educational needs or disabilities – may also have an impact on their understanding of consent and their vulnerability to nonconsensual situations.

(PSHE Association 2015: 4)

Pause for thought

Consider the guidance relating to consent, provided by the PSHE Association.

- Highlight the key elements that constitute informed consent.
- What factors might impede the ability to give consent?
- What pressures might an individual face when deciding whether to give consent? Are these immediate, contextual, external, internal or otherwise?

Sexual abuse and experimentation

It is not possible to explore issues relating to sexual abuse in detail in a chapter of this nature, but it is important to note that abuse, pornography and social media can each have a significant detrimental impact on the development of children and young people. How education professionals identify and address harmful sexual behaviours is an area that was explored earlier in the chapter.

Sexual abuse

Boyer and Fine (1992), Roosa et al. (1997) and Schloredt and Heiman (2003) highlight sexual abuse as a contributing factor to early sexual experimentation, with the education and perception of sex coming from negative experiences resulting in risky behaviour. Ashley, Jackson and Davies (2008) point out that childhood sexual abuse is an indicator for future unrestricted sexual behaviour caused by skewed perceptions of sex, impacting upon identity with the young person and using sexual activity to normalise the abuse experienced.

Pornography

It is becoming increasingly apparent that pornography is a significant source for children and young people when accessing information about sex. Due to its skewed, and often misogynistic, perspective on sex, pornography can give a concerning and even frightening perspective on sex for young people. It can suggest an ideal, or a norm of what sex involves which is far from the reality of most people's experience. This hegemonic perspective of dominant, heterosexual masculinity may also impact upon gender behaviours and reinforce patriarchy within social relationships, including within the education system (Connell 1995). This may then lead, as suggested by King-Hill and Barrie (2015), to a skewed perception of consent when considering sex, impacting upon how young people comprehend and rationalise their gender and sexual identity in terms of consenting relationships (McCarry 2010). Research has demonstrated that young people find it difficult to comprehend the legal definition of consent (Burton, Kitzinger, Kelly and Regan 1998; Burman and Cartmel 2005; Marston and King 2006; McCarry 2010; Beckett et al. 2013), constructing their own definition (Beckett et al. 2013). A survey on behalf of the National Association of Headteachers (2013) found that 83% of parents of secondary aged pupils want to see issues around pornography addressed in sex and relationship education in schools.

Social media

Social media and technology are an important part of contemporary Western life which adds to the complexity, for children and young people, of negotiating this safely. Social media makes it easy for personal information to be shared and an educator's role may now have to entail consideration for how this is to be approached and addressed within a classroom setting. Whilst internet safety is embedded in the National Curriculum (DfE 2014), it does not cover relationship elements and the dangers that surround them, for example 'sexting': the sending of explicit images or text to another. Whilst sexting is a concern mainly from early adolescence, it is worth considering introducing the concept of virtual boundaries from an early age. Indeed, a YouGov poll indicated that 91% of parents believe that pupils should receive PSHE lessons to teach about the risks of sexting, as well as the threat of stranger danger in online activity (DfE 2017).

Pause for thought

Consider the impact of social media and other technological sources on your own perceptions of sex and sexuality:

- What pressures does this create for you of those known to you?
- Are representations of sex and relationships realistic, idealised or sensationalised? What effect does this have?
- What pressures exist to engage in sexting or other risky behaviours using social media?

Moving forward

In order to develop inclusive practice in the area of sexual development and behaviour, we need to consider:

- What support and training is provided for teachers and other professionals working with children and young people.

- How these professionals can be enabled to identify both acceptable and risky sexual behaviours, according to the age and stage of those in their care.
- How the influence of the media can impact on young people, and what strategies can be used to support healthy development, including positive self-identity.
- What is meant by inclusive relationships and sex education.
- How prejudice, stereotyping and heteronormative assumptions can be tackled within the education system at all levels.
- How children and young people can be supported to make positive and appropriate choices, with an awareness of the meaning of consent.

Conclusion

Sex and sexuality continue to be subjects that people find difficult and sometimes embarrassing to discuss. This may be due to social or cultural norms, and can impact on perceptions of whether children and young people should be educated in these areas. Whilst some parents and carers may find the subjects difficult to broach, they may also have strong views on what should be included in the school curriculum: their views may stand in contrast to the views and needs of their children.

Enabling children and young people to understand the concept of consent, and to be equipped to make decisions based in a well-developed sense of self-identity, self-esteem and self-worth is essential if positive, healthy life choices are to be made. This chapter has raised particularly important questions: how and where are those providing relationships and sex education trained, and how do such educators identify the parameters of what constitutes healthy sexual development and behaviours? Whilst the answers have not yet been reached, developing the debate will help to work towards it.

Further reading

Brook, PSHE Association and Sex Education Forum (2014) *Sex and Relationship Education (SRE) for the 21st Century*. Available at: www.pshe-association.org.uk/sites/default/files/SRE%20for%20the%2021st%20Century%20-%20FINAL.pdf_0.pdf

Mason, S. and Woolley, R. (2011) *Relationships and Sex Education 5–11*. London: Continuum.

Morris, J. and Woolley, R. (2017) *Family Diversities Reading Resource: 150+ children's picture books to value children's families* (2nd edition). Lincoln: Bishop Grosseteste University. Available at: http://libguides.bishopg.ac.uk/childrensliterature

References

Alldred, P. and David, M. (2007). *Get real about sex: The politics and practice of sex education*. Maidenhead: Open University Press.

Arai, L. (2009). *Teenage pregnancy: The making and unmaking of a problem*. Bristol: Policy Press.

Ashley, N., Jackson, J. and Davies, S. (2008). Sexual Self-Schemas of Female Child Sexual Abuse Survivors: Relationships with Risky Sexual Behavior and Sexual Assault in Adolescence. *Archive of Sexual Behaviour*, 39, 1359–1374.

Beckett, H., Brodie, I., Factor, F., Melrose, M., Pearce, J., Pitts, J., Shuker, L. and Warrington, C. (2013). "It's wrong but you get used to it": A qualitative study of gang-associated sexual violence towards and exploitation of, young people in England. Sine loco: Office of the Children's Commissioner's Inquiry into Child Sexual Exploitation in Gangs and Groups.

Boyer, D. and Fine, D. (1992). *Sexual Abuse as a Factor in Adolescent Pregnancy and Child Maltreatment*, [Online]. Available at: http://jech.bmj.com/content/60/6/502.abstract

Brook. (2010). *Have Fun, Be Careful Campaign*, [Online]. Available at: www.brook.org.uk/contraception/have-fun-be-careful-campaign

Burman, M. and Cartmel, F. (2005). *Young people's attitudes towards gendered violence*. Glasgow: NHS Health Scotland.

Burton, S., Kitzinger, J., Kelly, L. and Regan, L. (1998). *Young people's attitudes towards violence, sex and relationships: A survey and focus group study*. London and Glasgow: Child and Woman Abuse Studies Unit, University of London; Media Research Unit, Sociology Department, University of Glasgow; Zero Tolerance Trust.

Connell, R. W. (1995). *Masculinities*. Berkeley: University of California Press.

Daguerre, A. and Nativel, C. (2006). *When Children become Parents*. Bristol: Policy Press.

DePalma, R. and Atkinson, E. (2009). 'No outsiders': Moving beyond a discourse of tolerance to challenge heteronormativity in primary schools. *British Educational Research Journal*, 35(6), 837–855.

DfE (2014). *National Curriculum in England: Framework for Key Stages 1–4*. Available at: www.gov.uk/government/publications/national-curriculum-in-england-framework-for-key-stages-1-to-4/the-national-curriculum-in-england-framework-for-key-stages-1-to-4

DfE (2017). *Policy Statement; Relationships Education, Relationships and Sex Education, and Personal, Social, Health and Economic Education*. Available at: www.gov.uk/government/uploads/system/uploads/attachment_data/file/595828/170301_Policy_statement_PSHEv2.pdf

Duncan, S. (2010). *Teenage Pregnancy*, Teenage Pregnancy Conference, Knightsbridge Hotel, London, 20th October 2010.

Duncan, S., Edwards, R. and Alexander, C. (2008). *Teenage parenthood: What's the problem?* London: The Tufnell Press.

Finkelhor, D. (1995). The victimization of children. *American Journal of Orthopsychiatry*, 65(2), 177–193.

Finkelhor, D., Ormrod, R. and Chaffin, M. (2009). Juveniles who commit sex offenses against minors. *Juvenile Justice Bulletin United States Department of Justice*, December, 1–12.

Guasp, A. (2012). *The school report: The experiences of gay young people in Britain's schools in 2012*. Cambridge: Stonewall. Available at: www.stonewall.org.uk/sites/default/files/The_School_Report_2012_.pdf

Hackett, S. (2014). *Children and young people with harmful sexual behaviours*. Dartington: Research in Practice.

Hackett, S. (2016). *Exploring the relationship between neglect and harmful sexual behaviours in children and young people: Evidence scope 3, NSPCC*. London.

Hackett, S., Phillips, J., Masson, H. and Balfe, M. (2012). *Recidivism, desistance and life course trajectories of young sexual abusers: An in-depth follow-up study, 10 years on SASS research briefing no. 7*. Durham: University of Durham.

Hackett, S., Phillips, J., Masson, H. and Balfe, M. (2013). Individual, family and abuse characteristics of 700 British child and adolescent sexual abusers. *Child Abuse Review*, 22(4), 232–245.

Hawkes, D. (2008). *Just what difference does teenage motherhood make? Evidence from the Millennium cohort study*. London: The Tufnell Press.

King-Hill, S. (2013). Teenage mothers' experiences of the transition to parenthood in relation to education: An interpretative phenomenological analysis. *MIDIRS Midwifery Digest*, 23(4), 426–434.

King-Hill, S. (2016). Implementing the Brook Sexual Behaviours Traffic Light Tool in Cornwall: An Evaluation. Commissioned by Brook and Cornwall Council and carried out by the University of Worcester. Sine loco: Unpublished.

King-Hill, S. and Barrie, R. (2015). Perceptions of consent in adolescents who display harmful sexual behaviour. *The British Journal of School Nursing*, 10(5), 221–225.

Legislation.gov.uk (2010). *Equality Act 2010*, [Online]. Available at: www.legislation.gov.uk/ukpga/2010/15/contents

MacVarish, J. and Billings, J. (2008). *Challenging the irrational, amoral and antisocial construction of the 'teenage mother'*. London: The Tufnell Press.

Mail Online (2010). *We'll Never End Our Teenage Pregnancy Epidemic Until We Admit What's Really Causing It*, [Online]. Available at: www.dailymail.co.uk/debate/article-1253631/BRENDA-ALMOND-Well-end-teenage-pregnancy-epidemic-admit-whats-REALLY-causing-it.html

Marston, C. and King, E. (2006). Factors that shape young people's sexual behaviour: A systematic review. *Lancet*, 368, 1581–1586.

Mason, S. and Woolley, R. (2011). *Relationships and sex education 5–11*. London: Continuum.

McCarry, M. (2010). Becoming a 'proper man': Young people's attitudes about interpersonal violence and perceptions of gender. *Gender and Education*, 22(1), 17–30.

McCrory, E., Hickey, N., Farmer, E. and Vizard, E. (2008). Early-onset sexually harmful behaviour in childhood: A marker for life-course persistent antisocial behaviour? *The Journal of Forensic Psychiatry and Psychology*, 19(3), 382–395.

NAHT (2013). *Research Commissioned by the National Association of Head Teachers (NAHT), Carried Out in April 2013 by Research Now*. Available at: www.naht.org.uk/welcome/news-and-media/key-topics/parents-and-pupils/parents-want-schools-to-manage-dangers-of-pornography-says-survey/

Office for National Statistics (2011). *An overview of sexual offending in England and Wales published by analysts from the Ministry of Justice, Home Office and Office of National statistics*. London: Ministry of Justice, Home Office and the Office for National Statistics.

PSHE Association (2015). *Teaching about Consent in PSHE Education at Key Stages 3 and 4*. Available at: https://www.pshe-association.org.uk/sites/default/files/PSHE%20Association%20guidance%20on%20teaching%20about%20consent%20at%20key%20stages%203%20and%204%20March%202015.pdf

Radford, L., Corral, S., Bradley, C., Fisher, H., Bassett, C., Howat, N. and Collishaw, S. (2011). *Child abuse and neglect in the UK today*. London: NSPCC.

Roosa, M., Tein, J., Reinholtz, C. and Angelini, P. (1997). *The Relationship of Childhood Sexual Abuse to Teenage Pregnancy*, [Online]. Available at: www.jstor.org/pss/353666

Ryan, G.D. and Lane, S.L. (1997). *Integrating theory and method*. San Francisco, CA: Jossey-Bass.

Ryan, G.D., Miyoshi, T.J., Metzner, J.L., Krugman, R.D. and Fryer, G.E. (1996). Trends in a national sample of sexually abusive youths. *Journal of the American Academy of Child and Adolescent Psychiatry*, 35(1), 17–25.

Schloredt, A. and Heiman, R. (2003). Perceptions of sexuality as related to sexual functioning and sexual risk in women with different types of childhood abuse histories. *Journal of Traumatic Stress*, 16, 275–284.

Sex Education Forum (2014). *New Survey Finds Children and Young People Aren't Being Taught about Consent in School*. Available at: www.sexeducationforum.org.uk/policy-campaigns/the-consent-issue.aspx

Smith, C., Allardyce, S., Hackett, S., Bradbury-Jones, C., Lazenbatt, A. and Taylor, J. (2014). Practice and policy in the UK with children and young people who display harmful sexual behaviours: An analysis and critical review. *Journal of Sexual Aggression*, 20(3), 267–280.

Smith, C., Bradbury-Jones, C., Lazenbatt, A. and Taylor, J. (2013). *Provision for young people who have displayed harmful sexual behaviour*. London: NSPCC.

SunOnline (2010). *Teenage Pregnancy Disaster*, [Online]. Available at: www.thesun.co.uk/sol/homepage/news/632581/Teen-pregnancy-disaster.html

Taylor, J.F. (2003). Children and young people accused of child sexual abuse: A study within a community. *Journal of Sexual Aggression*, 9(1), 57–70.

Woolley, R. (2010). *Tackling controversial issues in the primary school: Facing Life's Challenges with Your Learners*. London: Routledge.

11 Teaching Assistants and inclusion

Teresa Lehane

As a University tutor, I was observing a trainee teacher, during the final stages of a teaching placement in a school in which she had already secured a teaching post. The pupils in the group were all on the school's SEN D (special educational needs and disability) register. Partway through the lesson, a Teaching Assistant (TA) arrived from exam duties. When we discussed the lesson afterwards, the trainee teacher and I agreed that at around this point in time the students had become more relaxed, motivated and co-operative and the last part of the lesson was much the most successful. Where we differed was that the teacher had not noticed the TA joining the group.

Introduction

There are three main reasons for this chapter's focus on Teaching Assistants (TAs). First and foremost for this book, it is possible to learn a great deal about inclusion and how it is lived out in practice in our schools and educational provision from studying the work of TAs. Second, there is a good deal of research in this field, both in the UK and internationally, and this is a great example of how we can learn from very large-scale longitudinal studies as well as much smaller snapshots. Third, many of us work as TAs or work with TAs, and research-informed study of their work can help us and the learners we support.

What might we learn? Studying inclusive education can feel, as Allan (2008) has described it, full of 'platitudes' about 'celebrating' diversity and difference (Allan 2008: 65) as well as limited to endless changes in terminology and policy (Visser 2002: 71). The word inclusion itself is often criticised as a buzzword (Todd 2007: 8), and Slee suggests that 'all manner of thinking, discourse and activity' can sometimes 'pass itself off as inclusive' (2006: 111). It can be easy to assume that progress 'towards inclusion' is steady, but there is mounting evidence that this is not the case. Looking at the work of TAs enables us to apply critical imagination about inclusion to real practical situations. By *critical imagination*, we mean to help explore some hidden inverted commas. Hardy (2009) has described the almost 'obligatory' use of inverted commas in some writing to indicate that nothing is taken for granted and that the word within the inverted commas is, in some way, problematic and contested. However, too many inverted commas could be unhelpful in this book, given the number of times the words inclusion, inclusive or other problematic and contested terms such as SEN D are used. Looking thoughtfully at TAs can help us explore some of the 'taken for granted' nature of some ideas in education and inclusion and analyse why some of our imaginary inverted commas are still needed.

We will first look at the history of TAs, when and how so many people came to be deployed as TAs, as this history relates to the history of inclusion and probably sowed the seeds for some of today's successes and limitations and some of the contradictions and complexities in inclusive education. The education system in England will provide examples, although readers will wish to consider how practice varies in their own setting.

Numbers

Counting the numbers of TAs is not straightforward because schools are complex systems with varying job roles, and also because official counting systems change over time. However, growth in the numbers of TAs is well-established, with figures for full-time equivalent (FTE) TAs in publicly funded schools in England since 1997 approximately as shown in Table 11.1.

TAs represent around 25% of the total school workforce in England. Similar growth has taken place in the United States with the idea of 'para-educators' for individuals with disabilities enshrined in law (Shyman 2010: 828). Teacher assistant numbers have also increased in other countries, including Australia, Canada, Finland and Germany (Giangreco 2013: 94).

Roots in history

The historical background and policy context for this huge increase in TA numbers in England was driven by at least four strands of thinking which recur throughout the literature on TAs and which are important for our analysis.

The first strand is the idea of general assistance aimed at improving teaching and learning. This includes both indirect and direct roles. The first means TAs releasing teachers from more routine tasks so that they can focus on teaching; the second means direct pedagogical engagement or *teaching* by TAs (Blatchford, Russell and Webster 2012). The second main strand reflected in literature on TAs relates to ensuring the supply of teachers, retaining and supporting them in the profession (Bach, Kessler and Heron 2006). The third strand relates to pupils with SEN and/or disability. The fourth strand has been linked to policy initiatives and therefore alters over time. For example, at times policy appears more or less emancipatory and related to social justice. These four strands co-exist, closely affecting each other, and are lived out in schools often by the same people, the same TAs, in the same lesson.

The history of classroom assistance may be traced back at least as far as the 19th century pupil-teachers (Watkinson 2003; Watkinson 2008). In the 1920s, Margaret McMillan, in her pioneering

Table 11.1 Approximate numbers of full-time equivalent (FTE) TAs in publicly funded schools in England 1997–2015

1997	1998	1999	2000	2001	2002	2003
60,600	65,560	69,700	79,050	95,020	105,440	121,270
2004	2005	2006	2007	2008	2009	2010
132,240	147,250	153,510	163,800	176,990	183,700	213,900
2011	2012	2013	2014	2015		
219,800	232,300	243,700	255,100	263,000		

nurture schools, advocated employment of supplementary staff as well as teachers (Mansbridge 1932). The specific ancillary role probably originates in parent volunteers and paid school auxiliaries in the period after World War II (Hancock, Hall, Cable and Eyres 2010). However, the place of ancillaries in the school system is perhaps first explicit in the Plowden Report (DES 1967). In the context of trying to reduce class size and implement progressive plans for primary education, Plowden advocated the employment of ancillaries, assistants and teachers' aides. As well as the first strand or driver of improving classroom standards and the second of easing the load on (scarce) teachers, the third strand of TA work is also seen. In the section on education of handicapped children in ordinary classes, using terminology of the period, Plowden states that 'even one or two severely handicapped children add greatly to the responsibilities of a busy teacher in a large class. In such instances, some ancillary help may be essential' (DES 1967: 300).

The fourth strand of TA work in public policy initiatives can be glimpsed, at least in the US context, with emancipatory origins which Lewis (2003) locates in the civil rights and women's movements. Instructional aides, often women from minority groups, were recruited for HeadStart and to support bilingual learners, as a 'bridge to the poor' (Lewis 2003: 93) and as cultural brokers able to negotiate between majority and minority cultures (Lewis 2003). Lewis is one of many writers subsequently referring to TAs as having close links with parents, possibly living on the same estates and the same neighbourhoods and having social links through their own children (Lewis 2003; Roaf 2003; Mansaray 2006; Giangreco and Doyle 2007; Barkham 2008; Graves 2011; Blatchford, Russell and Webster 2012). While the cultural broker expectations are problematic, not least with TAs probably unprepared for such roles (Lewis 2003), this element of 'being in between' is also explored by Mansaray (2006) and others in the UK, including Alborz, Pearson, Farrell and Howes (2009). For example, the increase in TA numbers (as shown in Table 11.1) reflects, at least in part, the wider social aspiration of the New Labour period of UK public policy (1997–2010) which avowed, at least in principle, the idea that every child matters, with accompanying public expenditure (Bach, Kessler and Heron 2006; Veck 2009).

The recruitment of special needs assistants in England developed after the Warnock Report (DES 1978) and the 1981 Education Act (Swann and Loxley 1998; Watkinson 2003; Bach, Kessler and Heron 2006; Hancock, Hall, Cable and Eyres 2010; Blatchford, Russell and Webster 2012). Local Management of Schools, introduced in 1988, allowed headteachers 'creativity' in general staffing decisions through control of the budget (Watkinson 2003: 33) and generalist classroom assistants continued to be recruited in the 1990s, including staffing for a range of booster and intervention groups as the National Curriculum standards regime was implemented (Swann and Loxley 1998; Watkinson 2003; Mistry, Burton and Brundrett 2004; Bach, Kessler and Heron 2006; Hancock, Hall, Cable and Eyres 2010; Blatchford, Russell and Webster 2012).

Terms for and categories of TAs have varied (Swann and Loxley 1998; Watkinson 2003; Veck 2009), but the four strands of improving learning, supporting teachers, including pupils with SEN and a broader sense of social inclusion all continue with varying emphases and, crucially, still with little explicit discussion on how these strands inter-relate. Power is critical in all these strands; in the first two, power in relationship to teachers' professional boundaries. In the third and fourth strands, a great deal is asked of TAs where SEN provision (third strand) and social inclusion (the fourth) all depend to some degree on intervention by them, apparently without accompanying re-thinking of schooling, expectations or pupil assessment.

The New Labour period (1997–2010) saw a further sea-change in the TA field with the Workforce Reform policy. With key elements distilled in a National Agreement explicitly designed to address a teacher recruitment and retention crisis (Bach, Kessler and Heron 2006; Alexander 2010), Workforce Reform 'foregrounded the importance of assistants' (Cremin, Thomas and Vincett 2005: 413) through each phase of its implementation, including the reduction of teachers' routine bureaucratic and cover tasks and the introduction of planning, preparation and assessment time (PPA time) (Blatchford, Russell and Webster 2012). Many of the occupational standards linked to the subsequent Higher Level Teaching Assistant (HLTA) and cover supervisor status would once have 'only been associated with the responsibilities of qualified teachers' (Blatchford, Russell and Webster 2012: 12) and was deeply controversial, not least with the National Union of Teachers. You may want to think about these matters in a school context known to you.

The significance of Workforce Reform should not be underestimated for schools in general nor for the field of SEN D. The Training and Development Agency (TDA, undated) itself stated that this remodelling agenda underpinned other DfES initiatives and that 'remodelling is . . . fundamental to raising standards and will form the context for all other changes and developments' (TDA undated: 7). We cannot ignore Blatchford, Russell and Webster's (2012) view of public service modernisation as provision of cheaper workers and the 'systematic deskilling of teachers by central government' (Swann and Loxley 1998: 143). The growth of paraprofessional numbers in policing and health as well as education was explicitly presented as 'best practice' in modernising public services in general (Hancock, Hall, Cable and Eyres 2010; Smith 2012). Bach, Kessler and Heron (2006) indicate that this is part of the shift towards 'new public management', itself associated with Taylorisation of work where less skilled tasks are 'cheapened and delegated to support staff' (Bach, Kessler and Heron 2006: 4). Bach et al. argue that, despite this growth in public assistant roles, there is a dearth of analysis of the 'structure, operation and consequences' of them, with TAs, for example, presented 'very much as a means to an end' (Bach, Kessler and Heron 2006: 3). Writing from an industrial relations standpoint, Bach, Kessler and Heron (2006) indicate a long-standing tendency for employers to allocate tasks after workers have been recruited (Bach, Kessler and Heron 2006: 4). In Gunter's view (2007) of Workforce Reform, too, there was no attempt to use research evidence 'to locate the skills and knowledge of adults in schools with learners and learning' (Gunter 2007: 6), the base being 'organisational rather than pedagogic' (Gunter 2007: 7).

In summary, right from the outset, the work of TAs has been a point of intersection between different but related strands of educational thinking and policy. Whether inherent and unavoidable, a matter for celebration or even regret, the apparent lack of delineation, and even 'confusion' (Blatchford, Russell and Webster 2012: 13) between these strands seems uncontested.

What are the links with inclusion?

TAs hold a central position in the field of special educational needs (SEN) and are seen internationally as a 'primary tool' for inclusion (Hemmingsson, Borell and Gustavsson 2003: 88). It is often assumed that inclusive schooling automatically calls for TA input. Even allowing for an emphasis on physical disability, it is interesting to note how far it has become assumed that the education system can only be accessed through paraprofessionals. Allan (2008), citing Slee (2011), characterises this as $E = AR + D$. Equity [E] comprises the student with disability (D) plus additional resources (AR). Paliokosta and Blandford (2010), for example, note that that in a study of three 'very culturally different' secondary schools, additional adult support was seen as a prerequisite for inclusion (2010: 184), the same assumption being noted by Glazzard (2011) in a primary school. TA 'hours' have almost been perceived as 'currency' in which support is calculated (Roaf 2003: 222), and schools have tended to see the number of pupils with SEN as a key reason for growth in TA numbers (Blatchford, Russell and Webster 2012). There can be little doubt that TAs have contributed enormously to the successful 'mainstreaming' of many pupils with SEN D as well as to 'inclusion' in its fullest sense.

TA 'substitution' for teachers in the pedagogy of pupils with the SEN has also been noted over a long period (OfSTED 2004, Reindal 2008). Empirical studies such as that of Bedford, Jackson and Wilson (2008) found that in interviews/focus groups with around 41 teachers, TAs were often expected to have sole charge of some pupils with SEN. This phenomenon is also reported in the extensive review by Giangreco and Doyle (2007) and in the largest study available in this field, the five year systematic Deployment and Impact of Support Staff (DISS) project by the Institute of Education for the DCSF (Blatchford, Russell and Webster 2012). Blatchford et al. report that many pupils with SEN were routinely 'taught' for much of the time by TAs, rather than teachers (Blatchford, Bassett, Brown, Martin, Russell and Webster 2009: 6–7). The significance of the work of TAs for the education of such pupils seems beyond doubt (Armstrong 2016).

Research

The Deployment and Impact of Support Staff (DISS) research (Blatchford, Russell and Webster 2012) was included in the British Educational Research Association's (2014) 40th anniversary selection of 40 key studies to have had a significant impact on education since 1974. The very large size and careful design of the DISS research is beyond doubt and also rated as high quality evidence by the systematic EPPI (Evidence for Policy and Practice Information and Coordinating Centre) review (Alborz, Pearson, Farrell and Howes 2009). DISS was systematic, naturalistic and non-experimental work undertaken between 2003 to 2008 using questionnaires, time-logs, pupil achievement data, case studies, teacher ratings, observation and interviews. Their key finding was that 'the more TA support pupils received, the less progress they made' (Blatchford, Russell and Webster 2012: 46).

In short, the DISS researchers looked at the characteristics, conditions of employment, preparedness, deployment and practice of TAs and found each of these dimensions was demonstrated to operate less than optimally and affect the impact of TAs. For example, many support staff worked unpaid hours (Blatchford, Russell and Webster 2012). Variable levels of training and limited preparedness in both teachers and TAs and limited time for liaison were also noted and confirmed by questionnaires, case study and observation. Only 1 in 20 secondary teachers had timetabled time with a TA for planning, preparation and feedback. Crucially, pupils with SEN interacted more with TAs; those without SEN interacted more with teachers (Blatchford, Russell and Webster 2012). TAs were found, in practice, to be deployed in a direct instructional role, routinely supporting low attaining pupils and those with SEN with a substantial degree of separation from teachers and the rest of the class, both within but also away from the classroom. For example, almost all the team's observations of TA intervention for low attaining pupils in secondary schools took place away from the class and the teacher. Even when support was provided in class, Blatchford et al. noted the phenomenon of 'stereo teaching' where pupils tend to be exposed to two voices, the teacher and the TA, often talking about the same thing (2012: 87). In addition, some TAs felt 'vital information' regarding pupil engagement or progress did not feed back into planning (2012: 86). For Blatchford et al., then, all this is alternative rather than additional support. Finally, analysis of practice indicated substantive differences in this support in that, for example, TA talk tended to statements, prompts and task completion, closing down rather than opening up understanding, while teachers' talk tended more to explanation, cognitive focus and feedback on learning.

The findings of the DISS research do not stand in isolation and were not entirely unexpected, given both previous research in the UK and research in other countries. For example, Giangreco (2013), writing for an international audience, concludes that Australian research comes to similar conclusions as does US research on TAs. Drawing on international research, including DISS, he argues that there is an overarching problem 'that too often teacher assistants are not used wisely . . . but rather metaphorically as a bandaid for an injury that at least requires stitches and possibly major surgery' (2013: 94). Like the DISS researchers, Giangreco is clear that no blame attaches to TAs, that the research is not a reason to reduce their numbers (at least without a thoughtful alternative) and suggests that changes towards effective utilisation are not primarily their responsibility (2013: 94). Problems tend to arise when TAs are given 'an ill-defined, informal, instructional role' (Webster, Russell and Blatchford 2016: 127). Giangreco argues convincingly that 'overuse and misuse of teacher assistants is a symptom, not a cause' and relates to 'root issues within general and special education' (Giangreco 2013: 101). Thus, Giangreco and Doyle (2007) highlight the argument that the scenario of providing the least qualified personnel to 'provide primary instruction' to the most complex learners is not only illogical but would be unacceptable if applied to students without SEN (2007: 432). This is the heart of the matter: what do we want for pupils deemed to have SEN D?

Pause for thought

Do the findings of the DISS research surprise you?

- Do different standards apply to staff working with pupils with and without SEN D? Should different standards apply?
- What models of support and deployment have you seen in schools?

If you were a school pupil with special educational needs, what might your views be? What if you were a TA? What if you were a teacher?

- Is it right for a child with SEN D to be taught mainly by TAs?
- Why do TA expertise and effectiveness matter in successful inclusion?

We know that the vast majority of TA support has been for lower-attaining pupils and those with SEN (Blatchford, Russell and Webster 2012) and that this has an impact on their education. There is also some evidence that the SEN D system in schools is becoming more deregulated within a context of school diversity and choice, for example in the academy and free school movements, and moving towards a market model with private sector providers competing to offer services as commissioned, all within a context of austerity (Lehane 2017). It seems no coincidence that, after many years of such matters being considered, when a set of Professional Standards for Teaching Assistants was eventually published in 2016, they were non-mandatory and non-statutory. DISS team members, trade unions and others were involved in establishing the standards. While the Department for Education initially commissioned this work, they have made it clear that they are no longer involved with the document. Thus, while many TAs are well qualified, trained and prepared for their work, there is still no obligation at all to ensure qualifications, training or preparedness in TAs.

The DISS research has been described as a 'wake-up call', however, and researchers have taken up the challenge to improve matters. For example, Webster, Russell and Blatchford (2016), the leaders of the DISS team, have since carried out the EDTA (Effective Deployment of TAs) and MITA (Maximising the Impact of TAs) research to work with schools and pairs of teachers and TAs to develop and evaluate ways forward. A first and second edition of a book of guidance on better deployment have followed, developing materials to help schools think through, plan and evaluate, breaking firmly away from any remnants of the Velcro (dependency model) approach to TA deployment. Early signs of progress are encouraging.

Pause for thought

Reflecting on the discussion in the preceding paragraphs:

- Could statutory standards for Teaching Assistants help make inclusion more effective?
- Is it more important for schools to make changes which work for them?
- What are the key issues in a context known to you?
- Do these issues reflect the findings from research outlined in this chapter?

Case study

Jo, a teaching assistant, has a BA in Education (First Class Honours in Special Needs and Inclusion Studies) following a Foundation Degree in Learning Support. Her school is rated 'good' by the school inspection body Ofsted. Jo took part in a small research project (Lehane 2016) and reflected on her work as an Higher Level Teaching Assistant in her school's Learning Support Base for four years and three previous years spent in the 'mainstream' of the same school. Some of her comments include the following:

> students say can I stay up here with you, I don't wanna go back over there [to mainstream class] . . . please don't send me back . . .

> *[T]he Department probably hinders inclusion . . . [teachers say] you have them, I can't have them, rather than trying to include them in the classroom.*
>
> *[It is] one of those in between roles . . . caught in the middle sometimes and it's hard to find a place . . . looking after . . . special needs students comes back to us . . . some teachers might not have even looked at an IEP [Individual Education Plan].*
>
> *[It is] less formal over here . . . we still have rules . . . we're probably more consistent in a way . . . we never tell them off though or issue them with a consequence for not having a pen, we just give them one.*

Jo perceives substantial differences between 'mainstream' and base within her mainstream school, such as 'a big lack' of differentiation in 'mainstream' and the base providing a calmer ethos with benefits for pupil behaviour. Jo expresses a feeling of criticality about the nature of schooling, 'a very strange place to be . . . like a mini-prison for children . . . they have no choice to come here . . . locked up with loads of people they probably wouldn't be with'. Jo states that some teachers have expressed views like 'those kids . . . so weak, I can't teach them . . . you have them, I can't have them, rather than trying to include them in the classroom'. Jo compares, for example, rarely seeing lesson plans in the mainstream, but [in the base] 'I know exactly what I'm doing for the whole year'. Similarly, references to keeping herself 'out of the way' in mainstream or 'running around scribing' and assisting pupils to copy from the board contrast with her considerable responsibility levels in the base for leading groups, entering students for exams and organising annual reviews.

Jo gives the impression that as well as separation between 'mainstream' and 'base', there is some separation between teachers and TAs, albeit amicable. While some teachers communicate, 'some just say thanks, Miss, for the lesson and never kind of start any kind of conversation with you'.

In some respects, Jo is critical of teacher pedagogy; for example, with scribing simply to reproduce information from the board she states 'the teacher really hasn't . . . taken account of the full scope of learning needs in the classroom'. Some pupils are seen as a 'nightmare' in the mainstream: 'he's always mucking about, silly behaviour . . .' but 'when he's up here [in the Base], he's so delightful, works so hard' . . . 'angels up here . . . totally different children'. She does not contest the idea that 'teachers expect the knowledge and the understanding of students' to come from support staff, but there is evidence of understanding of the demands on teachers in catering for diverse needs, 'it's very hard . . . trying to differentiate that much . . . it's not easy'.

In this case study, there seem to be some parallels between the experiences of children deemed to have SEN D and those of the TAs working with them. To some extent, despite a great school and mainly happy working relationships, some pupils seem to be treated as 'other' and assumed to be different and all too easily despatched out of class. Jo refers to a clear delineation in attitudes and practice between mainstream and support base even inside her mainstream school and makes us think about why a pupil spending time in the Learning Support Base has told Jo: 'don't send me back'. Returning to the vignette at the start of the chapter, we may have some insights about why the (excellent) student teacher did not notice the TA's contribution to the lesson. Are there similarities between that TA and Jo?

Moving forward

In order to work towards inclusive practice in working as a Teaching Assistant or with Teaching Assistants, we need to consider:

- How learning support professionals are trained, prepared, supported and deployed and what the aims of learning support are. Research indicates that default and dependency models are likely to work less well. Models based on careful deployment and clear focus are likely to work more effectively.
- We are asking a huge amount from Teaching Assistants, and their professional work has evolved in a relatively ad hoc way, responding to different drivers, over the last 50 years or so. They have made and continue to make an enormous contribution. We need to think this through fully in the light of current research and knowledge and provide the support that is required.
- Giangreco (2013) suggests a range of alternatives to current approaches, including greater use of specialist teachers alongside the classroom teacher. What do you think?

Conclusion

The work of TAs, closely involved for at least 30, perhaps 50, years with the learning of pupils with special educational needs and disabilities, deserves careful study. We can see that, for much of that time, TAs have not been deployed as effectively as they might despite the best of intentions from all concerned. There is some evidence of parallels between the experiences of children deemed to have 'SEN D' and those of the TAs working with them. TAs themselves can feel 'othered' and less than included. The reasons for this are many and complex, and an underlying issue is our attitude to inclusion and to children with SEN D. We would probably not have tolerated such poor deployment and poor returns in the case of children who were not deemed to have SEN D. So perhaps it is really our attitudes we need to examine and keep re-examining. As Len Barton and others have long made clear, inclusive education is not a 'thing' but a complex struggle, not one amenable to easy or slick answers (Barton 2016: 156). In line with approaches such as the Index to Inclusion (Booth and Ainscow 2011), successful inclusion of families and of staff is pivotal in the inclusion of children and young people.

We continue to ask a great deal of TAs, as educators and stakeholders have done throughout the history of TAs. As discussed earlier, the ask includes enhancing teaching and learning for children, supporting teachers in all their role, supporting individuals across the range of special educational needs and/or disabilities and promoting social justice and inclusion. They are also now asked to achieve this in an increasingly deregulated and diverse range of schools in a context of fiscal austerity.

Webster, Russell and Blatchford (2016) state that neither the EDTA nor MITA projects on the work of TAs require schools to examine their SEN provision per se (Webster, Russell and Blatchford 2016). They carefully do not rule this out, however, and it would seem imperative to do so in the light of what is now understood.

Further reading

British Educational Research Association (2014), *A portrait of 40 years of educational research through 40 studies* www.bera.ac.uk/project/40at40
Webster, R. and Blatchford, P. (2012), Supporting learning? How effective are teaching assistants? Chapter 5 in Adey, P. and Dillon, J. (eds.), *Bad education: Debunking myths in education*. Maidenhead: Open University Press. pp. 77–92.
Webster, R., Russell, A. and Blatchford, P. (2016), *Maximising the impact of teaching assistants: Guidance for school leaders and teachers*. 2nd edition. London: Routledge.

References

Alborz, A., Pearson, D., Farrell, P., and Howes, A., (2009), The Impact of Adult Support Staff on Pupils and Mainstream Schools, Technical Report, *in*: *Research Evidence in Education Library*, London: EPPI – Centre Report 1702T, Social Science Research Unit, Institute of Education, University of London. http://eppi.ioe. ac.uk/cms/LinkClick.aspx?fileticket=97YoE2o3AGo%3d&tabid=2438&mid=4540 (Accessed 10.10.16).
Alexander, R., (2010), *Children, Their World, Their Education, Final Report and Recommendations of the Cambridge Primary Review*. London: Routledge Esmée Fairbairn Foundation.
Allan, J., (2008), *Rethinking Inclusive Education: The Philosophers of Difference in Practice*. Dordrecht NL, Netherlands: Springer.
Armstrong, F., (2016), Chapter 'Inclusive Education: The Key Role of Teaching Assistants' in Richards, G. and Armstrong, F. (eds.). *Key Issues for Teaching Assistants*. 2nd edition. Abingdon: Routledge, pp. 1–12.
Bach, S., Kessler, I., and Heron, P., (2006), Changing Job Boundaries and Workforce Reform: The Case of Teaching Assistants, *Industrial Relations Journal*, 37 (1) pp. 2–21. doi: 10.1111/j.1468-2338.2006.00387
Barkham, J., (2008), Suitable Work for Women? Roles, Relationships and Changing Identities of 'Other Adults' in the Early Years Classroom, *British Educational Research Journal*, 34 (6) pp. 839–853. doi: 10.1080/01411920802041558
Barton, L., (2016), Chapter 'Social Justice, Human Rights and Inclusive Education' in Richards, G. and Armstrong, F. (eds.). *Key Issues for Teaching Assistants*. 2nd edition. Abingdon: Routledge, pp. 156–161.
Bedford, D., Jackson, C.R., and Wilson, E., (2008), New Partnerships for Learning: Teachers' Perspectives on Their Developing Professional Relationships with Teaching Assistants in England, *Journal of In-Service Education*, 34 (1) pp. 7–25.
Blatchford, P., Bassett, P., Brown, P., Martin, C., Russell, A., and Webster, R., (2009), *Deployment and Impact of Support Staff Project*, DCSF Research Brief DCSF – RB 148, London: Institute of Education (DCSF funded) [online]. www.ioe.ac.uk/DISS_Research_Summary.pdf (Accessed 08.10.09).
Blatchford, P., Russell, A., and Webster, R., (2012), *Reassessing the Impact of Teaching Assistants*. Abingdon: Routledge.
Booth, T., and Ainscow, M., (2011), *Index for Inclusion: Delivering Learning and Participation in Schools*. 3rd edition. Bristol: Centre for Studies on Inclusive Education.
British Educational Research Association, (2014), *A portrait of 40 years of educational research through 40 studies*. www.bera.ac.uk/project/40at40
Cremin, H., Thomas, G., and Vincett, K., (2005), Working with Teaching Assistants: Three Models Evaluated, *Research Papers in Education*, 20 (4) pp. 413–432. http://dx.doi.org/10.1080/02671520500335881
DES, (1967), *The Plowden Report: Children and Their Primary Schools* (Chair: Lady Bridget Plowden). London: HMSO. www.educationengland.org.uk/documents/plowden/plowden1-00.html (Accessed 02.01.12).
DES, (1978), *Report of the Committee of Enquiry into the Education of Handicapped Children and Young People* (Chair: Mrs. H.M. Warnock). London: HMSO.
Giangreco, M.F., (2013), Teacher Assistant Supports in Inclusive Schools: Research, Practices and Alternatives, *Australasian Journal of Special Education*, 37 (2) pp. 93–106.

Giangreco, M.F., and Doyle, M.B., (2007), Chapter 'Teaching Assistants in Inclusive Schools' in Florian, L. (ed.). *The Sage Handbook of Special Education*. London: Sage, pp. 429–439.

Glazzard, J., (2011), Perceptions of the Barriers to Effective Inclusion in One Primary School: Voices of Teachers and Teaching Assistants, *Support for Learning*, 26 (2) pp. 56–63. doi: 10.1111/j.1467-9604.2011.01478

Graves, S., (2011), Performance or Enactment? The Role of the Higher Level Teaching Assistant in a Remodelled School Workforce in England, *Management in Education*, 25 (1) pp. 15–20.

Gunter, H., (2007), Remodelling the School Workforce in England: A Study in Tyranny, *Journal for Critical Education Policy Studies*, 5 (1) pp. 1–11.

Hancock, R., Hall, T., Cable, C., and Eyres, I., (2010), 'They Call Me Wonder Woman': The Job Jurisdictions and Work-Related Learning of Higher Level Teaching Assistants, *Cambridge Journal of Education*, 40 (2) pp. 97–112. http://dx.doi.org/10.1080/0305764X.2010.481382

Hardy, S., (2009), Chapter 'The New Pornographies: Reproduction or Reality' in Attwood, F. (ed.). *Mainstreaming Sex: The Sexualisation of Western Culture*. London: I.B. Tauris, pp. 3–18.

Hemmingsson, H., Borell, L., and Gustavsson, A., (2003), Participation in School: School Assistants Creating Opportunities and Obstacles for Pupils with Disabilities, *OTJR: Occupation, Participation and Health*, 23 (3) pp. 88–98.

Lehane, T., (2016), 'Cooling the Mark Out': Experienced Teaching Assistants' Perceptions of Their Work in the Inclusion of Pupils with Special Educational Needs in Mainstream Secondary Schools, *Educational Review*, 68 (1) pp. 4–23. http://dx.doi.org/10.1080/00131911.2015.1058753

Lehane, T., (2017), 'SEN's Completely Different Now': Critical Discourse Analysis of Three 'Codes of Practice' for Special Educational Needs (1994, 2001, 2015), *Educational Review*. http://dx.doi.org/10.1080/00131911.2016.1237478

Lewis, K.C., (2003), *Instructional Aides: Colleagues or Cultural Brokers?* Paper presented at the Annual Meeting of the American Educational Research Association, Chicago, Illinois [online]. www.adi.org/journal/ss04/Lewis.pdf (Accessed 10.10.16).

Mansaray, A.A., (2006), Liminality and In/Exclusion: Exploring the Work of Teaching Assistants, Pedagogy, *Culture and Society*, 14 (2) pp. 171–187. http://dx.doi.org/10.1080/14681360600738335

Mansbridge, A., (1932), *Margaret McMillan Prophet and Pioneer: The Story of Her Life and Work*. London: Dent and Sons.

Mistry, M., Burton, N., and Brundrett, M., (2004), Managing LSAs: An Evaluation of the Use of Learning Support Assistants in an Urban Primary School, *School Leadership and Management*, 24 (2) pp. 125–137. http://dx.doi.org/10.1080/1363243041000695787

OfSTED, (2004), *Special Educational Needs and Disability*. London: Ofsted [online]. www.ofsted.gov.uk/Ofsted-home/Publications-and-research/Browse-all-by/Documents-by-type/Thematic-reports/Special-educational-needs-and-disability-towards-inclusive-schools (Accessed 01.05.12).

Paliokosta, P., and Blandford, S., (2010), Inclusion in School: A Policy, Ideology or Lived Experience? Similar Findings in Diverse School Cultures, *Support for Learning*, 25 (4) pp. 179–186. doi: 10.1111/j.1467-9604.2010.01464.x

Reindal, S.M., (2008), A Social Relational Model of Disability: A Theoretical Framework for Special Needs Education? *European Journal of Special Needs Education*, 23 (2) pp. 135–146. http://dx.doi.org/10.1080/08856250801947812

Roaf, C., (2003), Chapter 'Learning Support Assistants Talk about Inclusion' in Nind, M. Rix, J., Sheehy, K. and Simmons, K. (eds.). *Inclusive Education: Diverse Perspectives*. London: Fulton, pp. 221–240.

Shyman, E., (2010), Identifying Predictors of Emotional Exhaustion among Special Education Paraeducators: A Preliminary Investigation, *Psychology in the Schools*, 47 (8) pp. 828–841. doi: 10.1002/pits.20507

Slee, R., (2006), Limits to and Possibilities for Educational Reform, *International Journal of Inclusive Education*, 10 (2–3) pp. 109–119.

Slee, R., (2011), *The Irregular School: Exclusion, Schooling and Inclusive Education*. London: Routledge.

Smith, M., (2012), *Hyperactive: The Controversial History of AD/HD*. London: Reaktion.

Swann, W., and Loxley, A., (1998), The Impact of School-Based Training on Classroom Assistants in Primary Schools, *Research Papers in Education*, 13 (2) pp. 141–160. http://dx.doi.org/10.1080/0267152980130203

TDA, Training and Development Agency for Schools, (no date), *Popular Questions on the National Agreement*. [online]. www.tda.gov.uk/upload/resources/doc/p/popular_questions_na.doc (Accessed 09.11.09).

Todd, L., (2007), *Partnerships for Inclusive Education: A Critical Approach to Collaborative Working*. London: Routledge.

Veck, W., (2009), From an Exclusionary to an Inclusive Understanding of Educational Difficulties and Educational Space: Implications for the Learning Support Assistant's Role, *Oxford Review of Education*, 35 (1) pp. 41–56. http://dx.doi.org/10.1080/03054980701782031

Visser, J., (2002), The David Wills Lecture 2001: Eternal Verities – the Strongest Links, *Emotional and Behavioural Difficulties*, 7 (2) pp. 68–84. http://dx.doi.org/10.1080/1363275020050707

Watkinson, A., (2003), *Managing Teaching Assistants: A Guide for Headteachers, Managers and Teachers*. London: Routledge Falmer.

Watkinson, A., (2008), *Leading and Managing Teaching Assistants: A Practical Guide for School Leaders, Teachers and Higher – Level Teaching Assistants*. Abingdon: David Fulton.

Webster, R., Russell, A., and Blatchford, P., (2016), *Maximising the Impact of Teaching Assistants: Guidance for School Leaders and Teachers*. 2nd edition. London: Routledge.

12 Inclusion and the arts

Simon Taylor

Sixteen-year-old Andy has been staying at the city's emergency accommodation centre for the last three weeks. Run by a local charitable trust, it supports young people who are homeless or at risk. He has been dealing with the boredom and frustration felt by many of the young people there through participating in some photography workshops led by Pete, a professional artist. Pete is employed by the local art gallery in the city and is encouraging Andy to create some self-portraits that might be included in an exhibition that will be open to the public. Andy is feeling a mixture of nervousness, excitement and pride that his work is being taken seriously and he has a chance to tell his own story for the first time.

Introduction

This chapter looks at the central role that creativity, and the arts more broadly, can play in inclusive education. Learners may become excluded from mainstream education for a variety of complex and often interlinked reasons; it is also important to understand the wide range of informal contexts in which learning through the arts is situated and innovative practice is taking place, including art galleries, museums, libraries, archives, theatres, community and day care centres, prisons, pupil referral units and other 'alternative provision'. We will first take a look at the broader picture, in particular the impact of Government and policy-makers, but also recent changes to our understanding of the arts and creativity, and their possible role in developing the culture and identity of our local communities and improving the life chances for young people like Andy.

Policy, inclusion and the arts

For many people, there is a feeling that the arts are 'not for me', and negative attitudes to art and creativity persist, sadly often based on their own far-from-positive experience in mainstream education. These groups or individuals are sometimes classified as 'hard to reach' by organisations and policy-makers, a term that is problematic for a number of reasons that we will look at later in this chapter. There is no denying that there are ongoing issues with elitism and accessibility within the arts but it is also interesting to observe the recent changes in policy from arms-length Government bodies such as Arts Council England (ACE), still the main source of financial support for the arts, museums and libraries, using money from the National Lottery via the Department for Culture, Media and Sport. In an effort to combat the traditional ideas that persist about elitist 'high culture', such as ballet, theatre and opera and 'low' or 'popular culture', such as contemporary music, film and television, ACE's most recent strategy document is entitled *Great Art and Culture for Everyone* (ACE, 2013). Chairman of ACE, Sir Peter Bazelgette, describes this publication as "both a manifesto and an action plan for all of us" (2013: 3). Interestingly, the tone throughout is accessible, inclusive and avoids the type of jargon usually found in policy documents, but the terms of reference are wide-ranging. It states:

> arts and culture play an important role in local regeneration, in attracting tourists, in the development of talent and innovation, in improving health and well-being, and in delivering essential services . . . We are one of many players within the arts and cultural ecology, which covers a very broad spectrum of activity, from films to opera, from rock music to library books.
>
> (2013: 14)

The language used here acknowledges that cultural production itself has seen a radical shift in recent years, from old hierarchies of 'high' and 'low' culture to the fragmentation and pluralism of contemporary 'DIY culture' with multiple voices, including those of young people, black and ethnic minorities, feminist voices and, more recently, voices representing gender and disability. The status of the arts and culture has also changed, with the end of 'grand narratives'; modernist ideas about the continual progress of Western civilisation being discredited, patriarchal stories of 'great works of genius' (usually by dead white European males) now questioned and alternative histories or new versions of history on offer. This gradual process of democratisation, a 'pick and mix' of increasingly diverse cultures, influences and beliefs over the last thirty years, is seen by many as a signifier of post-modernism, a term first coined by the French philosopher Jean-Francois Lyotard (1984).

In parallel with this democratic process, ironically, we have seen a marginalisation of arts subjects within mainstream state education in the UK and a sharp reduction in the number of students taking a creative subject, such as music or drama, at GCSE over the last few years. Latest figures from the Joint Council for Qualifications (JCQ) suggest that young people in England sat 44,000 fewer GCSEs in arts subjects in 2016. This 7.7% drop on the previous year is significantly higher than the 0.4% overall fall in the number of GCSEs taken. More worryingly, if the Government presses ahead with plans to make at least 90% of pupils take the English Baccalaureate or EBacc – a set of seven or eight GCSEs, which includes history or geography but not the arts – it will discourage young people's ambitions and may undermine the UK's creative industries (Arts Professional, 2016). At the same time, within the independent, fee-paying education sector, creative subjects are thriving and are valued for the way in which they encourage personal development, self-confidence and independent thinking amongst students, thus perpetrating privilege. These changes in emphasis, and the move away from a broad and balanced curriculum to one focussed on core knowledge and STEM subjects (science, technology, engineering and mathematics) may be reducing choices and closing down options for progression for many in the state sector. It could also be argued that it disproportionately affects vulnerable children, those with special education needs and young people at risk from exclusion. There is no doubt that recent changes in Government education policy have significantly reduced the vocational opportunities for those not so academically able or struggling with circumstances outside of their control.

Cultural capital

More broadly, some cultural commenters, most importantly French sociologist Pierre Bourdieu, have highlighted the significance of what is known as 'cultural capital' – a phenomenon in society where the arts seem to exist only for the enjoyment of the privileged few – a small elite of educated people who supposedly have innate 'taste' and can 'read' the cultural codes, despite that fact that these abilities are learned and should be available to everyone (Bourdieu, 1979). The danger is that, as Bourdieu puts it, "art and cultural consumption are predisposed, consciously and deliberately or not, to fulfil a social function of legitimating social differences" (Bourdieu, 1979, 1984: 7). Many high-profile professionals working in the arts and the wider creative sector today are aware of this danger and the powerful position that a certain level of cultural capital can put them in. David Anderson, former Head of Learning at the Victoria and Albert Museum in London, has spoken passionately about the multi-faceted nature of exclusion and the hurdles that face many people trying to access the arts and culture (in this case museums). He and many others have fought long and hard to protect free access to museums and galleries for the public in England. I would argue that the issues outlined by Anderson here apply just as much to those at risk of exclusion from mainstream education:

> There are many barriers to access . . . The principle ones are social class, poverty, educational disadvantage, ethnic and cultural background, disability and an individual's own attitudes. These factors often operate in combination, so that a successful strategy to overcome them requires a co-ordinated programme.
>
> (Anderson, 1999: 94)

Pause for thought

Reflecting on previous paragraphs, consider:

- How we can ensure that there is access to 'Great Art and Culture for everyone' and not just the privileged few?
- Whether the issue is really 'hard to reach' groups or, rather, 'hard to reach' cultural venues, inaccessible and daunting to enter?
- Should access to museums and galleries be free? Should public money be spent on outreach/education activities?
- What interventions might be successful in these circumstances?

Despite these issues being unresolved, it is now widely recognised that learning and development are lifelong processes and, in response, arts institutions and organisations must adapt to accommodate a broader spectrum of families, adults, children and young people, including those from excluded communities that do not have access to artistic and cultural institutions.

Cultural value

It is fair to say that social inclusion within the arts is a contested area in its own right, and there are dissenting voices from within the arts sector itself who worry about the dangers of populism or 'dumbing down' in an effort to appeal to ever broader audiences or wider demographics. John Holden is an academic who writes for the cultural think tank DEMOS. He sees the idea of cultural value as a struggle between the conflicting demands of instrumental value, that is, government funding agendas dictating the outcomes; institutional value, where arts organisations are merely preserving the status quo; and intrinsic value, or the importance of 'art for art's sake' (Holden, 2006). As an example of the instrumental use of the arts, during the era of New Labour (1997–2005) many UK Government-funded projects targeted supposedly 'hard to reach' communities or groups using arts-based interventions and partnerships, but these produced mixed results and limited evidence of success. In addition, there continues to be a stigma attached to young people labelled NEETs (Not in Education Employment or Training), and many communities resented being labelled 'socially deprived' when target groups were being identified.

Research

Research by the cultural writer and commentator Francois Matarasso entitled *Use or Ornament? The social impact of participation in the arts* (1997) identified the impact of participation in the arts through a range of case studies. Matarasso identified positive social outcomes in six main areas:

- personal development
- social cohesion
- community empowerment and self-determination
- local image and identity
- imagination and vision
- health and well-being

However, doubts were cast about Matarasso's methodology, in particular, questions about the influence of the social context and doubts about the capacity of the arts to tackle the root causes of social exclusion, such as long-term unemployment, poverty, crime or under-investment. Despite these criticisms, this was an influential report and the idea of promoting social cohesion, personal development, health and well-being through participatory arts has been gathering pace ever since.

A more recent research report entitled *Enriching Britain: Culture, Creativity and Growth* (Warwick Commission, 2015) was the result of a year-long investigation into the future of cultural value, undertaken by a diverse group of UK cultural leaders, supported by academics from the University of Warwick. Set against a backdrop of economic austerity, cuts in funding to the arts and a reduction in the status of arts subjects within state education, the report argues that the cultural and creative industries are one entity, an ecosystem, which is becoming increasingly important to British life, the British economy and Britain's place in the world. The analysis by the Commission calls for a joined-up approach to policy-making and a national strategy that could maximise cultural, economic and social return. The report is a challenge to all those who value how culture enriches people's lives and makes a range of recommendations, most importantly:

> The key message from this report is that the government and the cultural and creative industries need to take a united and coherent approach that guarantees equal access to

> everyone to a rich cultural education and the opportunity to live a creative life. There are barriers and inequalities in Britain today that prevent this from being a universal human right. This is bad for business and bad for society.
>
> (Warwick Commission, 2015: 8)

Reflecting on these two examples, consider:

- Can participation in the arts really solve long-term social problems?
- Is a 'top-down' approach ever justified to promote arts and culture?
- Should access to 'a rich cultural education and the opportunity to live a creative life' be a universal human right?

It is interesting to observe that much of the evidence put forward in this research is based on the economic argument of a 'return on investment' for Government subsidy, and uses the terminology of business. Perhaps this is a sign of the times. Can public funding for the arts only be justified in terms of the value to the wider economy, especially during times of austerity? Another interesting idea contained within the report is the importance of an 'arts ecosystem', where small-scale, local, grass roots cultural activity is encouraged and can be seen to benefit enormously from even a modest amount of start-up or 'seed' funding.

What is also significant, as highlighted by the Warwick Commission (2015), is the joint responsibility of Government and the creative industries to work together to ensure barriers and inequalities are removed, and to guarantee everyone 'a rich cultural education and the opportunity to live a creative life'. Whilst the implications for diversity and participation, education and skills are very welcome, questions could be asked as to whether this aim is actually shared by everyone, is realistic, or even sustainable.

The methodology that the Warwick Commission used is also worth analysis as it appears to have been a very collaborative approach, using a wide range of evidence-gathering tools. These included public debates and 'provocations', focus groups, written reports by strategic partners such as the Cultural Learning Alliance (2011) and interviews with leading figures in the arts and cultural sector. One criticism of this methodology could be that these cultural leaders and academics are the beneficiaries of a certain level of cultural capital and so are not representative of the population as a whole. However, perhaps conscious of this potential bias, the authors have included a section entitled 'Making the local matter', where they focus on the importance of encouraging communities to see themselves as 'co-commissioners' of their arts and cultural experiences. Here is a real emphasis on the arts, culture and heritage sectors bringing communities together in ways that reflect their expressions of identity and have a lasting impact.

Creativity in practice

In this section, we will explore in more detail what makes the arts and creativity so effective in inclusive practice, and the particular skills that can be developed when thinking and acting like an artist. Psychologist Mihaly Csikszentmihalyi (1996) explored ideas about the 'flow' of creativity. He talked to a wide range of professionals – artists, scientists, engineers, business people, writers and doctors – and found a common phenomenon. All these diverse individuals found contentment through the process of discovery, invention and activities that are intrinsically rewarding, rather than through material or financial gain. Exploring and inventing are basic human traits that were the drivers of our ancestors' evolution of culture. We have probably all experienced the feeling at some point of enjoying an activity so much that we lose track of time, are 'in the zone' or completely self-absorbed. This is the phenomenon of optimal experience or 'flow', and it is essential for creativity in whatever field you operate in, be that the arts, sciences, business or health and social care (Csikszentmihalyi, 1996).

Within the field of education, it is essential to create the conditions for 'flow'. This is particularly challenging with the demands of the school curriculum in its present form, timetabling of short lessons that do not allow time for the creative process, the emphasis on 'core subjects' and preparation for assessment that are collectively squeezing out creative subjects such as art, craft, design, dance, drama and music.

Thinking and acting like an artist

Contact with professional artists can help to reverse this decline, but this contact also brings other positives. Ofsted, in their advice for art and design subject specialists, asks teachers to focus on the benefits of "thinking and acting like an artist" (2012: 11). One of these benefits undoubtedly is a problem or enquiry-based approach, refining ideas and exploring answers to open-ended questions (known as Socratic questions, after Greek philosopher Socrates). These might include: what does this mean to you? why do we think in this particular way? how could we do this differently? why do we say that? what would this be like if . . . ? Arts practitioners are comfortable with ambiguity and uncertainty, happy to explore contradictions, opposing sides of an argument, multiple readings of a work and a multiplicity of meanings. These approaches have been described as 'habits of mind' by Guy Claxton and Bill Lucas from the Centre for Real World Learning at the University of Winchester. They believe these essential skills, what they term 'functional literacies', can be developed in a formal way through creative vocational education and will equip learners to better navigate the world of employment and challenges of an uncertain future (Claxton and Lucas, 2012).

Serious play

Using the arts also allows for collaborative partnerships and freedom from constraints. Theatres, museums, art galleries and other venues can and do operate innovative education programmes without the demands of a curriculum or an inspection regime (e.g. Ofsted). The education teams working in these contexts understand the importance of risk and experimentation, curiosity, serious play, trial and error, making mistakes and learning from them. In effect, developing a society of responsible risk takers. Importantly, arts venues like these are safe spaces in the real world where individuals can 'have a go', perhaps fail, but importantly learn from the experience and have a sense of personal progression that is not dependent on standardised assessment tests or exam results. Using the arts in this way has parallels with mentoring and coaching, where arts-based learning can deepen understanding and explore creative alternatives to logical and rational approaches to decision-making (Hughes, 2009). By creating a psychological space, the art activity allows the participant to stand back from their situation. With support from the artist or facilitator, the participant is then able to reflect on their situation and experiences. These creative activities are very effective in facilitating reflective practice, for instance, using clay to create three-dimensional sculptures as metaphors for organisational or personal change (Hughes, 2009).

Jean Lave and Etienne Wenger's theory of 'situated learning' is relevant here (1991). That is, the idea that learning is often unintentional and situated within authentic activity, context and culture rather than abstract ideas in the classroom. Lave and Wenger developed this further with the idea of 'legitimate peripheral participation' where social interaction and collaboration are essential components, just as they are within the arts. Learners (or arts practitioners) become involved in a 'community of practice' embodying certain beliefs and behaviours, and through regular interaction, slowly move from the periphery of the community to its centre, gradually assuming the role of an expert in their particular field (Lave and Wenger, 1991).

Many of these ideas have their origins in Vygotsky's theories about learning and creativity as a social process, closely related to an individual's social development (Vygotsky, 1978). For Wenger, the social construction of knowledge is dependent on the active participation of the individual in a community, and the construction of his or her identity is also enabled through these communities (Wenger, 1998). Rather than work in isolation in an artist's studio, for instance, creative adults often benefit from meeting or associating themselves with other like-minded individuals, often through a club, society, group exhibition, artists' co-operative or evening class, and surely children and young people are no different.

Pause for thought

Reflecting on ideas about learning and creativity, consider:

- How can educators create the right conditions to enable creativity and 'flow'? What conditions enable you to be creative?
- How might learners react to an approach of risk-taking and experimentation in the classroom?
- Do you find the idea of an 'open question approach' threatening or exciting?
- What could the benefits be of inviting artists, musicians or theatre practitioners into your setting?
- How can educators encourage a 'community of practice' where they are?

Making meaning

In this section, we will look at approaches that are commonplace within the arts but which could offer new opportunities within learning environments, especially for cultivating the ethical dimension of education – the core values and principles that underpin any inclusive approach. Much of the work of visual artists is about interpretation, dialogue and discussion, "encouraging flexibility, empathy, critical evaluation and creativity, especially the exploration of non-obvious solutions to real, difficult problems" (Claxton and Lucas, 2010: 169). These are not new ideas, however. In the 1960s the business guru and academic Edward de Bono introduced the idea of creative, lateral thinking: "in any self-organising system there is an absolute mathematical necessity for creativity" (de Bono in NACCCE, 1999: 55). Artists, in whatever art form or media they employ, are encouraging the viewer or participant to engage in the 'making of meaning', to make connections with one's own lived experience and create personal understanding.

However, our current systems of education are not set up to encourage this. Researchers have observed that children's capacity for creative or divergent thinking reduces over time as they move through formal education and are increasingly 'taught for the test' (Robinson, 2010). In an effort to combat this decline, proponents of the 'Learning Sciences' are combining the latest neuroscience research with educational philosophy. Guy Claxton's 'Building Learning Power' programme (Claxton, 2002) offers practical ways in which dispositions of resilience, imagination (visualisation) and concentration can be stretched and strengthened. With his colleague Bill Lucas, he has developed new ideas about our individual ability; that ability is not fixed, but that intelligence is 'expandable' (Claxton and Lucas, 2010). This has echoes in the work of American psychologist Carol Dweck and her belief that children can only really fulfil their potential by being encouraged to have a 'growth mindset' rather than a 'fixed mindset'. In this way, children realise that what matters is not their supposed level of intelligence, but the process they use and how they apply themselves to a particular problem. Dweck's assertion is that effort activates ability (Dweck, 2007), and I believe artistic ability itself is not necessarily 'a gift' but rather a set of skills that have to be activated by hard work and sheer determination. The importance of process rather than outcome cannot be emphasised enough in terms of using the arts in educational contexts. Letting children experiment, with say paint or clay, in an open-ended way rather than working towards a prescribed outcome is the best way forward to develop their visual literacy, tactile skills and self-confidence.

If we accept the idea that intelligence is not fixed, but can take multiple forms or is even expandable, then creative or practical intelligence can be developed through using the arts. There are a wealth of opportunities for experiential learning (Kolb, 2015) or learning through immersive 'hands-on' experience and participation, whether via music, theatre productions, visual art, craft workshops or dance performances. Some early years settings, most notably the pre-schools of Reggio Emilia in Northern Italy, have turned this experimental 'free flow' approach into a pedagogy that uses the model of artist's studios ('ateliers') staffed by artist-teachers ('atelieristas'). The 'Reggio Approach', as it has become known, is particularly notable for its cross-curricular innovation that combines art, science, physics, digital learning tools and environmental concerns in a playful and creative way (Cagliari et al., 2016).

Also important is the development of tacit knowledge, that is, learning a particular skill through touch and repetition until it becomes almost unconscious or instinctive. A good example of this is the young musician endlessly practicing scales on the piano in an attempt to achieve 'mastery' of their instrument and their musical skills. It is generally accepted that it takes 10,000 hours to achieve this level of 'mastery' in any skill, whether that be throwing a clay pot, playing the flute, cooking a meal, dancing capoeira or programming 'open source' computer software (Sennett, 2008) (note: 10,000 hours is equivalent to three hours a day for approximately ten years).

The idea of practical intelligence links to theories of embodiment and the emerging discipline of embodied cognition (Claxton and Lucas, 2010). Art forms such as dance, drama and music are excellent examples of how learners use and understand their bodies in an intelligent way, not separate from their intellectual abilities, but in a way that means their learning and creativity is literally 'embodied' in their performance (Addison et al., 2010). On a day to day level, using the arts can develop a different set of physical skills and expertise, understanding bodily feelings and emotions, cultivating imagination and children's sense of the possible (Bruner, 1966). Early experiences of music, dance, drama and the crafts can help to unlock children's potential, develop empathy and stimulate curiosity through sensory exploration in a way that passive learning and traditional didactic methods often do not.

Using the arts in criminal justice

In this section, I want to focus on a specific group that is excluded from mainstream society but can still benefit from an approach to education that uses the arts – those serving custodial sentences in prisons, young offender institutes and other secure units.

The current prison population in the UK stands at 85,457, of which just under 4,000 (a mere 4.5%) are female. A large number (45%) are serving short to medium term sentences but, shockingly, 50% of inmates lack basic skills in literacy and numeracy. As a result, many do not have the capacity they need to find employment after release and re-offending rates remain high. Prison staff refer to this phenomenon as the 'revolving door', where no sooner has an ex-offender been released than they are back in custody serving another short-term sentence. This is often due to an inability to find employment, re-integrate with society or change self-destructive patterns of behaviour. In an attempt to address recidivism or re-offending rates, some of the more enlightened Prison Governors in England have used the skills of local arts educators and voluntary organisations, or even offered inmates the opportunity to take part in national schemes and competitions as part of their rehabilitation.

Case study

Gary is serving a six-month prison sentence and has signed up for the weekly education classes, rather than attend the gym or work in the laundry, which doesn't appeal to him and won't necessarily help with his anger management issues. During his first session, the tutor asks for volunteers who might be interested in acting in a play with the visitors from a local theatre company, to be performed in front of the other inmates and Prison Officers at the end of the week. The people from the community theatre do a brilliant short piece using masks as an ice-breaker to get everyone talking and discussing the issues the inmates might want to communicate to their audience . . . time is short, the pressure is on, but Gary is looking forward to the rehearsals and the welcome distraction away from time in his cell.

Geese Theatre Company, based in the Midlands in England, is a team of arts practitioners who present interactive theatre and facilitate drama-based group work, staff training and consultation for the probation service, prisons, young offender institutions, youth offending teams, secure hospitals and related agencies throughout the UK and abroad. Commissioned by, amongst others, the UK Government's Ministry of Justice, Geese Theatre uses drama performances to explore key issues, problems and challenges in prisons.

One example, as highlighted in the case study of Gary above, is a series of plays and workshops that have been developed with violent offenders, using masks to adopt characters (that include their victims) and allowing inmates to act out violence, examine its consequences and the cognitive processes behind it. "A performance can mirror behaviours – audiences are invited to observe behaviours and situations that may be familiar and have an opportunity to witness the impact of particular behaviours on other people" (Geese Theatre, 2016: available at www.geese.co.uk). Drama productions like this offer the opportunity to explore raw emotions in prison and provide a means of mastering issues such as violence and preventing it from turning outwards, or inwards. This applies equally to mainstream education contexts, where the arts "allow young people to explore emotions and fears in a safe, controlled situation. They are able to look at difficult and painful situations by externalising them and putting them into the third person" (NACCCE, 1999: 61). As well as the therapeutic effects on individuals, the arts in prison also build self-confidence and self-esteem in a context where "routine prison education classes often do the opposite, confronting prisoners with their disabilities" (Carey in Koestler Trust, 2012: 42). Sessions like this, led by trained arts educators, are accessible and often provide the first positive experience of education for many learners (see also Chapter 13 on Restorative Justice). The self-confidence inmates gain can improve performance in numeracy and literacy and goes some way to proving the importance of building trust and positive one-to-one attention. This can be a transformative experience.

Case study

Paul has recently been released from prison after serving a short-term sentence. He is preparing a portfolio of his artwork and photography ready for an interview at a local FE College and hopes to secure a place on the one-year Art Foundation Course. Whilst inside, he entered his drawings in the annual Koestler Awards and won a prize. The art tutor from the prison's education department has put his name forward for a mentoring scheme where Paul receives a year's worth of one-to-one advice and coaching from a professional artist already working in the creative sector. The meetings have been going well and Paul feels positive about his chances of securing a place at college.

Many offenders have benefitted from the chance to share the work they produce with a wider audience whilst incarcerated. The Koestler Awards Scheme is an annual exhibition of artwork and writing from prisons, secure hospitals, young offender institutes and people on probation. Established in 1962, Arthur Koestler's original intention was to make the prisoner's life more bearable, to help the process of rehabilitation, and perhaps to discover hidden talents. His own experience of political imprisonment during the Spanish Civil War (1936–39) informed his view that "the prisoner's worst enemy is boredom, depression, the slow death of thought" (Koestler Trust, 2012: 6). Entries to the Koestler Awards number more than 8,000 each year and feature a wide range of media including painting, drawing, sculpture, pottery, music composition, creative writing and drama. Award-winning pieces are displayed at London's Southbank Centre, whilst regional exhibitions in community galleries have been curated by young people from Intensive Supervision and Surveillance teams within the Youth Offending Service, with training and guidance from professional art curators.

Possibly the greatest challenge for this hugely successful scheme is how to continue the engagement with the arts beyond prison. Not only do ex-offenders struggle to find materials, but there is again the issue of accessibility:

> the arts feel accessible in prison because of personal contact with writers and artists. But on release ex-offenders find the art world 'elitist', and its 'posh buildings' intimidating . . . while prisoners engage actively in the arts on the inside, this is rarely continued beyond prison.
>
> (Carey in Koestler Trust, 2012: 45)

To address this problem, a pilot mentoring scheme was established in 2007, now funded by the Paul Hamlyn Foundation. Trained professional artists, writers and musicians are matched with offenders for one year after release. These mentors provide invaluable advice and guidance on career progression and opportunities for further study, addressing the sense of loss and abandonment that offenders often experience on release.

Pause for thought

Reflecting on the case studies of Gary and Paul, and the wider discussion about the arts in prison settings, consider:

- How can the arts offer a legitimate route back into society for excluded individuals?
- How can participation in arts activities be used to explore different viewpoints and to develop empathy?
- What scenarios can be used to stimulate conversation and discussion about past experiences in a group situation?
- How can creative writing and drama change self-perceptions and alter habitual ways of living and looking at things?
- How can the arts help to challenge preconceptions about certain groups in society?
- How can we stimulate enthusiasm in disaffected learners or those who have been failed by mainstream education?
- What local opportunities are there for excluded learners to share their work with a wider audience? How could public spaces be used more imaginatively (e.g. office reception areas, empty shop units, community centres, station concourses etc.)?
- What mentoring opportunities can you offer? How can you encourage links between learners and practicing professionals?

Moving forward

In order to work towards inclusive practice using the arts we need to consider:

- a 'safe space': participatory arts can offer a non-threatening environment to explore issues and cultivate imagination;

- agency: the arts can help excluded individuals develop autonomy, self-expression and their own voice;
- freedom from constraints: arts organisations as collaborative partners are free to experiment and take risks without the demands of a curriculum or an inspection regime;
- dialogue and discussion: the arts and artists are good at questioning things and opening up debate; 'what if . . . ?', 'why does this happen?', 'how might things be different?', 'what do we mean by . . . ?';
- interpretation: arts experiences and artworks can encourage the development of personal opinions, empathy and appreciation of other points of view;
- being comfortable with ambiguity and debate: there is no wrong answer!;
- experiential learning and making meaning: the arts help excluded learners with the co-construction of meaning based on their own lived experience;
- unexpected outcomes: using the arts can have wider significance to excluded learners beyond educational progression and development, including social skills, cultural identity, economic status, health and well-being.

Conclusion

This chapter has explored using the arts to encourage inclusion and empower individuals in a broad range of informal learning contexts. These individuals may be marginalised or excluded from mainstream education for a number of complex and often interlinked reasons. It is the job of educationalists and creative professionals to enable a more democratic participation in the arts and the development of cultural capital amongst people and communities that may have been labelled 'hard to reach'.

The benefits of such participation and experiences are wide ranging but often difficult to quantify or measure. These wider benefits may include development of a practical intelligence, embodied cognition and a sense of our place in the world.

Particular skills and 'habits of mind' can be developed through 'thinking and acting like an artist', and contact with professional arts practitioners can encourage a more questioning approach and the making of meaning. The importance of developing both visual literacy and a tactile literacy has been explored, as well as the dispositions of empathy, resilience, imagination and concentration or 'flow'.

We have explored how the arts can help to reintegrate excluded learners and provide alternative routes back into mainstream education, but could arts-based interventions be preventative? As professionals, we must believe in the possibility of rehabilitation and improving life chances through education. There is no fixed path.

Consider the short vignette that opened this chapter. Experiences like Andy's, of working with a professional artist, could be a powerful vehicle for offering children and young people a sense of agency and a voice. Perhaps by using the arts and visual communication tools such as photo essays, digital photography, film and video, "young people can become agents in the transformation of society through a pedagogy of hope" (Giroux in Addison et al., 2010).

Useful resources

Arts Council England: *www.artscouncil.org.uk/why-culture-matters*
Cultural Learning Alliance: *www.culturallearningalliance.org.uk*
Early Arts: *www.earlyarts.co.uk*
Geese Theatre: *www.geese.co.uk*
Koestler Trust: Arts by Offenders: *www.koestlertrust.org.uk*

Further reading

Cultural Learning Alliance (2017), *ImagineNation: The value of cultural learning*. London: CLA.
Dewey, J. (1938), *Experience and Education*. New York: Macmillan.
Eisner, E. (1998), *The Enlightened Eye: Qualitative Enquiry and the Enhancement of Educational Practice*. Upper Saddle River, NJ: Merrill.
Leavy, P. (2015), *Method Meets Art: Arts-Based Research Practice*. New York: Guilford Press.
Louise, D. (2015), *The Interpretation Matters Handbook: Artspeak Revisited*. London: Black Dog Publishing.
Pringle, E. (2006), *Learning in the Gallery: Context, Process, Outcomes*. Sine loco: Engage/Arts Council England.
Tims, C. (ed.) (2010), *Born Creative*. London: DEMOS.

References

Addison, N., Burgess, L., Steers, J. and Trowell, J. (2010) *Understanding Art Education: Engaging Reflexively with Practice*. Oxford: Routledge.
Arts Council England (2013) *Great Art and Culture for Everyone*. London: Arts Council England.
Bourdieu, P. (1984) *Distinction: A Social Critique of the Judgement of Taste*. Cambridge, MA: Harvard University Press.
Bruner, J. (1966) *Toward a Theory of Instruction*. Cambridge, MA: Harvard University Press.
Cagliari, P., Castagnetti, M., Giudici, C., Rinaldi, C., Vecchi, V. and Moss, P. (eds.) (2016) *Loris Malaguzzi and the Schools of Reggio Emilia*. London: Routledge.
Claxton, G. (2002) *Building Learning Power*. Bristol: TLO.
Claxton, G. and Lucas, B. (2010) *New Kinds of Smart: How the Science of Learnable Intelligence Is Changing Education*. Maidenhead: Open University Press.
Claxton, G. and Lucas, B. (2012) *How to Teach Vocational Education: A Theory of Vocational Pedagogy*. London: Centre for Skills Development, City & Guilds.
Csikszentmihalyi, M. (1996) *Creativity: Flow and the Psychology of Discovery and Invention*. New York: Harper Collins.
Cultural Learning Alliance (2011) *ImagineNation: The Case for Cultural Learning*. London: Cultural Learning Alliance.
Dweck, C. (2007) *Mindset: The New Psychology of Success*. New York: Ballantine Books.
Holden, J. (2006) *Cultural Value and the Crisis of Legitimacy*. London: DEMOS.
Hughes, S. (2009) 'Leadership, management and sculpture: How arts based activities can transform learning and deepen understanding', *Reflective Practice*, Vol. 10, No. 1, February 2009, 77–90.
Koestler Trust (2012) *Doing Time with the Arts: The Koestler Trust at 50*. London: Koestler Trust.
Kolb, D. (2015) *Experiential Learning: Experience as the Source of Learning and Development* (2nd ed.). Upper Saddle River, NJ: Pearson Education.
Lave, J. and Wenger, E. (1991) *Situated Learning: Legitimate Peripheral Participation*. Cambridge: Cambridge University Press.
Lyotard, J.-F. (1984) *The Postmodern Condition: A Report on Knowledge*. Manchester: Manchester University Press.
Matarasso, F. (1997) *Use or Ornament? The Social Impact of Participation in the Arts*. Stroud: Comedia.
National Advisory Committee on Creative and Cultural Education (NACCCE Report) (1999) *All Our Futures: Creativity, Culture & Education*. London: DCMS & DfEE.
Ofsted (2012) *Making a Mark: Art, Craft and Design Education*. London: Ofsted.
Robinson, K. (2010) *Changing Education Paradigms*. London: RSA. Available at: www.ted.com/talks/ken_robinson_changing_education_paradigms Accessed 27/9/16.

Sennett, R. (2008) *The Craftsman*. London: Penguin.

Vygotsky, L. S. (1978) *Mind in Society: The Development of Higher Psychological Processes*. Cambridge, MA: Harvard University Press.

Warwick Commission (2015) *Enriching Britain: Culture, Creativity and Growth: The 2015 Report by the Warwick Commission on the Future of Cultural Value*. Warwick: University of Warwick.

Wenger, E. (1998) *Communities of Practice: Learning, Meaning and Identity*. Cambridge: Cambridge University Press.

Websites

Arts Professional: www.artsprofessional.co.uk/news/gcse-results-confirm-drop-take-arts-subjects. Accessed 9/11/16.

Geese Theatre: www.geese.co.uk. Accessed 12/7/16.

13 Restorative justice

Gwenda Scriven

> The future is not a result of choices among alternative paths offered by the present, but a place that is
> created – created first in the mind and will, created next in activity. The future is not some place we are
> going, but one we are creating. The paths are not to be found, but made. The activity of making them
> changes both the maker and their destination.
>
> John H. Schaar (Goodreads.com: undated)

Introduction

The need to re-think the way in which wrongdoing is dealt with has been identified by Zehr (1990, 2002, 2014), a pioneer of restorative justice who has highlighted the need for a paradigm shift away from the belief in a punitive approach to justice towards a restorative approach. Zehr suggests that the adoption of a punitive approach by most modern societies has created a lens through which the world is viewed; this lens has shaped the thinking and understanding of reality and, subsequently, determined the way in which offending behaviour is dealt with. Other advocates of restorative justice (Braithwaite, 1989; Graef, 2002; Marshall, 1999; Umbreit, Coates, and Vos, 2007; Wachtel, 2003; Zehr, 1990, 2002, 2014) also agree that modern societies need to move away from a retributive paradigm of justice predicated upon vindictiveness and revenge and move towards a restorative paradigm which focuses on repairing harm and restoring community. A key theme echoing through all these views is the identification of the fatally flawed belief that a society can deal with wrongdoing by meting out punishment and expecting this to be a means through which to deter future wrongdoing; such a view is, according to McCold (1996), an age-old myth that is rarely challenged. The aim of this chapter is to review existing material relating to youth justice and restorative practices. It provides an overview of historical and current material relating to youth crime and wrongdoing.

The general acceptance that punishment bestowed by those with the power to administer it is the most efficacious means of challenging and changing behaviour is pervasive; it has traditionally underpinned many spheres of British society, including the judicial system, schools, children's residential settings and parent-child relationships. Rosenberg (2003), in his examination of the costs and consequences of adopting a punitive approach, points out that punishment can in some cases be effective, but the overall effect is a negative rather than a positive one. He illustrates this through an historical example he witnessed of a teacher who scolded and slapped a pupil for hitting a smaller boy. Within this example, Rosenberg identifies several layers of learning; the offending pupil learns that it is possible to justify the use of violence (the slap); he learns that it is unwise to hit another pupil when he may be caught, so he will become a more covert offender; he learns that one can achieve one's aims through the use of force (punishment from the teacher).

Crime and punishment

Punitive sanctions are deemed necessary, argues Rosenberg (2003), because as humans we tend to accept 'Creep Theory', which incorporates the generally held view that people are basically selfish and violent and therefore, to control these tendencies, we need to punish those who deviate from the accepted norms. Although Rosenberg's work focuses primarily on non-violent communication (NVC) there is a strong relationship between the use of language and restorative justice (Rosenberg, 2003); a clear parallel between restorative justice and NVC can be identified in the questions addressed within these approaches. Advocates of restorative justice and NVC would tend to accept that in some circumstances punishment might change behaviour, but they also recognise the need to focus on addressing underlying needs in order to positively change and sustain desired behaviours. Rosenberg (2003) identifies the question addressed within the punitive approach as 'What do we want the other person to do differently?'; if this question is asked and underpinned with punishment the wrongdoer may behave differently but, as identified in the teacher example above, the *desired* outcome may not be achieved. Changing the question to 'What do we want the other person's reasons to be for doing what we want them to?' will still mean that punishment will not work, but requirement to punish is removed in a restorative approach in which the predominant aim is to repair harm, change subsequent behaviour and restore community.

Restorative approaches are not affiliated to any specific system of spiritual belief, but the basic principles of restoration and healing underlie a number of world faiths and, as a practicing Christian, I identified with the parallel Zehr (1990) draws between biblical teaching and restorative justice. Shalom, God's will for peace for humankind, is, argues Zehr, rooted in biblical justice and relates to meeting the needs of others rather than seeking revenge. Although not without its flaws, a significant example of the way in which restorative justice can bring peace and restore community is that of the South African Truth and Reconciliation Commission (TRC), chaired by the Reverend Desmond Tutu. The TRC, rather than seeking to punish those responsible for the wrongs and atrocities inflicted during the apartheid era, effectively adopted a restorative approach to repair the harm done (Roche, 2006). What the TRC experience tells us is that even in situations where significant harm has been inflicted and communities shattered by injustice, the adoption of a restorative approach can help heal and rebuild broken relationships. Since the time of the TRC similar approaches have been taken in the establishment of truth commissions in other parts of the world, perhaps a testament to restorative justice and confidence in the belief that healing and restoration can triumph over the need for retribution.

Graef (2002) argues that the major concern of the justice system in Britain lies in the processing and punishment of offenders. In his view little, if any, consideration is given to the improvement of the offender or the needs of those affected by the crime. Newburn (2002) echoes this focus on the punitive aspects of the justice system but, at the same time, acknowledges that to some extent there has been a degree of recognition of the wellbeing of young offenders. In his view, the justice system has been simultaneously characterised by an 'uneasy balance . . . between welfarism [policies and practices associated with a welfare state] on the one hand and a punitive tendency on the other' (2002: 559). In his tracing of this 'uneasy balance' through the emergence of youth justice (enshrined in the

Youthful Offenders Act 1854), the development of reformatories, the creation of juvenile courts and the recognition that juvenile cases needed to be separated from adult crime (the 1908 Children Act), he highlights the way in which the incarceration of young people has been, and still is, an important element of Britain's approach to youth crime (and crime in general). Punishment in the form of detention certainly does represent the ongoing punitive approach to crime but, as highlighted by Newburn, there are clear elements of welfarism within much of the past and present legislation.

Historical perspectives

The nineteenth century witnessed both the identification of youth offending as a specific problem and the subsequent development of a justice system that reflected the growing distinction between youth and adult offending. The identification of young people as distinctly different is highlighted by Shore (2002), who argues that the whole notion of juvenile delinquency was invented in the nineteenth century, a time during which increasing numbers of children were appearing in courts, with punishment for young offenders being left to the discretion of the judge, resulting in the outcome of custody frequently being the preferred option. This incarceration of the young is a clear reflection of the way in which accountability and punishment have been regarded as necessary aspects of the justice system; there is clear evidence of Newburn's (2002) 'uneasy balance' in the political debates of the 1820s and 1830s regarding the extent to which the justice system should be punitive or reformative (Shore, 2002).

Both punitive and reformative elements were present in the subsequent legislation of the nineteenth and twentieth centuries. The custody of young people has remained, but there has been intrinsic acknowledgement within government thinking that young people who offend should not be dealt with in the same way as adult criminals. This was present, for example, in the 1854 Youthful Offenders Act, which led to provision of reformatories for young people (Pitts, 2003). The needs of the young were further established in the Gladstone Report of 1894, which identified the need not simply to punish offenders but to reform and rehabilitate them (Newburn, 1995). The subsequent 1898 Prison Act (Howard League for Penal Reform, undated) separated young offenders from adult prisoners; a separation which might suggest an understanding of the need to take into account factors such as age, understanding and welfare. Newburn, however, tempers these apparently humanitarian aspects of Acts such as this in his citation of Humphries (1981), who suggests that the real underlying reason for such developments lay not with the needs of the young but rather in the desire to quell rebellious youth. A similar point is made by Pitts, who identifies within such legislation an apparent emphasis on the deeds rather than the needs of young offenders.

Whilst recognising the role of the justice system in dealing with the deeds of young offenders, Muncie, Hughes and McLauglin (2002) suggest that the vulnerability of the young and the need to provide for their welfare was acknowledged through nineteenth-century legislative developments. A forceful argument given that the mid-nineteenth century marked a turning point for juvenile justice as the separation of provision for adult and child offenders was established. However, such developments were not solely based upon the welfare of the young and, as identified by Muncie et al., the separation of adult and child offenders today still runs in parallel with the notion that offenders should be held accountable for their wrongdoing.

Legislative developments in the first part of the twentieth century, according to Pitts (2003), witnessed a change of emphasis from the deeds to the needs of offenders and witnessed, according to Newburn (1995), milestone legislation such as the Children Act 1908, which led to establishment of juvenile courts. The later Children and Young Persons Act 1933 (Ministry of Justice, 1933) which, in Part IV, set in place separate detention facilities for young people and, in Part III, ensured that there would be no capital punishment for those under the age of eighteen, further established the need for special consideration of the welfare needs of young people. Newburn argues that the 1933 Act, together with the Criminal Justice Act 1948, incorporated the welfare aspects and the setting up of social services for children expressed in Children Act 1948, all of which include an acknowledgement of the welfare needs of the young.

By the late 1960s Newburn's (2002a) 'uneasy balance' between welfare and punitive sanctions is again highlighted in the opposition to the implementation of the 1969 Children and Young Persons Act relating to juvenile justice. The Act, which if fully implemented would have resulted in a radical move away from punitive sanctions and the adoption of 'a more explicitly "welfare" oriented jurisdiction' (Bottoms, 2002: 217), was regarded as too permissive and welfare minded with too strong an emphasis on the role of the social worker. Leading up to the Act there was opposition by the Conservative Party, supported by the Magistrates Association and some lawyers and probation officers, to Labour Party proposals relating to the establishment of an essentially 'decriminalising' (Bottoms, 2002: 216) juvenile justice system. The force of opposition to the Labour proposals eventually led to the concession of the retention of juvenile courts. The Act itself was never fully implemented and there has been no large scale replacement of punitive sanctions.

The gradual move away from welfarist principles within the Youth Justice system continued in the 1970s and led to a stronger emphasis on 'correction through discipline and punishment' (Gelsthorpe and Morris, 2002: 239). Rising crime rates in the 1980s resulted in a reassertion of discipline and authority amid prevailing notions of the seriousness of crime and the threat this posed (Gelsthorpe and Morris). The government response to these developments was the introduction of large scale prison building and, according to Newburn (1995), the introduction of the Criminal Justice Act 1982, which represented a significant attack upon welfarist principles; an attack that was particularly evident in the move from social worker decision-making to that of judicial decision-making; a move that had been actively pursued by youth justice professionals, civil servants and criminologists (Pitts, 2003). Newburn regards these developments as a significant turning point because they signal the replacement of the notion of the child in need to that of the juvenile delinquent. A view echoed by Angus (2008), who describes the range of reforms taking place as 'a dichotomous policy approach to children's issues' (2008: 52) because at the same time as prioritising the care and protection of children, children who offend are 'dealt with robustly' (2008: 52).

Pause for thought

Reflecting on the historical developments outlined above, consider:

- the general purpose of the justice system, including notions of punishment and rehabilitation;
- your own view of the role of this justice system, and what purpose(s) it serves; and
- whether you feel that young people should be treated any differently to adults. Do you feel that age should be a factor when sentencing those who are found guilty of committing a crime?

Matthews (2003) identifies an increasing punitiveness among politicians and the general public in the 1980s and 1990s, a period that witnessed both an increasing concern about the apparent growth in youth crime and delinquency and a growing acknowledgement that alternatives to prison were required in order to slow the inexorable rise in the prison population (Downes, 1998; Matthews, 2003). These high-profile issues provided ammunition for the political 'battle' that was being waged over which party was most able to effectively deal with crime (Downes, 1998; Gelsthorpe and Morris, 2002; Goldson, 2002; Newburn, 2002; Pitts, 2003). Slogans such as 'tough on crime' and 'tough on the causes of crime' became key features of political speeches as political parties sought to establish themselves as the party which could effectively deal with crime and criminal behaviour.

This was a time, according to Pitts (2003), in which there was a replacement of both the principles of welfare and those of justice with 'a third model of youth justice' (2003: 82), which he describes as 'corporatism'. A development, institutionalised in the Criminal Justice Act 1991, that is based upon the management of offenders rather than their rehabilitation or their punishment. Key changes in terms of youth offending within the 1991 Act were that juvenile courts became youth courts with jurisdiction extended to 17-year-olds. The restriction in custodial sentencing enshrined the acknowledgement that most young people grow out of crime and that within custodial sentencing there are inherent dangers for young people that can result in a subsequent criminal pathway (Newburn, 1995).

Within this 'new penology' identified by Pitts (2003: 83), the aim was not to reduce crime or reintegrate offenders but simply to ensure, as far as possible, that the dangers they may pose to wider society are reduced through the management of offenders. Embedded within these changes is also a shift in emphasis as the victim, rather than the offender, became the central focus of attention (Angus, 2008). In terms of restorative practices, this shift of emphasis holds apparent promise but, as will be discussed later in this chapter, victim focus without victim involvement might not be as beneficial as it might initially appear.

Restorative practices

Although restorative practices were already present within some educational and youth justice settings in the 1990s, since the 'No More Excuses' document (Home Office, 1997), which introduced concepts of responsibility, restoration and reintegration (Gelsthorpe and Morris, 2002) and the recommendations set out in the Youth Justice and Criminal Evidence Act 1999, regarded by Crawford and Newburn (2003) as a radical overhaul of the Youth Justice System (2003: 1), restorative practices have been gradually introduced into a wider range of settings. This move away from exclusionary punitive justice towards a more inclusive restorative approach represents a significant value shift by recognising both the social context of wrongdoing and, importantly, the participation of all those affected by the wrongdoing (Crawford and Newburn, 2003).

Inclusive approaches to the resolution of wrongdoing, although frequently regarded as a new approach, have their roots in much older justice systems and are only 'new' in the sense that they represent a new way of dealing with what is considered to be wrongdoing in many industrialised Western societies. Graef (2002), who describes restorative justice as the 'bedrock of tribal justice for several millennia' (2002: 9), argues that in Britain restorative justice dates back to Saxon times and may be found in some of the earliest written laws. This system of justice was not superseded until the Norman Conquest, when wrongdoing became a crime against the monarch and state rather than a local community issue. This is still the case today as legal proceedings incorporate references to Regina vs. the accused. Much of the contemporary restorative practice as we know it has emerged from pre-modern forms of justice found in traditional approaches within, for example, First Nation communities in Canada, Maori communities in New Zealand and Australian aboriginal communities (Braithwaite, 1989; Gelsthorpe and Morris, 2002; Wearmouth, McKinney, and Glynn, 2007; Weitekamp, 1999; Zehr, 2002, 2014). These traditional forms of community justice focus on the wellbeing of the community rather than simply the punishment of the wrongdoer and incorporate practices which place great value upon the maintenance of the community and putting right the harm that has been done. In traditional Maori culture, for example, much value is placed upon harmony and restoration of the community, values that can be upheld by collective responsibility for the resolution of wrongdoing and the reintegration of the wrongdoer into the community (Wearmouth, McKinney, and Glynn 2007). The importance of community is also highlighted by Morrison and Ahmed (2006), who argue that in communities where a higher level of importance is placed upon the violation of relationships than the violation of rules, 'restorative justice seeks to harness the power of relationships to strengthen accountability and support mechanisms within civil society' (2006: 210). Traditional values of community and restoration are at the heart of current restorative practice and, when effectively established, represent a radical alternative to the punitive sanctions frequently used to address wrongdoing.

Case study

In a project undertaken in schools in the East of England (2015–2018), GR8 AS U R, a not-for-profit organisation with charitable aims, has been piloting resources to help to stop bullying before it starts.

Using a structured approach, easily memorable for children aged 4–7 years, the children have been learning about self-esteem and self-worth as well as strategies to gain support when they encounter a difficult situation. Central to this approach is the 'heal not hurt' approach, which is founded in restorative practices.

The project outlines why this restorative practice is particularly appropriate for and effective in schools (GR8 AS U R, 2015: 2):

- Because hurting others doesn't help resolve issues; it usually makes things worse.
- Hurting others causes anger, which is often followed by the desire for revenge, which in turn can lead to more aggression, violence and negative behaviour – and so the cycle continues and worsens.
- Healing others, treating them fairly and with respect, on the other hand, brings people closer together without leaving one party feeling hard done by, angry and in need of revenge.
- Healing is the best way to communicate, build relationships and resolve issues, for everyone.

It achieves this through STAR Steps (GR8 AS U R, 2015: 6–7):

- *S*tand up – developing personal power and advocacy;
- *T*alk to someone – sharing power with others;
- *A*lways help – enabling the power of action, and;
- *R*emember everyone – bringing the power of inclusion.

It provides a structure for the person who has been hurt, enabling them to address the situation and to consider its impact:

- What did you think when you realised what had happened?
- How has this affected you and others?
- What has been the hardest thing for you?
- What do you think needs to happen to make things right?

(GR8 AS U R, 2015: 15)

In addition, it scaffolds the experience of the person that has hurt someone (GR8 AS U R, 2015: 16):

- What happened?
- What were you thinking at the time?
- Who was affected by what you did?
- In what way were they affected?
- What do you think needs to happen to make things right?

Project evaluator Dr Richard Woolley from the University of Worcester highlights that:

the approach avoids asking why something happened, as very often individuals do not know the answer to this question. Rather, they are enabled to focus on their feelings, and the impact of their behaviour, and to begin to repair the relationships though a restorative approach.

This project, aimed initially at 4–7 year olds in sixteen pilot schools, has already been extended to cover primary education (ages 4–11 years) due to the perceived effectiveness within the schools involved.

Although process is present in both the punitive approach and the restorative approach to wrongdoing, the difference lies in the way in which process occurs. Within the punitive approach, the assumption is that the imposition of an unpleasant sanction or punishment will result in behavioural change, but punishment for wrongdoing does not necessarily achieve the desired results. As Amstutz and Mullet (2005) suggest, punitive approaches may be effective for some people in the short term, but they do not teach a real understanding of the effect of negative behaviour nor do they foster the skills necessary for behavioural change. Punitive sanctions rely heavily on humiliation and discomfort, or to put it in more personalised terms, attempting to rectify harm by inflicting harm on the wrongdoer. Amstutz and Mullet capture this succinctly in their citation of Nelson, Lott and Glenn (undated) who pose the question 'where did we get the crazy idea that to make people do better we first have to make them feel worse?' (undated: 11). There is further support for this view from Cavanagh's (2005) school-based research, which also highlights the 'harm' that may arise from adopting a punitive (retributive) approach to wrongdoing; Cavanagh makes the point that zero-tolerance approaches to wrongdoing are disempowering because they do not provide a means through which conflicts can be resolved in a non-violent way. The result, he argues, is that the student response is to also become retributive. Where harm has been done, relationships on all sides are adversely affected (Hopkins, 2004), and it is important, therefore, to recognise that punitive approaches which deal with the wrongdoing in isolation are unlikely to repair the harm that has been done. The example of GR8 AS U R outlined above (and also included in Chapter 1) is an example of effective restorative practice being engendered with young learners, which shows that there are possibilities for this approach to be developed with a broad age range in schools and other settings.

Promoting participation and engagement

Restorative approaches, in which all those affected are able to participate, unlike punitive approaches, address these issues by offering opportunities for all those involved to feel heard and understood (Graef, 2002; Hopkins, 2004; Wearmouth, McKinney, and Glynn, 2007; Zehr, 2002, 2014).This distinction between approaches is concisely identified by Morrison and Ahmed (2006), who suggest that where traditional approaches value state accountability and punishment, restorative approaches value healing and restoration. Whilst broadly in agreement with this view, Amstutz and Mullet (2005) argue that accountability is a feature of both punitive and restorative approaches. Both approaches are concerned with appropriate consequences for behaviour, but within the restorative approach, the emphasis is upon repairing the harm done rather than simply punishing the wrongdoer.

Trail blazers in the field of restorative justice and restorative practice such as Amstutz and Mullet (2005); Braithwaite (1989); McCold (1999); Wachtel (2003); and Zehr (2002, 2014) have, since the late 1970s, challenged punitive models of justice and during this time many countries throughout the world have incorporated some elements of restorative practice within their justice systems but, by and large, it has been offered in the form of choices alongside existing systems of justice rather than as a predominant model of justice. The exception to this is New Zealand, which has incorporated restorative justice into its legal structure by making it the core of its juvenile justice system (Amstutz and Mullet, 2005; Gelsthorpe and Morris, 2002; Graef, 2002; Roche, 2006; Zehr, 2002, 2014). The developments in New Zealand are a testament to what can be achieved when restorative justice is incorporated into the youth justice system and consistently applied.

Implementing restorative justice

The implementation of restorative justice and practices in Britain has been on a much more piecemeal basis than in New Zealand. This may at least in part be due to the fact that restorative practices do not fall neatly into an easily defined set of activities, and although there is some similarity of principle and practice within the range restorative strategies, with many practices sharing ideas and principles, no underlying single theoretical base or agreed definition of what constitutes a restorative practice has emerged. Rather, there is a wide range of practices purporting to be restorative which have, according to Marshall (1999), been 'branded' as 'restorative justice'. Zehr (2002, 2014) recognises this diversity of programmes and practices and suggests that as more programmes identified as restorative justice emerge, 'the meaning of [restorative justice] is sometimes diluted or confused' (6). He goes on, however, to suggest that what authentic restorative practices have in common is a set of principles and a guiding philosophy.

As identified above, the foundation of the principles and guiding philosophy of restorative justice are rooted in community cohesion and restoration by placing greater importance upon repairing harm and restoring relationships than upon assigning blame and imposing punishment. All participants, including the harmed person who is given a 'central role' (Graef, 2002: 18), have the opportunity to talk about how they have been affected. Restorative practices work on a 'feelings' level in which all participants freely express how they feel and have the opportunity to listen to and acknowledge the feelings and views of others. Genuinely restorative practices provide wrongdoers with an opportunity to understand the consequences of their actions and behaviours and how this has affected others, as identified in the example from GR8 AS U R (2015). This is not a 'soft option' nor does it mean that the wrongdoer is 'let off'; indeed, research (Strang and Sherman, 2003; Braithwaite, 1989) suggests that in terms of the stress (related to shaming) experienced the wrongdoer frequently feels that restorative approaches are more challenging than conventional judicial processes.

The powerful nature of such challenging experiences which can generate 'empathy and remorse' (Strang and Sherman, 2003: 40) and lead to a reduction in re-offending, can be located within the theory of reintegrative shaming (Braithwaite, 1989) which plays a crucial part in the restorative process. The early restorative work undertaken in New Zealand by pioneers such as O'Connell (O'Connell, Wachtel, and Wachtel, 1999) provided a basis on which Braithwaite drew in the establishment of a theoretical framework in which shaming is associated with the actions (wrongdoing) of an individual rather than with the individual per se. Braithwaite highlights the way in which in many societies wrongdoers are stigmatised and excluded without being given an opportunity to repair the harm that has been done. Enshrined in Braithwaite's work is the notion that shame should be reintegrative rather than alienating; he argues that reintegrative shaming inhibits further wrongdoing because it separates the deed from the doer and, crucially, restores the individual to the community rather than ostracising them as happens within punitive justice systems.

A key element of restorative practice is the principle of 'fairness' (Strang and Sherman, 2003; Umbreit, Coates, and Vos, 2007). This is an important principle because participants, whether wrongdoers or those affected by wrongdoing, are more likely to comply with and feel satisfied with processes that are deemed to be fair. Chan Kim and Mauborgne (1997) argue that fairness builds trust and commitment which in turn produces voluntary co-operation enabling participants to reach a shared understanding and identify creative solutions. Chan Kim and Mauborgne are referring more specifically to the world of business here, but fairness is a concept that applies to any situation of human interaction and the key points they identify can be seen at the heart of restorative practices. As identified by the Restorative Practices Training Association (RPTA) (2006), fair process is about interacting with others and allowing them to tell their stories in a way where they are heard and treated with dignity and respect.

Both Chan Kim and Mauborgne (1997) and Umbreit, Coates, and Vos (2007) conclude that, win or lose, individuals who feel that the process has been fair are much more likely to be satisfied with the outcome. This view is supported by research into procedural fairness undertaken by Jackson and Fondacaro (1999), who found that fairness and being treated with dignity and respect are more likely to result in the decisions made by others being perceived as legitimate. This perceived legitimacy is a factor in subsequent reduction of undesirable behaviours. Fairness, dignity and respect all feature highly in restorative practices.

In supporting their claim that restorative justice is effective Sherman and Strang (2007) argue that low rates of success identified in some restorative justice schemes could be related not to restorative justice per se, but to hastily introduced programmes which are delivered without adequate planning or follow up. They conclude that measures of effectiveness which do not incorporate consideration of the extent to which good practice is present represent a real weakness in the research. A fundamental point, which echoes the calls for the adherence to authentic restorative practices (Amstutz and Mullet, 2005; Braithwaite, 1989; Wachtel and McCold, 2004; O'Connell, Wachtel, and Wachtel, 1999; Zehr, 2002, 2014), is being made here, namely that the imperative to deliver authenticity of practice necessarily entails the need for genuine commitment to restorative practices, appropriate training and effective, rather than token, delivery of restorative programmes. As has been already discussed, restorative justice can and does encompass a wide range of practices and the fact that it can be effectively applied to many situations is a wholly positive feature. The crucial factor, however, is that where this authenticity is not present, then what is being delivered should not be 'branded' as restorative justice.

Case study

Evaluation of projects aimed at young people and delivered by appropriately trained professionals have been generally very positive. Boulton and Mirsky (2006) recorded significant improvements in all aspects of behaviour in a special school for boys with emotional and behavioural difficulties following the whole school introduction of restorative practices, and Mirsky (2005), in her study of a residential home for looked-after children, found that the implementation of sanctions was reduced by 59% and offending levels by 33%.

What has become clear from studies of restorative practices applied to settings for young people is that restorative approaches to wrongdoing are most effective when practitioners focus on the creation of environments conducive to values of restorative practice within a whole setting context. (Hopkins, 2002, 2004). A positive institutional dynamic and the commitment from those in leadership is also vital in sustaining restorative programmes.

Given the community roots of restorative practices and the importance placed upon community involvement and links to community integrity and inclusion rather than exclusion discussed earlier in this review, these prerequisites are not surprising.

Example case studies are available through the *Relational Schools Project* (www. relationalschools.org), which focusses on the quality of human relations between teacher and student, in contrast to a traditional model of discipline and didactic delivery, and the *Forgiveness Project* (http://theforgivenessproject.com/), which presents real life stories to consider alternatives to resentment, retaliation and revenge.

Moving forward

In order to develop inclusive practice in the area of restorative justice, we need to consider:

* Putting the key decisions in the hands of those most affected by the wrongdoing.
* Promoting a victim-oriented approach in which s/he takes an active role in the restorative process.
* Ensuring that the concerns of the victim are central.
* Helping the wrongdoer take ownership and responsibility for their own actions.
* Developing a focus upon repairing the harm that has been done.
* Facilitating opportunities for dialogue.
* Making sure the proceedings and agreements are voluntary.
* Ensuring the whole process is rooted in respect for others.
* Supporting the reintegration of the wrongdoer into the community.
* Making sure that both the victim and the wrongdoer achieve closure.

(Adapted from: Amstutz and Mullet, 2005; Graef, 2002; Zehr, 2002, 2014)

Conclusion

Returning to the vignette included at the beginning of this chapter, it is important to note that restorative practices involve a journey. In contrast to a prison sentence or similar punishment, they are evolutionary in nature, and seek to bring healing and closure and transform behaviours to facilitate a more positive future. The process may not be clear-cut, and is not always simple, but the intention is to nurture rather than destroy (see also the discussion of the use of the arts in the rehabilitation of offenders in Chapter 12). The efficacy of a restorative approach is clearly articulated by Sherman and Strang (2007), who argue that a restorative approach to wrongdoing is, for both victims and wrongdoers 'a more humane and respectful way to respond' (2007: 24).

Not only does restorative justice provide a greater degree of procedural fairness for victims and wrongdoers, it is also effective in the reduction of re-offending (Sherman and Strang 2007; Shapland et al., 2007). A reduction in wrongdoing among young people, particularly that which is deemed to be criminal, is vital if as a society we want to improve the longer term outcomes for those growing into adulthood.

Acknowledgements

Thanks are expressed to Bill Scriven, Gwenda's husband, for allowing her work to be edited and included in this book. Thanks must also be expressed to Jacqueline Hitchcock-Wyatt, Founder and CEO of *GR8 AS U R* for permission to include information from the National Lottery *Reaching Communities* – funded pilot project. Further details about the work of this organisation are available at www.gr8asur.com.

Further reading

Shapland, J., Robinson, G. and Sorsby, A. (2011) *Restorative Justice in Practice*. London: Routledge.
Wallis, P. (2014) *Understanding Restorative Justice: How Empathy Can Close the Gap Created by Crime*. Bristol: Policy Press.
Zehr, H. (2014) *The Little Book of Restorative Justice*. New York, NY: Good Books.

References

Amstutz, L. and Mullet, J. (2005) *The Little Book of Restorative Discipline for Schools*. Intercourse, PA: Good Books.

Angus, S. (2008) Children as Victims of Crime. In Kennison, P. and Goodman, A. (Eds.), *Children as Victims (Transforming Integrated Services)*. Exeter: Learning Matters, pp. 49–60.

Bottoms, A. (2002) On the decriminalisation of English juvenile courts. In Muncie, J., Hughes, G. and McLauglin, E. (Eds.), *Youth Justice Critical Readings*. London: Sage, pp. 216–227.

Boulton, J. and Mirsky, L. (2006) *Restorative Practices as a Tool for Organizational Change: The Bessels Leigh School*. Todmorden: International Institute for Restorative Practices.

Braithwaite, J. (1989) *Crime, Shame and Reintegration*. New York: Cambridge University Press.

Cavanagh, T. (2005) *Creating Safe Schools Using Restorative Practices in a Culture of Care*. Hamilton, NZ: Fulbright Foundation in association with The University of Waikato.

Chan Kim, W. and Mauborgne, R. (1997) Fair process: Managing the knowledge economy. *Harvard Business Review*, 75(4), 65–75.

Crawford, A. and Newburn, T. (2003) *Youth Offending and Restorative Justice: Implementing Reform in Youth Justice*. Devon: William Publishing.

Downes, D. (1998) Back to the future: The predictive value of social theories of delinquency. In Holdaway, S. and Rock, P. (Eds.), *Thinking about Criminology*. London: UCL Press, p. 73.

Gelsthorpe, L. and Morris, A. (2002) Restorative youth justice: The last vestige of welfare? In Muncie, J., Hughes, G. and McLauglin, E. (Eds.), *Youth Justice Critical Readings*. London: Sage, pp. 238–254.

Goldson, B. (2002) New punitiveness: The politics of child incarceration. In Muncie, J., Hughes, G. and McLauglin, E. (Eds.), *Youth Justice Critical Readings*. London: Sage, pp. 386–400.

GR8 AS U R (2015) *GR8 AS U R Journey Book: Heal Not Hurt Approach*. Norwich: GR8 AS U R. Details available from www.gr8asur.com

Graef, R. (2002) *Why Restorative Justice? Repairing the Harm Caused by Crime*. London: Calouste Gulbenkian Foundation.

Home Office (1997) *No More Excuses: A New Approach to Tackling Youth Crime in England and Wales*. London: Crown Copyright.

Hopkins, B. (2002) Restorative Justice in Schools. *Support for Learning*, Vol. 17(3), 144–149.

Hopkins, B. (2004) *Just Schools: A Whole School Approach to Restorative Justice*. London: Jessica Kingsley Publishers.

Humphries, S. (1981) *Hooligans or Rebels?: An Oral History of Working-class Childhood and Youth 1889–1939*. Oxford: Blackwell.

Jackson, S. and Fondacaro, M. (1999) Procedural Justice in Resolving Family Conflict: Implications for Youth Violence Prevention. *Law and Policy*, Vol. 21(2), 101–127.

Marshall, T. (1999) *Restorative Justice: An Overview*. London: Home Office.

Matthews, R. (2003) Rethinking penal policy: Towards a systems approach. In Matthews, R. and Young, J. (Eds.), *The New Politics of Crime and Punishment*. Cullompton: Willian Publishing, pp. 223–249.

McCold, P. (1996) Restorative Justice and the Role of the Community. *Restorative Justice: International Perspectives*, Vol. 85, 86.

McCold, P. (1999) *Restorative Justice Practice: The State of the Field 1999*. Paper presented at the Building Strong Partnerships for Restorative Practices Conference, Burlington, Vermont.

Ministry of Justice (1933) *Children and Young Persons Act 1933 Part III & IV Protection of Children and Young Persons in relation to Criminal and Summary Proceedings (Youth Courts) Section 45*. London: Crown Copyright [Online]. Available at: www.statutelaw.gov.uk Access date: 14.3.17.

Mirsky, L. (2005) *From Sanctions to Support: Restorative Practices Transform Homes for Looked after Children*. Todmorden: International Institute for Restorative Practices.

Morrison, B. and Ahmed, E. (2006) Restorative Justice and Civil Society: Emerging Practice, Theory and Evidence. *Journal of Social Issues*, Vol. 62, pp. 209–215.

Muncie, J., Hughes, G. and McLauglin, E. (2002) *Youth Justice Critical Readings*. London: Sage.

Newburn, T. (1995) *Crime and Criminal Justice Policy*. Harlow: Longdon.

Newburn, T. (2002) Young people, crime and youth justice. In Maguire, M., Morgan, R. and Reiner, R. (Eds.), *Oxford Handbook of Criminology* (3rd edition). Oxford: Clarendon Press, p. 3.

O'Connell, T., Wachtel, B. and Wachtel, T. (1999) *Conferencing Handbook*. Pipersville: The Piper's Press.

Pitts, J. (2003) Youth justice in England and Wales. In Matthews, R. and Young, J. (Eds.), *The New Politics of Crime and Punishment*. Cullompton: Willian Publishing, pp. 71–99.

Restorative Practices Training Association (RPTA) (2006) *Trainers Handbook*. Todmorden: IIRP.

Roche, D. (2006) Dimensions of Restorative Justice. *Journal of Social Issues*, Vol. 62(2), pp. 217–238.

Rosenberg, M. (2003) *Nonviolent Communication: A Language of Life*. Encinitas, CA: PuddleDancer Press.

Schaar, J. H. (undated) Available at: www.goodreads.com/quotes/279924-the-future-is-not-some-place-we-are-going-but Accessed date: 14.3.17.

Shapland, J., Atkinson, A., Atkinson, Chapman, B. H., Dignan, J., Howes, M., Johnstone, J., Robinson, G. and Sorsby, A. (2007) *Restorative the Views of Victims and Offenders*. London: Ministry of Justice.

Sherman, L. and Strang, H. (2007) *Restorative Justice: The Evidence*. London: The Smith Institute in association with The Esmee Fairbairn Foundation.

Shore, H. (2002) Reforming the juvenile: Gender, justice and the child criminal in nineteenth century England. In Muncie, J., Hughes, G. and McLauglin, E. (Eds.), *Youth Justice Critical Readings*. London: Sage, pp. 159–172.

Strang, H. and Sherman, L. (2003) Repairing the Harm: Victims and Restorative Justice. *Utah Law Review*, Vol. 1 pp. 15–42.

Umbreit, M., Coates, B. and Vos, B. (2007) Restorative Justice Dialogue: A Multi-Dimensional, Evidence-Based Practice Theory. *Contemporary Justice Review*, March 2007, Vol. 10(1) pp. 23–41.

Wachtel, T. (2003) *Restorative Practices in Schools: An Antidote to Zero Tolerance VOMA Connections, Winter 2003, No 13* [Online]. Available at: www.voma.org Access date: 14.3.17.

Wachtel, T. and McCold, P. (2004) *From Restorative Justice to Restorative Practices: Expanding the Paradigm*. Conference Paper from Building a Global Alliance for Restorative Practices and Family Empowerment. The IIRP Fifth International Conference on Conferencing, Circles and Other Restorative Practices, Vancouver, British Columbia Canada, August 5–7, 2004.

Wearmouth, J., Mckinney, R. and Glynn, T. (2007) Restorative Justice in Schools: A New Zealand Example. *Educational Research*, Vol. 49(1) pp. 37–49.

Weitekamp, E. (1999) *Research on Victim-Offender Mediation, Findings and Needs for the Future*. Paper for the First Conference of the European Forum for Victim-Offender Mediation and Restorative Justice, Leuven, Belgium, October 27–29, 1999.

Zehr, H. (1990) *Changing Lenses: A New Focus for Crime and Justice*. Scotsdale: Herald Press.

Zehr, H. (2002) *The Little Book of Restorative Justice*. Intercourse, PA: Good Books.

Zehr, H. (2014) *The Little Book of Restorative Justice*. New York, NY: Good Books.

14 Leadership and inclusion

Leela Cubillo and Richard Woolley

Stefan was an ordinary looking boy with nothing especially notable to distinguish him from the other nine- and ten-year-olds in his class. Even the fact that he was a second-language speaker whose family were recent immigrants was unremarkable in a school where there were at least seventeen different languages spoken. But he was different. He appeared to have no friends and kept very much to himself, and he had a way of staring at you with a fixed gaze that you could not fail to notice. On questioning, his classmates said that he made them feel uncomfortable. They reported that any efforts made to include him were met with little response other than a resounding 'No' . . . and his steely gaze.

In class, his behaviour was inconsistent, occasionally replying to direct questioning by the teacher and at other times appearing to be disinterested and displaying disruptive behaviour (such as knocking on the desk and muttering loudly to himself). Teachers attributed his behaviour and lack of communication to a lack of comprehension of the language. The school tried to provide appropriate language support, but without much success. As the term wore on his behaviour became progressively worse, and in one teacher's class in particular, he started to become physically disruptive. In accordance with the school's behaviour policy, he was then excluded from the class and, following repeated offences, reported to the headteacher.

Introduction

This chapter looks at leadership for effective inclusion in schools, the role of the headteacher in leading the inclusive school and the added demands and responsibilities placed on the leadership of an inclusive school in order to achieve successful performance. It then moves on to present some conclusions from the book overall.

Ensuring inclusive education for all is one of the major challenges facing school leaders today. As definitions of inclusive education have progressed from a narrow concept of serving children with disabilities in an educational setting to a broader one that embraces diversity and seeks to provide an education for all learners, understanding the nature of the leadership within the organisation becomes even more critical if we are to achieve those aims.

In this chapter, current and past leadership practice and development in leadership theory are presented, in order to provide a contextual understanding of theory and practice, along with a review of significant studies on the development of school leadership. Much of the early literature on school leadership was based on an assumption of a causal link between school leadership and successful school performance, despite a lack of robust evidence to support it at the time. With advances in research and new understandings of leadership practice, the significance of effective leadership for school effectiveness is acknowledged, but with attention paid to the limitations of the influence of leadership alone. Significant to this discussion is the fact that many of the initial studies on the impact of leadership on learning and school effectiveness failed to take account of the context of the school in terms of its social environment or the diversity of its learners.

The chapter will also reflect on some models of leadership in schools and recent thinking on what constitutes successful leadership. The different approaches to leadership that schools take in regard to the inclusion agenda are considered, as they move away from traditional and hierarchical models to more collaborative and distributed approaches to leading schools. The chapter also points to other factors that may influence leading for inclusion such as the culture of the school organisation, motivation, values and the way in which the school responds to and manages change. Readers are invited to reflect on and challenge current thinking on leadership practice for inclusion in schools and explore strategies for leading inclusive education.

Pause for thought

Reflecting on your own experience of the education system, as a child or an adult, a pupil or an employee, consider:

- What aspects of the leadership of the school affected its ethos and the potential for a sense of inclusion?
- What practices exhibited by teachers and school leaders can you recall that supported a sense of inclusion?
- What behaviours, systems or other attributes of the school undermined or limited the inclusion of all learners, staff and other stakeholders?

Leadership in education

The last two decades have seen the emergence of a variety of new perspectives and approaches to the study of educational leadership. While these new perspectives have produced a more diverse understanding of the theory and practice of leadership in educational settings, the term 'leadership' and its definition is still a disputed concept. A point of contention is the distinction between 'management' and 'leadership'. Bush (2007, 2008a, 2008b) provides a constructive analysis based on the premise that the fundamental concern of educational leadership and management, unlike other disciplines, has to be with 'the purpose or aims of education' (Bush, 2007: 391). Influence, vision and purpose are often identified as central to leadership while management is seen as associated with maintenance, systems and the development of people. It is important to note that while there are differences between the terms, both are seen as essential to the effective operation of the school and one set of activities is not given prominence over the other (Bush, 2008a: 4).

There are a number of approaches to classifying leadership, one of which appears to be a dichotomy between those who focus on the leaders themselves and those who focus on the leadership itself. This approach makes a distinction between those who associate leadership with the individual and others who view leadership primarily as an interaction between leaders and those being led. Much of early theory focussed on the qualities of the leader, as in trait theory, the so-called 'great man' theory, which suggests an inborn capacity to lead based on the assumption that leadership rests upon the knowledge, competencies and personal attributes of individuals who are placed in positions of power and authority (Stogdill, 1974). However, associating leadership with the individual without regard to the social environment or context has limited value in providing an understanding of the nature of leadership. The second approach focusses on the concept of leadership itself rather than the individual as leader. The definitions in this latter group pay attention to the function of leadership and examine the role of leadership within organisational settings (Beare et al., 1997; Southworth, 2002).

The challenge to respond to changes in educational policy and practice nationally and globally has highlighted the need to educate for leadership and social responsibility. Educational leadership can no longer be seen as a singular task with a limited function, but a plural and multi-functional activity that takes account of context and culture. In their commentary on the state of research in educational leadership and management, Heck and Hallinger (2005) reported on the numerous aspects of leadership that appear to have attracted the attention of researchers such as values, cognitive perspectives, dilemmas of management and social justice. The dominance of these ideologically driven perspectives point to a move towards the construction of leadership as a moral and social endeavour (Sergiovanni, 1992, 2005; Grace, 1995). Also apparent in the leadership literature is a narrative that now includes questions about culture, identity and difference, and the role of democracy in leadership and education (Southworth, 2002; Starratt, 2004).

It is evident that there are many different, and often contested, conceptualisations of leadership. Bush (2008a: 277), drawing attention to Yukl's (2002: 3) assertion that leadership involves a social influence process, suggests that defining leadership as influence rather than authority 'provides support for the concept of distributed leadership and for constructs such as senior leadership teams'. The notion of distributed or shared leadership is one that has been readily adopted by the educational community as a means of sharing the task of leadership and extending the influence of leadership (Gronn, 2008; MacBeath, 2009; Harris, 2009). Despite any limitations of distributed leadership (Crawford, 2012; Lumby, 2013), it offers a useful strategy for dealing with the multiplicity and complexity of the leadership role and remains widely used in current educational practice. Where one takes a stance in these broad understandings of leadership has implications for perceptions of what constitutes 'successful' leadership. Discussions regarding successful or effective leadership imply value judgements being made, which must take account of context to be meaningful.

Pause for thought

Reflect on your own views on the aims and purposes of education, and the resultant responsibilities of school leaders.

Consider which of the following should, in your opinion, be prioritised:

- The individual needs and differences of pupils.
- The school's ranking in league tables.
- Contribution to the local community, including to providing educational opportunities to local residents.

Leela Cubillo and Richard Woolley

- Maintaining an orderly and calm school environment, where educational excellence can be achieved.
- Developing an inclusive school community in which children learn to accept, appreciate and celebrate one another's differences.

Reflect on the tensions between these aspects of the life and ethos of a school. Are there other areas that you feel school leaders should be making a priority, and why?

The importance of school leadership for successful schools

Studies on the characteristics of successful schools have consistently stressed the importance of the quality of a school's leadership on the school's performance. From a major study of primary schools in the UK several decades ago which identified 'purposeful leadership of the staff by the headteacher' as one of twelve key factors contributing to effective schooling (Mortimore et al., 1988) to more recent studies, the belief that effective leadership is a key characteristic of effective schools is widely supported. The establishment of a National College for School Leadership in England in 2001 illustrated the conviction in the importance of school leadership, and particularly that of the headteacher. In spite of moves to broaden the context of leadership towards notions of shared or distributed leadership, the prime responsibility for the performance of the school is firmly placed with the headteacher.

Despite the widespread belief in a causal link between school leadership and school effectiveness, the ambiguity of the empirical knowledge base at the time prompted several researchers to seek further evidence. A helpful contribution to the debate was provided by Hallinger and Heck (1999) in a publication synthesising the findings from previous reviews of empirical literature investigating perspectives on school leadership and principal leadership effects. They examined the assumption that school leadership has a significant positive impact on student performance, and posed the question 'Can leadership enhance school effectiveness?' The question was answered in the affirmative but with a note of caution. The writers reported that while their review supports the belief that school leadership does indeed influence school effectiveness, these effects are achieved only indirectly through their influence on school and classroom processes which themselves have a direct impact on student learning.

A systematic review on school leadership carried out to examine the impact of school leadership on student outcomes reported that, while effective leadership is centrally important, the nature and focus of leaders' actions were either contested or unclear (Bell et al., 2003). The review did, however, serve to highlight the complexity of the relationship between school leadership and school performance and supported the belief in the centrality of the role of school leadership to school effectiveness. Harris (2004: 3), commenting in an editorial for the 'School Leadership and Management' journal, notes that, 'Whatever else is contested, the contribution of school leadership to securing and sustaining school improvement is not'.

A significant report published by Leithwood et al. (2006), for the National College for School Leadership, provides robust evidence for what they called 'seven strong claims about successful leadership'. The report concluded that leadership has very significant effects on the quality of school organisation and on pupil learning. As far as we are aware, there is not a single documented case of a school successfully turning around its pupil achievement trajectory in the absence of talented leadership.

(Leithwood et al., 2006: 5)

Case study

Leithwood et al. (2006) identified seven strong claims about successful leadership, namely:

- School leadership is second only to classroom teaching as an influence on pupil learning.
- Almost all successful leaders draw on the same repertoire of basic leadership practices.
- The ways in which leaders apply these basic leadership practices – not the practices themselves – demonstrate responsiveness to, rather than dictation by, the contexts in which they work.
- School leaders improve teaching and learning indirectly and most powerfully through their influence on staff motivation, commitment and working conditions.
- School leadership has a greater influence on schools and students when it is widely distributed.
- Some patterns of distribution are more effective than others.
- A small handful of personal traits explains a high proportion of the variation in leadership effectiveness.

(Leithwood et al., 2006: 3)

Consider Leithwood et al.'s claims. Reflecting on your own experience of school leadership, whether as a pupil, member of staff, parent, governor or in another role, how important do you consider each claim to be? What examples from your experience support your views?

Leadership for inclusion

Any discussion on the effectiveness of leadership in the context of an inclusive school must consider the aims of social inclusion alongside the nature of the educational provision. It is now widely accepted that education for social inclusion must mean education for all regardless of personal circumstances or background, and that inclusion should be about respecting and valuing diversity rather than simply assimilating it. Raffo and Gunter (2008: 399) point out that this perspective 'shifts the lens from a fixed situation where there is an interest in fairness in representation to a dynamic process of how diversity is recognised and valued'.

However, the government's agenda for educational reform and social inclusion seems to be in contradiction to the raising standards agenda, as schools seem to be under ever-increasing pressure to improve educational attainment (Ainscow et al., 2004; Farrell and Ainscow, 2012). These apparently opposing demands create particular challenges for the leadership of the inclusive school. As Farrell and Ainscow (2012) point out, differentiated provision for pupils in order to achieve higher academic standards would not be compatible with an inclusive philosophy. It is clear therefore that there is a need for new strategies to resolve the problem.

Pause for thought

Consider the experience of Stefan, outlined in the vignette at the start of this chapter.
Consider:

- How Stefan's demeanour and observed behaviour might affect the way in which he was included in class or in the wider school.
- What factors might be impacting on his ability to engage with activities in school.

Now reflect on this additional information about Stefan's circumstances, and consider how the leadership of the school, its policies relating to inclusion and the leadership roles of a variety of staff might impact on Stefan's inclusion:

> The school had a newly appointed headteacher who was keen to actively promote a strong inclusive ethos across the school and did not believe in excluding any child, even as a temporary measure. He decided he needed to get to the root of the problem and gathered a team of staff to help him. What transpired as a result of their investigation was that Stefan had a profound level of deafness. Unfortunately, a negative experience in his native country had left him not wishing to make that fact known to anyone. He was actually quite an able student who relied on lip reading to communicate, which in a second language presented even more of a challenge. And as for the class in which he became disruptive, it seemed that the teacher tended to stand with her back to the window while teaching which completely obscured the view of her face. In frustration therefore, he decided that he would rather not be in the class at all than be there and not be able to engage with it.

Consider what measures might be introduced within the school to support Stefan and to address his needs.

- How might the school's leadership team help to support his engagement with education, the school community and life beyond the classroom?

Facets of inclusive leadership

Inclusive leadership requires reflection on the social, moral, ethical and legal situation in which it takes place. If we consider the population of an educational establishment, such as a nursery, school, college or university, there are a wide range of individuals with myriad needs and identities who need to be included in the overall development of an inclusive and appreciative community. Reflecting on the development of the values statements for a new school established in the East Midlands of England, one child contributed the acrostic: Together Everyone Achieves More (TEAM). That this mantra has probably been found in many places, but it was adopted as a part of the school's mission statement and overall aims: together we were stronger, and together everyone was valued and appreciated (or at least that was the intention and aspiration).

Case study

Neil Griffiths, children's author and champion of Storysacks, reflects on his aspirations for the role of education and the impact that he hoped would be experienced by the learners in his school (Taylor and Woolley, 2013: 212–213):

> As a teacher of 34 years I have long been haunted by the idea attributed to Mark Twain that he never let his schooling interfere with his education.
>
> Endless statutory dictums from successive governments and their ever changing Secretaries of State have only compounded my fears that most of our education does indeed happen beyond the boundaries of our schools. Often left feeling impotent and unable to make the positive difference to children's lives they deserved, I have regularly asked myself what should primary education seek to achieve?
>
> As a headteacher I had a clear aim in mind, that each child should leave us liking themselves, liking others and being liked by others. I set myself the challenge to shift the emphasis in our curriculum from memorising endless facts (many of no true value) to employing memorable practitioners who provided the children with memorable experiences that would stay with them and influence them positively throughout their lives.
>
> I hoped that during their time with us we would contribute to and develop in them seven important Cs:

- Curiosity
- Character
- Confidence
- Communication
- Caring
- Contentment
- Condition (physical well-being).

> Most of all, I hoped that as children left us, they would look over their shoulders with sadness at the departing and in the coming years look back and say: 'the days at my primary school were some of the happiest of my life'.

Reflecting on the views of Neil Griffiths, consider:

- How the values and vision he presents might support the development of an inclusive learning experience.
- How important you consider the elements of developing self-esteem, self-value and self-respect.
- How the reporting requirements of the education system (e.g. pressures from external inspection bodies, league tables and the need to be compliant with policy and procedures) might impact on a school's own vision for what and who it values.

In the post-Equality Act (Legislation.gov.uk, 2010) era in the education system in England, together we are on a spectrum of gender identities, on a spectrum of ages, a range of abilities and disabilities, from homes with different senses of social class, income, aspiration, ambition and capital, of diverse sexual orientations, married, single, divorced, with or without children, exploring whether our gendered identity reflects that with which we were assigned at birth, experiencing racism, homophobia, facing bullying because of perceived differences or because of our association with others with real or perceived differences, experiencing disabilities or supporting those with different abilities and disabilities. The list is extensive, important and significant to us personally and as a society, and in this summary is inevitably incomplete. Readers will wish to add their own dimensions of the notion of difference.

Leaders need to consider how this range of differences can be taken into account in order to ensure that all those eligible for inclusion in the school community and the children's workforce can be included, developed, encouraged and enabled to achieve to the best of their potential for the good of all in the school community. This is a challenge, particularly in societies where racism, homophobia, sexism, ageism and any other inappropriate labelling can be found.

There is a tension here, for some of those who find themselves in leadership positions have chosen to identify, or not to identify, as being in minority or other groups. This can bring personal pressure, alongside a personal aspiration to provide an inclusive environment for others.

Pause for thought

Reflecting on your own experience, consider:

- Times when you have felt particularly included in a workplace or learning setting.
- What factors made you feel included, and why this particular situation was different or special compared with others you have experienced.
- What aspects of the leadership within that workplace or setting helped to create an inclusive atmosphere, ethos and environment.

In England, the school inspection body Ofsted considers the effectiveness of the overall leadership and management in a school with regard to

> how well leaders and governors promote all forms of equality and foster greater understanding of and respect for people of all faiths (and those of no faith), races, genders, ages, disability and sexual orientations (and other groups with protected characteristics [as defined in the Equality Act]), through their words, actions and influence within the school and more widely in the community.
>
> (Ofsted, 2015: 39)

This provides a very clear focus on the breadth of issues relating to inclusion outlined in this book, although we have also included socio-economic issues, social and cultural capital and career aspirations. Although the term inclusion is used in a narrow sense in a variety of settings, as has been noted in earlier chapters particularly with a focus on special educational needs and at times disabilities, here the government's inspectors present a broad and wide-ranging summary.

There are tensions with any discussion about inclusion, where it takes on such a broad interpretation. Whilst the authors of this book have explored a diverse range of experiences of inclusion, they are writing in a world where racism, terrorism, a rise in nationalism and a hatred for difference make headline news on a daily basis. At the time of writing, leaders in United Kingdom are grappling with the impact of the referendum decision to leave the European Union (Brexit). The world is also coming to terms with the implication of the election of President Donald Trump in the USA. Following both public votes there was a rise in reported hate crime, particularly relating to ethnicity and immigration, and incidents of homophobia (Barker, 2016; BBC, 2016; Lusher, 2016; Townsend, 2016; Al Jazeera, 2016; Barros, 2016; Jamieson, 2016; Mathias and Abbey-Lambertz, 2017; Reilly, 2016; Singh, 2016). In such a setting it is perhaps more important than ever to address issues relating to diversity, equality and inclusion with children in schools, in order to enable them to live respectful and harmonious lives with those in their communities and wider society, and so that they are able to question and challenge those with intolerant views (each of which relates particularly to Cole's (2008) notion of 'isms' and 'phobias', 'including classism, racism/xeno-racism and xenophobia, sexism, disablism, homophobia and Islamophobia' (Woolley, 2010: 1)). One current area for concern is the torture and killing of gay men in Chechnya. Those who have studied the Holocaust of the mid-twentieth century in Europe, and subsequent genocides, will identify parallels in history.

Returning to the survey of student teachers introduced in Chapter 1, it is notable that one student teacher observed:

> I don't believe that enough training is given on developing children as a whole person. I feel that my training has focused almost entirely on their academic development to the detriment of helping to prepare children for life. Preparing children for life is important, especially in a world of ever-increasing problems, and it is this that I think will be hard to deal with.
>
> *Male undergraduate (3 year degree), training to teach children aged 3–7 years,*
> *East Midlands of England*

We may reflect on the problems that have been faced in the world in our own lifetimes. These may relate to economic, social, political, religious and other situations that have caused tension, division and unrest. This particular student teacher has a sense that children need to be prepared and equipped to live in a world with such complexities, and, we would argue, children and young people need school leaders at all levels to support them in developing resilience to face an ever changing, complex world.

Moving forward

In order to develop effective practice in leadership for inclusion, we need to consider issues that have repeatedly permeated aspects of this book:

- How school leaders are prepared and equipped to understand, appreciate and celebrate difference in their schools.
- How teachers and other education professionals can be enabled to look beyond the obvious or superficial, and see the real needs of children, young people and their families.
- How managers can be facilitated to become leaders, taking forward policies, principles, values and ethos, for the benefit of all stakeholders in a community.
- How education can be appreciated and celebrated as a transformative experience that enables all people (learners and staff) to feel valued as unique individuals, and to develop in a safe and supported environment.

Conclusion

A concept key to this book, but not addressed overtly until now, is that of social justice. As human beings, we exist in community and relate through shared social and cultural experiences. Even imagining a world where we could be isolated and live in total solitude on a deserted island, we would still be influenced by pollution in the air and water around us. There is nowhere on earth where we can exist and not be affected by others.

Being human is essentially about living in relationship with and in relation to other people. They may be our fellow school pupils, our work mates, neighbours, those who provide our food or give service in shops or through delivery services. We are continually relating to others, interpreting such relationships, evaluating them and working out how we fit in. Even when completing this chapter, there is a thought in our minds of how it will be received, what will readers think and whether there will be positive or negative reactions to its content.

In this book, our interpretations of inclusion and inclusive practices have been broad, many of them drawn from the stories of individuals shared in each chapter. The power of individual story in expressing individual need should never be underestimated.

In Chapter 2, Tyler helped us to consider how accessing a university education might make a significant difference, even though he was from a non-traditional background and self-taught. In Chapter 3, we explored how personal and individual stories, properly understood, can develop deep appreciation of individual needs and differences. In Chapter 4, Tariq and Molly helped us to think about layers of learning and depth. In Chapter 5, Ms Merrick challenged the organisation of her classroom and explored ways of overcoming barriers to learning for those with language differences. In Chapter 6, Morgan's exchange experience in a UK university provided insights into how religion and beliefs can be discussed in a safe and secure space, supported by academic processes. The experience of Sharon's weekend break with her husband in Chapter 7 illustrated how assumptions can easily get in the way of including someone with mobility needs that are not immediately visible. In Chapter 8, Ruth highlighted how something as apparently simple as going to the bathroom can be made difficult when binary gender labels are applied. In Chapter 9, the limitations placed on us by those who give careers advice and guidance were highlighted, as were the opportunities afforded to those with social networks for life-enhancing work experience. In Chapter 10, we reflected on the opportunities available to Lucy once her baby was born, and hoped that she would be able to pursue her career in engineering. Chapter 11 presented a challenge to consider how support staff in schools can be used to maximise learning, without creating exclusion or withdrawal and unintentionally undermining the inclusion agenda. In Chapter 12, we considered how developing creativity and artistic endeavour in prison environments might lead to future success and prosperity, rather than raising false hopes and aspirations. In Chapter 13, Gwenda helped us to consider how to mend relationships and encourage healing, without demonising or ostracising individuals. Finally, this chapter has raised some issues about leading, managing and inspiring approaches to inclusion in order to take forward the agenda and make a difference to individual lives. At the very start of the book the stories of Richard, Jake and Carline made us consider how where you live, how your life chances develop and how you identify yourself impact on the ways in which you feel included and accepted by those around you. We have explored some powerful stories along the way, and each of the accounts reflects an individual journey towards being included.

The sense of social justice, of acceptance, of being treated fairly and having positive and realistic chances in life permeates the stories of those individuals highlighted in the chapters of this book. Each person is unique and illustrates special individual characteristics: as do each one of us as readers of, and contributors to, this book.

We are all different and special, worthy of respect and individual value. The quest is to establish how our individual differences can be accepted and celebrated. Are we committed to and working towards inclusion; towards understanding what inclusion means in a broad sense; and striving towards a fairer, accepting, tolerant and respectful society where all feel valued?

This is the nature of understanding inclusion.

Further reading

Ainscow, M., Dyson, A., Goldrick, S. and West, W. (2012) 'Making schools effective for all: Rethinking the task', *School Leadership & Management*, 32(3), 197–213.

Legislation.gov.uk. (2010) *Equality Act 2010*. [online] Available at: www.legislation.gov.uk/ukpga/2010/15/contents

References

Ainscow, M., Booth, T. and Dyson, A. (2004) 'Understanding and developing inclusive practices in schools: A collaborative action research network', *International Journal of Inclusive Education*, 8(2), 125–139.

Al Jazeera (2016) Reports of racist attacks rise after Donald Trump's win: Victims take to social media to recount physical and verbal abuse as rights groups call on president-elect to act, 11 November 2016. Available at: www.aljazeera.com/news/2016/11/reports-racist-attacks-rise-donald-trump-win-161111035608375.html

Barker, I. (2016) Teachers warn Nicky Morgan of racism in schools following Brexit vote. Times educational supplement online, 1 July 2016. Available at: www.tes.com/news/school-news/breaking-news/teachers-warn-nicky-morgan-racism-schools-following-brexit-vote

Barros, A. (2016) Increased anxiety seen among LGBT youth since presidential election. VOA online, 13 December 2016. Available at: www.voanews.com/a/increased-anxiety-seen-among-lgbt-youth-since-presidential-election/3635000.html

BBC (2016) Race and religious hate crimes rose 41% after EU vote. BBC News online, 13 October 2016. Available at: www.bbc.co.uk/news/uk-politics-37640982

Beare, H., Caldwell, B. and Millikan, R. (1997) 'Dimensions of leadership', in M. Crawford, L. Kydd and C. Riches (eds.) *Leadership and Teams in Educational Management*. Buckingham: Open University Press, pp. 24–39.

Bell, L., Bolam, R. and Cubillo, L. (2003) 'A systematic review of the impact of school leadership and management on student/pupil outcomes', in *Research Evidence in Education Library*, Issue 1. London: EPPI-Centre, Social Science Research Unit, Institute of Education. Available at: www.eppi.ioe.ac.uk

Bush, T. (2007) 'Educational leadership and management: Theory, policy and practice', *South African Journal of Education*, 27(3), 391–406.

Bush, T. (2008a) *Leadership and Management Development in Education*. London: Sage Publications.

Bush, T. (2008b) 'From management to leadership: Semantic or meaningful change?', *Educational Management, Administration and Leadership*, 36(2), 271–288.

Cole, M. (2008) 'Introduction', in M. Cole (ed.) *Professional Attributes and Practice: Meeting the QTS Standards*, 4th edition. Abingdon: David Fulton, pp. 1–22.

Crawford, M. (2012) 'Solo and distributed leadership: Definitions and dilemmas', *Educational Management, Administration and Leadership*, 40(5), 610–620.

Farrell, P. and Ainscow, M. (Eds.) (2012) *Making Special Education Inclusive*. London: Routledge.

Grace, G. (1995) *School Leadership: Beyond Education Management*. London: Falmer Press.

Gronn, P. (2008) 'The future of distributed leadership', *Journal of Educational Administration*, 46(2), 141–158.

Hallinger, P. and Heck, R. (1999) 'Can school leaders enhance school effectiveness?', in T. Bush, L. Bell, R. Bolam and P. Ribbins (eds.) *Educational Management: Redefining Theory, Policy and Practice*. London: Paul Chapman, 178–190.

Harris, A. (2004) 'Editorial: School leadership and school improvement: A simple and complex relationship', *School Leadership and Management*, 24(1), 3–5.

Harris, A. (2009) 'Distributed leadership and knowledge creation', in K. Leithwood, B. Mascall and T. Strauss (eds.) *Distributed Leadership According to the Evidence*. London: Routledge, 253–266.

Heck, R. and Hallinger, P. (2005) 'The study of educational leadership and management: Where does the field stand today?', *Educational Management Administration and Leadership*, 33(2), 229–244.

Jamieson, A. (2016) 'They are scared: Teachers grapple with fear and bullying after Trump victory', *Guardian Online*, 20 November 2016. Available at: www.theguardian.com/us-news/2016/nov/20/donald-trump-schools-election-students-bullying

Legislation.gov.uk (2010) *Equality Act 2010*. [online] Available at: www.legislation.gov.uk/ukpga/2010/15/contents

Leithwood, K., Day, C., Sammons, P., Harris, A. and Hopkins, D. (2006) *Seven Strong Claims about Successful School Leadership, DfES*. London: NCSL, Nottingham.

Lumby, J. (2013) 'Distributed leadership: The uses and abuses of power', *Educational Management, Administration and Leadership*, 41(5), 581–597.

Lusher, A. (2016) 'Homophobic attacks rose 147 per cent after the Brexit vote', *Independent Online*, 9 October 2016. Available at: www.independent.co.uk/news/uk/home-news/brexit-hate-crime-hatred-homophobia-lgbt-147-per-cent-rise-double-attacks-on-gays-lesbians-a7352411.html

MacBeath, J. (2009) 'Distributed leadership: Paradigms, policy and paradox', in K. Leithwood, B. Mascall and T. Strauss (eds.) *Distributed Leadership According to the Evidence*. London: Routledge, 41–58.

Mathias, C. and Abbey-Lambertz, K. (2017) 'There's been an "Outbreak" of nearly 900 hate incidents since Trump's win', *Huffington Post Online*, 21 February 2017. Available at: www.huffingtonpost.com/entry/donald-trump-hate-incidents_us_583dd8bfe4b0860d6116bf95

Mortimore, P., Sammons, P., Stoll, L., Lewis, D. and Ecob, R. (1988) *School Matters: The Junior Years*. London: Open Books.

Ofsted (2015) *School Inspection Handbook*. Available at: www.gov.uk/government/publications/school-inspection-handbook-from-september-2015

Raffo, C. and Gunter, H. (2008) 'Leading schools to promote social inclusion: Developing a conceptual framework for analysing research, policy and practice', *Journal of Education Policy*, 23(4), 397–414.

Reilly, K. (2016) 'Racist incidents are up since Donald Trump's election: These are just a few of them', *Time Magazine*, 13 November 2016. Available at: http://time.com/4569129/racist-anti-semitic-incidents-donald-trump/

Sergiovanni, T. (1992) *Moral Leadership: Getting to the Heart of School Improvement*. San Francisco: Jossey Bass.

Sergiovanni, T. J. (2005) 'The Virtues of Leadership', *The Educational Forum*, 69(2), 112–123.

Singh, R. (2016) 'Britain warned racist violence and bullying will rise after far-right groups hail Donald Trump's election win', *Independent Online*, 10 November 2016. Available at: www.independent.co.uk/news/uk/home-news/britain-racist-violence-bullying-rise-far-right-groups-hail-donald-trump-election-win-a7409771.html

Southworth, G. (2002) 'Lessons from successful leadership in small schools', in K. Leithwood and P. Hallinger (eds.) *Second International Handbook of Educational Leadership and Administration*. London: Kluwer, pp. 451–484.

Starratt, R. J. (2004) 'Leadership of the contested terrain of education for democracy', *Journal of Educational Administration*, 12/2004, 42(6), 724–731.

Stogdill, R. M. (1974) *Handbook of Leadership: A Survey of the Literature*. New York: The Free Press.

Taylor, K. and Woolley, R. (2013) *Values and Vision in Primary Education*. Maidenhead: Open University Press.

Townsend, M. (2016) 'Homophobic attacks in UK rose 147% in three months after Brexit vote', *Independent Online*, 8 October 2016. Available at: www.theguardian.com/society/2016/oct/08/homophobic-attacks-double-after-brexit-vote

Woolley, R. (2010) Tackling Controversial Issues in the Primary School: Facing Life's Challenges with Your Learners. London: Routledge.

Yukl, G. A. (2002) *Leadership in Organizations*, 5th edition. Upper Saddle River, NJ: Prentice-Hall.

INDEX

Italic page references indicate boxed text and figures.